Texts in Transit II

Kenneth M. Shaffer, Jr.
and
Graydon F. Snyder

Brethren Press
Elgin, Illinois

Texts in Transit II

Kenneth M. Shaffer, Jr. and Graydon F. Snyder

Copyright © 1991 by Kenneth M. Shaffer, Jr. and Graydon F. Snyder

Brethren Press, 1451 Dundee Avenue, Elgin, Illinois 60120

This is a revised and expanded edition of *Texts in Transit: A Study of New Testament Passages That Shaped the Brethren*, copyright © 1976 by the Brethren Press.

Biblical quotations, unless otherwise noted, are from the New Revised Standard Version of the Bible, copyrighted 1989 by the Division of Christian Education, National Council of Churches, and are used by permission.

Other biblical quotations are new translations by Graydon F. Snyder and designated as the Believers' New Testament (BNT).

Cover design by Jeane Healy

ISBN 0-87178-837-3

Manufactured in the United States of America

Contents

Introduction

The first *Texts in Transit*, published in 1976, focused on thirteen New Testament scriptures central to the Brethren and their understanding of the faith. Fifteen years later, authors Graydon Snyder and Kenneth Shaffer present a revised and expanded version, *Texts in Transit II*, with 26 studies of New Testament passages: thirteen revised studies and thirteen new ones.

Typically, the Brethren revisit biblical texts eager for new understanding, ready to hear the authority of the Scripture in a changing world. Fifteen years after the publication of *Texts in Transit*, the church must ask new questions about faith and life and look to the New Testament for instruction. In the period between publications, for instance, the Brethren have grappled at Annual Meeting with the question of biblical authority, the issue of church and state, and the problem of substance abuse, none of which were addressed in the first study.

Texts in Transit II differs slightly in organization from the earlier version. Each study begins with two translations of the original Greek, the New Revised Standard Version replacing the RSV and Graydon Snyder's translation designated the Believers' New Testament (BNT), which brings out nuances of meaning important to the free church or Believers' Church tradition. Sections on exegesis, Brethren use of the text historically, and contemporary application remain with revisions. The section titled "Suggestions for Study" has been replaced with case studies for group discussion.

New challenges in life and the need for biblical guidance prompted this revision of *Texts in Transit*. More precisely, the living texts summon us to search for their endless meaning. These are "favorites," not because we like them, but because they speak to us of what we are to be about as a church. Every turn of events sends us back to the Scriptures to read them anew. In many ways, they will be new scriptures to us, new in our understanding. We and the texts are truly in transit.

Session 1

On Divorce and Remarriage

Matthew 5:27-32 (NRSV)

"You have heard that it was said, 'You shall not commit adultery.' [28]But I say to you that everyone who looks at a woman with lust has already committed adultery with her in his heart. [29]If your right eye causes you to sin, tear it out and throw it away; it is better for you to lose one of your members than for your whole body to be thrown into hell. [30]And if your right hand causes you to sin, cut it off and throw it away; it is better for you to lose one of your members than for your whole body to go into hell. [31]It was also said, 'Whoever divorces his wife, let him give her a certificate of divorce.' [32]But I say to you that anyone who divorces his wife, except on the ground of unchastity, causes her to commit adultery; and whoever marries a divorced woman commits adultery."

Matthew 5:27-32 (BNT)

You have heard that it was said, "Do not commit adultery." [28]But I say to you that every man who continuously looks at a woman with desire has already committed adultery with her in his heart. [29]And if your right eye offends you, take it out and cast it from you. For it is better for you if one of your members be destroyed than that your whole body be cast into Gehenna. [30]And if your right hand offends you, cut it off and cast it from you. For it is better if one of your members be destroyed than that your whole body be cast into Gehenna. [31]And it was said, "Whoever divorces his wife, let him give to her a certificate of divorce." [32]But I say to you that every man who divorces his wife causes her to commit adultery, unless it were already a matter of unchastity, and whoever marries a divorced woman commits adultery.

The Text in Its Biblical Setting

The first four of the texts we are studying belong to a section of the Gospel of Matthew which we usually label the "Sermon on the Mount." This sermon consists of sayings of Jesus collected in a topical sequence. To what extent this actually represents a sermon cannot be determined. (In Luke the parallel sayings are found in several different places throughout the gospel.) There is no question, however, that Matthew intended this teaching to carry great authority, for it is given on a mountain. That is to say it stands as the Christian equivalent to the teaching given by Moses from the mountain in Sinai (Exod. 19—34).

The "old tradition" refers not only to that ancient revelation given on Mt. Sinai, but also to the oral tradition which had grown up around the law of Moses. There are six references to the old tradition in the Sermon on the Mount (5:21, 27, 31, 33, 38, and 43). These are introduced by the phrase "it was said." Jesus introduces his own understanding of the law with the phrase "but I say to you." These are technical phrases used in the transmission and interpretation of tradition. Jesus repeats the tradition as he received it and then gives his interpretation. Jesus did not do away with the Jewish law. He did not say, "The Jewish law is one thing but the 'Christian' quite another." Rather he gave a new understanding of the ancient law, an understanding which became the Christian teaching on such matters. Because Jesus did so reinterpret the law, we then can understand his insistence that every jot and tittle of the law would be fulfilled (Matt. 5:17-18). For the most part Jesus emphasizes the intention rather than the act. So, for example, Moses forbade murder, but Jesus says anger has the same effect.

In this passage we hear Moses forbade adultery, but Jesus says anyone who keeps looking with desire has already done it. In another comparison with Judaism, Jesus says the Jews allowed divorce, but he says divorce, especially remarriage, creates adultery.

The Greek makes it clear that the admonitions are addressed to the man, or husband. It is the man who looks at the woman with desire, and it is the man who errs if he divorces his wife. The teaching on divorce occurs frequently in the New Testament (Matt. 19:1-12; Mark 10:2-12; 1 Cor. 7:10-11). In both Mark and 1 Corinthians there is an additional admonition directed toward the wife. Presumably Matthew was written in a social milieu where women could not have initiated a separation.

For both Jesus and Paul the key to righteousness lies in the wholeness of relationship rather than obedience to outward laws. That is
why Jesus could say anger destroys relationships as surely as does
murder. In the same way adultery was defined by law as illicit
intercourse, but Jesus defined it as continued desire for someone
other than your spouse. (If a single moment of attraction had been
meant, the Greek aorist tense would have been used.) If adultery is
defined as multiple primary sexual alliances, then the continued
desire would be as much adultery as intercourse itself.

The "cut it off" passages come from a series of apocalyptic "better
than" sayings found primarily in Mark 9:42-50. "Better than" sayings
are found throughout Hebrew wisdom literature. One thinks, for
example, of a saying like Ecclesiastes 4:6, "*Better* is a handful of
quietness *than* two hands full of toil and a striving after wind." But in
the New Testament and Jewish intertestamental writings, "better
than" sayings became unreal end-time threats. It would be better for
some terrible thing to happen to you than for you to do this unethical
action. The millstone saying and the cut it off or pluck it out sayings
(Mark 9:42-50) belong to this category. According to the Jesus tradition
it would be better to avoid or eliminate a problem than to let it destroy
you. The issue is not so much avoidance of temptation as it is to break
those patterns which might destroy relationships.

Since, for the Jesus tradition, the source of ethics lies in primary or
covenant relationships (rather than law), divorce does not become an
option. We must be very careful here. To say that divorce is not an
option means that a primary relationship like marriage cannot be
erased. According to the Judeo-Christian perception of life, we are
created as persons by family and close social relationships. One does
not jettison the process of learning which occurs in these ties. We work
through them. So honoring mother and father is a way of saying that
we must deal with the context that has created us. The same is true of
marriage. This primary relationship cannot be dissolved. Even if legal
divorce does occur, the relationship will not have been erased. It
cannot be.

If that is true then any separation of a wife and husband must be
done with the awareness that the "two have become one flesh" (see
the parallel passage in Matt. 19:3-9). Furthermore, any remarriage of
either husband or wife means that the new partner marries also the
original spouse. That marriage of the second husband or wife to the
original pairing is called adultery by Jesus. So a husband who divorces his wife causes her to be an adulteress when she remarries.
And a man who marries a divorced woman commits adultery with

her (causes her to form two primary relationships). Other texts say the same of the wife (Mark 10:12).

Of all the New Testament texts on the subject of divorce, only this one includes the famous exclusion clause: except for unchastity. The clause has been widely used as the one exception to the rule of no divorce. If that is true then the author of Matthew has misunderstood the Judeo-Christian understanding of marriage and "one flesh." Furthermore, such a legal approach to the marriage relationship contradicts what we have learned in the Sermon on the Mount about friends (5:21-26), men and women (5:27-31), power (5:33-37), and even enemies (5:38-48). For these reasons some readers suspect the so-called exception has been added at a later date to help Christians in a legal setting. The BNT translation keeps the clause but attaches it to a probable remarriage, not divorce. So the wife who divorces an unchaste husband does not cause him to commit adultery when he remarries. He has already done that.

The early church held so tightly to this view of marriage that even loss of a partner by death did not warrant a remarriage. Paul urges widowers and widows not to remarry but concedes it might be better than to confuse relationships in the faith community (1 Cor. 7:8-11).

The Text in Brethren Life

Alexander Mack (1679-1735), the leader of the first eight Brethren baptized in 1708, wrote about marriage and divorce in his *Rights and Ordinances* (1715). While he does not mention Matthew 5:27-32, he does quote Matthew 19:4-5 to show that God instituted marriage. It is clear from Mack's writings that marriage is for life. Separation is permitted only if an unbelieving spouse initiated it or if the unbelieving spouse "were to break out into all kinds of outrage and adultery."[1] When separation occurs under such circumstances, the believer is not permitted to remarry. Mack's primary text for his views on marriage and divorce is 1 Corinthians 7.

Between 1789 and 1907, many articles appeared in the minutes of Annual Meeting concerning marriage, divorce, remarriage, adultery, and fornication. In three instances Matthew 5:32 is cited and in one instance the verse is quoted. Article 8 of the 1842 Annual Meeting minutes states: "Considered, that according to the Word of God, Matt. 5:32; 19:3-10; Mark 10:2-12; Luke 16:18, and 1 Cor. 7:10, 11, 39, a person cannot marry again while the first companion lives, and that the

Gospel condemns not only the person that would marry again after being divorced, but also the person who would marry the divorced party."[2] In article 10 of the 1860 minutes, verse 32 is quoted to support the idea that a person cannot obtain a divorce for any cause except *fornication* (KJV). The 1898 Annual Meeting cited verse 32 to reaffirm that fornication is the only grounds for divorce and then went on to indicate that the church could accept as a member a person who remarries after a divorce if that person was the innocent party in a divorce due to fornication. This was a major shift from the earlier understanding that remarriage was not permitted on any ground after divorce. Finally, in 1902, Annual Meeting interpreted the word *fornication* in Matthew 5:32 to apply to both married and single persons.

The 1898 shift in attitude about divorce and remarriage was not popular with all Brethren. In 1899 Isaac J. Rosenberger (1842-1923), a noted Brethren evangelist, published a booklet at his own expense titled *An Exegesis on Marriage and Divorce*. Rosenberger's purpose in publishing the booklet was to show that the Annual Meeting decision of 1898 was not biblical. In particular he argues that the verb *put away* in Matthew 5:32 (KJV) does not mean the same thing as divorce. In the preceding verse (31), Jesus quoted the law of Moses which permitted divorce, but the law of Christ does not permit divorce. Says Rosenberger: "Moses' law had divorce following the putting away; but Christ's law is the putting away for one cause [fornication]; with no provision for divorce; divorce is not even implied."[3] Christ does not permit divorce, according to Rosenberger, so as to allow for reconciliation between the husband and wife (1 Cor. 7:11). Obviously if divorce is not permitted, then remarriage under any circumstances is not a question to be considered.

In 1932 Annual Conference was asked again to consider the question of divorce and remarriage. A committee of three was appointed to report back the next year. In their report, which was passed by the 1933 conference, they cited Matthew 5:27-32 as one of Jesus' teachings on divorce. The report had three major sections. The first section affirmed the position that Jesus forbids divorce and remarriage. In the second section the church is called to uphold the sacredness of marriage. The third section deals with the exceptions, particularly with the question of whether divorced persons who remarry while their former spouse is still living can be received as members of the church. The report indicates that such persons may be members of the church if they show evidence of repentance. However, neither they nor the divorced person who does not remarry are eligible for the offices of deacon or minister. This position is based on 1 Timothy 3:2, 12 and Titus 1:6. The report concludes with this sentence: "In receiving or retaining such persons as members, the church is not ignoring the Christian ideal of marriage but is making an exception for the truly repentant, giving them the advantage of church membership and commending them to the mercy, love and grace of God—as it seems evident that the apostolic church sometimes did."[4]

By the mid-twentieth century, the 1933 conference action no longer reflected Brethren practices or understandings. In 1962 two queries came to Annual Conference asking for a new study of divorce and remarriage. One of the queries specifically stated that the practices among Brethren pastors varied as to who would officiate at the remarriage of a divorced person. Furthermore, the query stated that "refusal to remarry divorced persons most frequently prevents the church from exercising its redemptive ministry."[5] In response to the queries, a committee of five was appointed. The committee reported at the 1963 conference, but the report was recommitted. An in-depth report was presented and approved at the 1964 conference. In the '64 report both Matthew 5:27-32 and 19:3-9 are included among the biblical teachings on divorce and remarriage. The report emphasizes that Jesus' words in the two Matthew texts must be understood in the context of the fact that the Pharisees were attempting to trap Jesus in their own debate over Jewish laws. Furthermore, the report calls for the Brethren to understand Jesus' words in light of the whole mind of Christ, which includes compassion for those who break the law (John 8:2-11). With these understandings the report affirms marriage as lifelong and indissoluble and then goes on to recognize the possibility of divorce and remarriage. Conditions are given to guide pastors as to when they might perform a marriage involving a divorced person. These include (1) evidence of the divorced person's penitence, (2) evidence that the couple is committed to true Christian marriage, and (3) continued opportunity for the pastor to provide guidance after the marriage. The report also outlines a premarital counseling program in the church and calls for improved educational resources on Christian marriage.

At the 1977 conference a paper titled "Marriage and Divorce" was adopted. This paper was prepared by a committee of five and basically affirms the positions on divorce and remarriage in the 1964 paper. No mention is made in the paper of Matthew 5:27-32. There is, however, a special emphasis on the theological understanding of marriage, particularly its covenantal nature. In the section on divorce and remarriage, there is a special call for church members to support the people involved rather than be judgmental. "The task of individual church members is to surround the divorcing persons with love and concern. Divorce as a tragedy is not to be judged, but is to be seen with sorrow and compassion . . . . We . . . urge members of the church to be loving rather than judgmental with regard to remarriage."[6]

In the "Human Sexuality from a Christian Perspective" paper, adopted by the 1983 Annual Conference, Matthew 5:28 is cited twice. These two citations occur in the section on married persons and sexuality. In both cases verse 28 is used to affirm that fidelity in marriage is "a matter of attitude as well as action."[7]

A detailed survey of divorce and remarriage up to 1969 is found in a two-part article by Eugene F. Roop titled "The Brethren and Church Discipline." While Roop's primary concern in the article is church discipline, he uses divorce and remarriage as a case study on discipline. In his discussion of divorce and remarriage, Roop points out the key role played by both Matthew 5:28 and 5:32. While the Brethren of the nineteenth century were fairly consistent in not allowing divorced persons to be members of the church, verse 32 did not permit them to make the practice into an absolute law. Furthermore, verse 28, coupled with 1 Corinthians 7:15, "forced the Brethren to moderate their position on divorce."[8] Thus it was due in part to the biblical text that queries kept coming to Annual Meetings in the nineteenth and twentieth centuries and the Brethren kept modifying their position.

Notes

1. Alexander Mack, *Rights and Ordinances*, in *European Origins of the Brethren*, comp. and trans. Donald F. Durnbaugh (Elgin, IL: Brethren Press, 1958), 392.

2. *Classified Minutes of the Annual Meetings of the Brethren: A History of the General Councils of the Church from 1778 to 1885* (Mt. Morris, IL: The Brethren's Publishing Company, 1886), 220-21.

3. Isaac J. Rosenberger, *An Exegesis on Marriage and Divorce* (Covington, OH: the author, 1899), 11.

4. *Minutes of the Annual Conferences of the Church of the Brethren, 1923-1944*, comp. and ed. H. L. Hartsough, J. E. Miller, Ora W. Garber (Elgin, IL: Brethren Publishing House, 1946), 97.

5. *Minutes of the Annual Conferences of the Church of the Brethren, 1955-1964*, comp. and ed. Ora W. Garber (Elgin, IL: Brethren Press, 1965), 319.

6. *Minutes of the Annual Conference of the Church of the Brethren, 1975-1979*, comp. Phyllis Kingery Ruff (Elgin, IL: Brethren Press, 1980), 305.

7. *Minutes of the Annual Conference of the Church of the Brethren, 1980-1984*, comp. Phyllis Kingery Ruff (Elgin, IL: Brethren Press, 1985), 582.

8. Eugene F. Roop, "The Brethren and Church Discipline (I)," *Brethren Life and Thought* 14 (Spring 1969): 101.

The Text in Today's World

The reader of the Bible must be careful to discern the kind of material being read. While most would agree that everything in the Bible has some relevance for us in our time, not everything has the same value or authority. Nor is the relevance the same throughout. The average reader knows this. Christians may (or may not) read the sections on sacrifice or priestly dress in Exodus and Leviticus and are aware that the sections are not immediately applicable to them as Christians in the twentieth century. Other passages deal with problems specific to that time and, therefore, must be applied in an indirect way. For example, we do not have food offered to idols (1 Cor. 8), but we do have other practices which can divide us.

We need to be particularly thoughtful when we read the Sermon on the Mount. Through the centuries a number of Christians have read the Sermon as a new Christian law. Others have rejected the Sermon on the Mount because, in their mind, no one could measure up to its highly demanding ethic (for example, the "interim ethic" proposed by Albert Schweitzer). The Lutheran tradition, taking the Sermon as law, tends to say Jesus gave it to us to make us know the depth of our sin. In that way we are ready to receive the grace of God given on the cross.

For others this seems to be a misunderstanding of law. Neither the revelation on Mount Sinai nor the Sermon on the Mount should be considered legally. Both are descriptions of reality rather than community laws. Scholars sometimes call such laws apodictic. There is no specific punishment connected with them. They simply describe the basic truths about covenantal life (ontological descriptions). So one cannot exist in the community if one disregards primary formation (honoring parents). One cannot live in covenant and, at the same time, murder a covenant partner. No penalty is mentioned, but a truth has been stated.

Though words of Jesus may be sharper than those of Moses, the same is true of the Sermon on the Mount. The basic statements are truths rather than laws. To be sure, murder still destroys covenant relations, but so does disdain, prejudice, and hatred.

The teaching of Jesus about divorce and remarriage fits in this category. It is a truth, not so much a law, that divorce is impossible. When a man and woman leave their primary formation community, they create a new community (one flesh). Just as one cannot disregard one's primary community (parents), neither can one void the secondary (marriage) community. What happens between a husband and wife cannot be erased.

I sometimes use my own marriage as an example. As a young man I was considered, and tested out as, a musical ignoramus. But I married someone who loves music. Over the years she has instilled in me a love for opera and symphonies that otherwise had been missing. If something happened to her, that love of operas and symphonies would not disappear. She has re-formed me. If I wished to remarry, that re-formation would still be a part of me. Or, to put it crassly, anyone who married me would also marry Lois.

The teaching of Jesus and the earliest church expresses this truth about marriage. It speaks very much to our day. We are troubled by a mindset which supposes people can walk into relationship and then walk away. When we understand that we are who we are because of those close relationships in which we are involved, then we realize that they cannot be erased.

Such teaching is not a law. We all know of marriages which do not and possibly cannot work. The intimate relationship may destroy rather than enhance. As an example, a young man may want a mother, perhaps, and a young woman may want a little boy. If they marry they may only perpetuate a thwarted childhood. Unless someone were wise enough to discourage the marriage, it may be divorce will be the only solution. Nevertheless, according to the words of Jesus, they have become one flesh. That is, their personalities have been re-formed in a negative way. If they divorce, that negative re-enforcement will still be there. Divorce will not in itself "cure" the problem. Indeed, in remarriage both parties will carry the difficulties with them, and both new partners will "marry" the old disastrous marriage. Christians may find it necessary to be divorced, or even to remarry, but it defies reality to do so without full awareness of what it means to be one flesh.

If, on the other hand, persons who were joined in a negative marriage can form other redemptive relationships, as in the faith community, then what was negative may be altered. In such redemptive situations the divorced person may enter a new marriage with grace and hope.

Case Study

A man who previously had not been a Christian asked to be baptized into a congregation in Illinois. When he made the decision to become a Christian, his common-law wife, also not a Christian, left him. About two years later the man asked the pastor of the congregation to marry him and a woman of that same congregation. She had not been previously married. Up to that time, the congregation had not allowed a remarriage of two of its own members to be consecrated by the pastor and the congregation. In its discussion of the issue, the church's executive committee raised the following questions:

1. Do the words of Jesus about divorce and remarriage apply to this case?

2. Had the man actually been married?

3. Regardless of the answer to the second question, should the man be counseled as if he had been married?

4. Should the woman be counseled as if her husband-to-be had been previously married and divorced? What would that mean?

5. Did the church have an obligation to the common-law wife who still lived in the community?

What do you think, and what decision would you have made?

Session 2

On Taking Oaths

Matthew 5:33-37 (NRSV)

"Again, you have heard that it was said to those of ancient times, 'You shall not swear falsely, but carry out the vows you have made to the Lord.' [34]But I say to you, Do not swear at all, either by heaven, for it is the throne of God, [35]or by the earth, for it is his footstool, or by Jerusalem, for it is the city of the great King. [36]And do not swear by your head, for you cannot make one hair white or black. [37]Let your word be 'Yes, Yes' or 'No, No'; anything more than this comes from the evil one."

Matthew 5:33-37 (BNT)

"Again you have heard that it was said in the old tradition, 'Do not perjure yourself, but keep any oath taken in the name of the Lord.' [34]But my position is that you should not swear at all, neither by heaven, because that is the throne of God; [35]nor by earth, because that is his footstool; nor by Jerusalem, because it is the city of the great Ruler. [36]Nor should you swear by your head, because you are not able to make one hair white or black. [37]But let your word be, 'Yes, that is true,' or 'No, it is not.' Anything more than that would be demonic."

The Text in Its Biblical Setting

Since the "old tradition" (again you have heard in the old tradition, v. 33) was a living tradition at the time of Jesus, we cannot expect to find the precise form of the statement on oath-taking in the Hebrew Scriptures. However, the original form surely was Leviticus 19:12 and possibly Numbers 30:2 or Deuteronomy 23:21-23. These texts deal with perjury-falsification under oath. Jesus reinterprets the tradition to mean there should be no oathtaking at all.

What follows then in verses 34b-36 admittedly confuses the issue. Having advised us not to take *any* kind of oath, Jesus then proceeds to enumerate specifically which oaths are unacceptable. Presumably, what he mentions must be oaths taken by Jews at that time. We know from contemporary literature (the Shebu'oth in the Talmud) that Jewish teachers were much concerned about the form of an oath and its binding nature. Apparently most verbal agreements were sealed with an oath. Any oath or vow made to the Lord was, of course, totally binding. But oaths taken on other things apparently were less certain. Jesus points out that nothing escapes the involvement of God. Anything in heaven is God's because that is the location of the court of God (Job 1:6-7); anything on earth is God's because the earth is subject to God's will (Psa. 8:6). Presumably the reference to both heaven and earth, so frequent in the Gospel of Matthew (6:10, 19-20; 16:19; 18:18) would cover all possibilities, and James' version of this saying leaves it at that (Jas. 5:12). But here Jesus mentions two more: an oath on the future (the new Jerusalem), which, however, belongs totally in the hands of God; or an oath on one's own self, which also lies outside our own control and, therefore, is useless as the guarantee of an oath. (An example of an oath on one's self might be: May my hair turn gray if . . . .)

Verse 37 returns to the original concern. Jesus advocated abolishing oath-taking altogether. The parallel passage in James 5:12 indicates this was indeed the concern rather than perjury or false witness. Jesus is saying that persons should always be true to themselves and others. There are no occasions when dishonesty or ambivalence are appropriate. That being true, there are no occasions when one might say, "This time I am telling the truth, I swear to it." Persons who are decisive to God and to each other can say simply "yes" or "no" without equivocating.

In intertestamental Judaism and early Christianity, it was popularly supposed that there were two urges in each of us: one to do right and one to do wrong. When faced with a decision, the important task is to know the difference between the way of life and the way of death. And one must have the will to say "yes" to the good impulse and "no" to the evil impulse. Not to know the difference is sinful and to waver would be disaster. James speaks of such wavering persons as double-minded (1:8; see Session 23). Jesus speaks of them as persons whose vision does not point to a single goal (Matt. 6:23) or as persons who attempt to serve two masters (Matt. 6:24). The Christian is one who has a singleness of purpose, knows the will of God, and is true to it. In relating to other persons, the Christian can express that same honesty and decisiveness. The inability to say "yes" or "no" means that a person is living under the influence of the evil impulse or the evil one. And persistent fluctuation or indecisiveness destroys one's credibility and trustworthiness so that the community itself can be destroyed. Jesus says such lack of singlemindedness comes from the evil one. It is therefore demonic.

The Text in Brethren Life

From their beginnings the Brethren have objected to the practice of swearing an oath as proof that one is telling the truth or as assurance that one will abide by an agreement. Alexander Mack (1679-1735) writes in his *Rights and Ordinances* (1715) that a government can depend more upon citizens who affirm with yes and deny with no than upon citizens who insist upon swearing oaths. Refusal to swear the oath, according to Mack, is "in accordance with the teaching of Christ."[1] Without doubt Mack was basing his position on Matthew 5:34-37.

During the American Revolution the oath of allegiance required by state governments presented problems for Brethren. These problems, however, had more to do with the Brethren beliefs concerning the relationship of church and state (see session 6) than with the Brethren refusal to swear an oath, since the law allowed a person to affirm the oath instead of swearing.[2] Even so, in 1785, only two years after the revolution, Annual Meeting specifically referred to Matthew 5:37 when dealing with the issue of oaths: "As to the swearing of oaths, we believe the word of Christ, that in all things which we are to testify, we shall testify what is yea, or what is true with yea, and what is nay, or not true with nay; for whatsoever is more than these cometh of evil."[3]

Peter Nead (1796-1877), the leading Brethren theologian of the nineteenth century, quotes Matthew 5:33-37 in the section on swearing oaths in *Primitive Christianity* (1834), his first major publication. After the quote Nead states that the commandment is so plain as to need no further comment and then expresses astonishment that so many Christians either overlook or willfully disobey the commandment.[4] Lewis Teeter (1845-1927), the only Brethren to publish an entire commentary on the New Testament (1894), presents the Brethren doctrine on swearing oaths in his comments on Matthew 5:33-37. Teeter understands verse 33 as a command to avoid swearing falsely and verse 34 as a command to avoid swearing oaths at all. In commenting on verse 37, he says that the Christian is to testify to the truth rather than perform any kind of oath.[5]

One of the most detailed discussions of the Brethren objection to the swearing of oaths is found in a tract by S. Z. Sharp (1835-1931) titled "Are Christians Allowed to Swear?"[6] Sharp, a Brethren educator who served as the first president of McPherson College, uses as his texts Matthew 5:33-37 and James 5:12. According to Sharp these texts have nothing to do with the subject of profanity. Furthermore, he states that they do not apply to anyone who is not a professed Christian. Sharp understands the two texts as commands from the Savior forbidding the Christian to swear any kind of oath. To prove this he states and refutes three arguments used by some to condone the swearing of oaths. Then he presents four arguments to prove that a Christian should not swear. The major thrust of the four arguments is that the law of Christ forbids the Christian to swear an oath, even in a court of law.

Otho Winger (1877-1946), who was president of Manchester College for thirty years, uses Matthew 5:33-37 as the basis for the Brethren objection to the taking of a civil oath in his book *History and Doctrines of the Church of the Brethren* (1920). Winger ends his discussion of oaths with the following observation: "The Brethren have generally been noted for their truthfulness and their honor for their word. It was formerly said that 'a brother's word was as good as his bond.' It is a matter of regret that the betrayal of this trust on the part of many has caused the respect for all to suffer."[7]

Vernard Eller, writing about the Brethren belief of integrity in *Church of the Brethren Past and Present* (1971), begins by quoting the slogan "A Dunker's word is as good as his bond." According to Eller the Brethren refusal to swear oaths is an attempt to live out the demands of Christian discipleship. This refusal is based upon three questions of integrity: "(1) whether the state has either the competence or authority to administer oaths in the name of God . . . ; (2) whether an oath commands any power either to help one to tell the truth or to guarantee that what he is telling is the truth; (3) whether what oath-taking implies is legitimate, namely that integrity is obligatory only under special conditions." Eller concludes by saying: "The Christian's commitment to integrity is part and parcel of his commitment to discipleship, and the integrity he shows he credits to the help of Christ; to grant status to an oath is to confuse the truth of this situation."[8]

Dale W. Brown, in *Church of the Brethren: Yesterday and Today* (1986), includes a discussion of oaths among the Brethren ordinances derived from admonitions in the New Testament. He points out that some Brethren have come to feel that legalistically following these ordinances creates a contemporary Phariseeism. Others, however, regard them as having instructional and symbolic value. Specifically concerning the refusal to swear an oath, Brown states: "More than literalistic adherence to the letter has been involved. More basic has been the pedagogical and symbolic value of pointing to a style of basic integrity, a higher allegiance than civil authority, and to the refusal to compartmentalize the sacred from the secular."[9]

The most recent Brethren writing concerning the swearing of oaths is found in Harold S. Martin's *New Testament Beliefs and Practices (A Brethren Understanding)*, 1989. In this book Martin elaborates on Brethren beliefs and practices as found in the 1923 summary which became known as the Brethren's Card. This summary includes opposition to "every form of oath" and cites Matthew 5:33-37 and James 5:12 as the biblical basis. Interestingly, Martin, unlike Sharp, understands Matthew 5:34 as prohibiting profanity as well as the taking of a civil oath.[10]

Notes

1. Alexander Mack, *Rights and Ordinances,* in *European Origins of the Brethren,* comp. and trans. Donald F. Durnbaugh (Elgin, IL: Brethren Press, 1958), 376.

2. Donald F. Durnbaugh and Dennis D. Martin, eds. *Brethren Encyclopedia* (Philadelphia: The Brethren Encyclopedia, Inc., 1983), s.v. "Revolutionary War, American," by Donald F. Durnbaugh.

3. *Minutes of the Annual Meetings of the Church of the Brethren, 1778-1909* (Elgin, IL: Brethren Publishing House, 1909), 10.

4. Peter Nead, *Primitive Christianity, or a Vindication of the Word of God* (Staunton, VA: Kenton Harper, Printer, 1834), 109-110.

5. Lewis W. Teeter, *New Testament Commentary* (Mount Morris, IL: The Brethren's Publishing Company, 1894), 1:24-25.

6. S. Z. Sharp, "Are Christians Allowed to Swear?" in *The Brethren's Tracts and Pamphlets* (Elgin, IL: Brethren Publishing House, 1900), Tract No. 275.

7. Otho Winger, *History and Doctrines of the Church of the Brethren* (Elgin, IL: Brethren Publishing House, 1920), 220.

8. Vernard Eller, "Beliefs," in *Church of the Brethren Past and Present,* ed. Donald F. Durnbaugh (Elgin, IL: Brethren Press, 1971), 48-49.

9. Dale W. Brown, "Worship," in *Church of the Brethren: Yesterday and Today,* ed. Donald F. Durnbaugh (Elgin, IL: Brethren Press, 1986), 73.

10. Harold S. Martin, *New Testament Beliefs and Practices (A Brethren Understanding)* (Elgin, IL: Brethren Press, 1989), 89-91.

The Text in Today's World

The saying on oath-taking has suffered considerable loss of influence over the years for at least two reasons. First, as has been noted, there exists some confusion about the direction of the text, because it speaks both about taking oaths and about general integrity in speech. At times Brethren have stressed honesty and integrity. But the second reason for the demise of the text's influence would be more important. As shown in the discussion of the text in its biblical setting, Jesus' prohibition of oaths was set in a community context. Jesus called for integrity in speech because lack of integrity can and does destroy that trust which is necessary for a covenantal society. But over the years we have lost the social dimension of the text. We have made of it a point of personal piety not to take an oath. Consequently, governmental agencies have printed forms to accommodate those of us who will not "swear." And we have often reduced the call to social integrity to simply the personal virtue of retelling the facts of the case.

If we return to the original intention of the passage, it does indeed have a number of things to say to our time. Some of these have already been noted in the section on Brethren use of the text. First, the passage calls for a consistency in speech and conversation which does not allow the possibility of an oath or any indication that now (for sure) the truth will be told. There should be no occasion when we could say, "Now I am really giving it to you straight." The importance of speaking the truth consistently does not derive from a sense of our own "purity" but from being known to the social community as a person who would not interpret data in a way that is destructive to the social fabric.

Secondly, the prohibition against vows taken on lesser elements of the creation such as Jerusalem or the Temple means that we, too, should not fall into the trap of giving ultimate significance (as in vows) to lesser things. For example we ought not assign godlike status to the state. From time to time and place to place, persons who work for the government are asked to make an oath of allegiance. The Christian cannot give ultimate allegiance to the state and so would not take or support such "vows."

Finally, we need to recognize the saving effect of community honesty. Persons can be destroyed because no one had the courage or the love to speak to them honestly. In Jesus Christ, God encountered us with truth. We too should encounter each other in "truth spoken in love." The failure of the church to speak honestly has created the necessity for other support groups such as Alcoholics Anonymous, Single Parents, and other group-process structures to help people discover openness in human relationships. But this is a church function which the Brethren have practiced in the past. In a community where love is present it is possible to speak openly of attitudes, habits and actions which hurt the person and the community. In terms of Matthew 5:33-37, that would be integrity of speech.

Case Study

A Jewish organization recently recognized a Polish woman now living in the United States. During World War II, as a teen-age girl in Poland, she saved the lives of at least four Jews who escaped from Auschwitz. She hid them under the barn floor and slipped food to them every day. In order to do that she falsified ration requests and even took excess food from her family without their knowledge. Several times she had to tell German officers she had seen no escapees. For her daring and compassion, she was honored as a heroine.

1. Was this a case where falsification was necessary and right?

2. Does falsification for even a good reason create patterns of living in untruth?

3. Under what conditions would you consider it right to falsify?

4. Does swearing or affirming to tell the truth have meaning for you? If you felt it necessary to falsify, would you also tell an untruth under "oath" (perjure yourself)?

On Retaliation

Matthew 5:38-48 (NRSV)

"You have heard that it was said, 'An eye for an eye and a tooth for a tooth.' [39]But I say to you, Do not resist an evildoer. But if anyone strikes you on the right cheek, turn the other also; [40]and if anyone wants to sue you and take your coat, give your cloak as well; [41]and if anyone forces you to go one mile, go also the second mile. [42]Give to everyone who begs from you, and do not refuse anyone who wants to borrow from you. [43]You have heard that it was said, 'You shall love your neighbor and hate your enemy.' [44]But I say to you, Love your enemies and pray for those who persecute you, [45]so that you may be children of your Father in heaven; for he makes his sun rise on the evil and on the good, and sends rain on the righteous and on the unrighteous. [46]For if you love those who love you, what reward do you have? Do not even the tax collectors do the same? [47]And if you greet only your brothers and sisters, what more are you doing than others? Do not even the Gentiles do the same? [48]Be perfect, therefore, as your heavenly Father is perfect."

Matthew 5:38-48 (BNT)

"You have heard that it was said, 'An eye for an eye and a tooth for a tooth.' [39]But my position is that you should not try to even the score when someone provokes you. But if anyone hits you on the right cheek, risk a slap on the other cheek too. [40]And if someone sues you for your coat, offer in addition your undergarment. [41]And if anyone forces you to go one mile, go an extra mile as well. [42]Give to the one who asks you, and do not turn down the one who wants to borrow money from you.

[43]"You have heard that it was said, 'Love your neighbor and hate your enemy.' [44]But my position is: Love your enemies and pray for those who persecute you. [45]In that way you become children of your heavenly Father, for his sun shines on the evil as well as the good, and he sends as much rain for the unrighteous as for the righteous. [46]For if you love all those who love you, what

good does that do you? Tax collectors would do even that, would they not? [47] And if you love members of your family only, what is so great about that? Even the unbelievers would do that, would they not? [48] So be openhearted to all, as your heavenly Father is openhearted to all."

The Text in Its Biblical Setting

The text Matthew 5:38–48 includes the last two of the six reinterpretations ("but I say to you . . . ") given by Jesus in the Sermon on the Mount. In biblical literature a series of sayings or teachings such as these often has a meaning which is more than the meaning of each individual saying. We can notice this especially in the prophets. For example, in Amos 6:4-7 we find a series of items such as "lying on beds of ivory" or "singing idle songs," which define Amos 6:1 ("those who are at ease in Zion"). Quite probably the wealthy of Zion did do such things, and quite likely Amos would have been happy if they ceased engaging in such activities. But that is not his primary point. At the end of the series, Amos says that the wealthy have no concern for the ruin of the house of Joseph (6:6b), and *that* is the crucial issue. Each element of the series has meaning, but the larger meaning can be seen only at the end of the series.

It is highly likely the six reinterpretations in Matthew 5 have the same intent. Each has meaning, but there is a progression of meaning which finally culminates in the last verse (5:48). A summary of the six sections of Matthew 5:21-48 indicates we are dealing with such a progression on several levels:

Verses 21-26: How people within the community of faith deal with conflict.

Verses 27-30: How people within the community of faith deal with seduction.

Verses 31-32: The integrity of the family within the community of faith.

Verses 33-37: The integrity of people within the community of faith.

Verses 38–42: How *individuals* within the community of faith deal with antagonism from people outside the community of faith.

Verses 43-47: How the *community* of faith deals with people and groups antagonistic to itself.

At least two progressions are immediately apparent. One is that the first four reinterpretations deal with the internal life of the community and the last two deal with conflicts between the faithful and "outsiders." Secondly, there is a progression from two reinterpretations dealing with the community as a whole, to the two dealing with families and individuals in the community, to the one dealing with individuals in relation to "outsiders," to the concluding section dealing with the whole community in relation to other types of communities. Both progressions lead to the same point: Ultimate godlikeness lies in the grace to treat all persons with respect and love. The point of the final teaching surely catches up the intent of the other five. Consequently, we should look to 5:48 as the verse providing the key for interpreting the entire section 5:21–47.

The fifth reinterpretation (vv. 38-42) involves the law of retaliation (*lex talionis*). This law embodies a very ancient system of justice found often in the Old Testament. It occurs almost precisely in this form in Exodus 21:24 and Leviticus 24:20. The function of the law of retaliation was to prevent excessive violence. There was no attempt to reconcile the conflicting parties, but only to keep the injured party from seeking unlimited revenge. The need for a law of retaliation is expressed in the story of Lamech, who killed a young man for scratching him (Gen. 4:23). Under the law of retaliation, Lamech would have been severely punished for exacting a penalty out of proportion to the offense committed. The law of retaliation seems crude but when followed would serve to prevent the violence of feuds and wars. Nevertheless, Jesus asked for more. His position was that we should not even try to exact revenge in a conflict situation.

Of considerable importance in verse 39 is the meaning of "evildoer" (NRSV). Since the underlying Greek word is preceded by a definite article (the), it cannot be evil in a general sense. It could refer to a corrupt or depraved person. But since the context is that of conflict with persons not of the community of faith, it seems more likely that the word translated evildoer refers simply to a person who has not responded to God. In Matthew 12:33-37, people who do not respond to God are called evil. A whole generation which refuses to repent can be called evil (Matt. 12:39). In 2 Thessalonians 3:2, persons who do not have faith are described as wicked and evil. Perhaps even more along the lines of the Sermon on the Mount, 2 Timothy 3:13 describes those who have left the faith as evil. We might therefore translate the words of Jesus: "Do not respond in kind to the provocations of those who are outside the community of faith."

Jesus then gives four successive examples of provocation: physical insult, legal action, political pressure, and financial rip-off. Again we are dealing with a series. Any one of these provocations could have happened to a Palestinian in Jesus' day. The real importance of the illustrations, however, is to point listeners to their own difficulties with persons who do not share their faith perspective. Whatever that situation might be, the faithful are to reject the route of seeking retaliation.

The sixth reinterpretation presents more difficulties. Nowhere in the Old Testament do we find a specific admonition to hate one's enemy. Apparently this was a problem contemporary with Jesus and the early church. "Hate" can mean the passion as we know it (Tit. 3:3), but more than likely it is used here in a religious sense of "rejection." "Love" is loyal following while "hate" is rejection and disobedience (Matt. 6:24; John 15:23). To reject a certain style of life is to hate it (Rom. 7:15). The world disdains Christians, therefore they are hated (Matt. 24:9; John 15:19). It may be necessary for Christians to reject (hate) their parental religion (Luke 14:26). And above all, Christians must reject (hate) their own self-interests (John 12:25; Luke 14:26).

What Jesus is saying then in 5:43 is: "You have heard that you should love those in your faith community and reject those who oppose your community." His reinterpretation of this tradition is that we are to love and pray for those who oppose us, showing them the same signs of friendship (love, greeting) as shown to a neighbor (member of our own community). The reason for this is that God does not act selectively, but treats all alike (Job 40:10-14; Acts 10:34). True disciples, likewise, do not reject those who reject them but unilaterally treat all the same, thereby becoming sons and daughters of (that is, becoming like) God.

The passage ends with the formula from Leviticus 19:2: You shall be thus . . . for the Lord your God is thus. The term often translated "perfect" *(teleios)* also means complete or mature (Eph. 4:13; 1 Cor. 2:6). Here it means mature in the sense of discipleship developed beyond the point of protecting our own self-interests. We are to be "openhearted to all," even as God is.

The Text in Brethren Life

The first Brethren writer to discuss Matthew 5:38-48 systematically was Peter Nead (1796-1877). He begins his discussion by comparing the children of God to sheep. Like sheep they are harmless; like sheep they are clean; and like sheep they provide wool each year for their owners. The doctrine taught by Jesus, says Nead, does not allow Christians "to retaliate or seek redress for their grievances. Under the law, retaliation was allowable, but not so under the Gospel of Jesus Christ."[1] Nead understands verses 38-48 as statements of a Christian's duty toward all men and women, to be put into practice in everyday life. When faced with the question as to what a Christian might do when injured by another, Nead simply says that a Christian must suffer. That's what Christ had done, that's what all subjects of the kingdom have done through all the ages, and that's what anyone wishing to be a child of God must do. In answer to people who said that such an understanding of Matthew 5:38-48 meant that Christians are opposed to the civil powers, Nead says:

> Not so—for I say it is right, and agreeable to the will of God, that as long as there are lawless and disobedient persons on the earth, that there should exist a civil authority; and when I say that the children of God are not under the law, I mean that they are not to make use of the law, so as to compel any of their fellow mortals into measures, or to bring any of them unto punishment. No, no—the children of God must not take vengeance on any man. To establish this assertion, we have the precepts and examples of Jesus Christ and his apostles.[2]

Two notable Brethren practices based on the refusal to retaliate when injured (nonresistance) are: (1) the refusal to appeal to a court of law for redress of injuries; and (2) the refusal to take the life of another person for any reason (pacifism).

As early as 1810, Annual Meeting stated that Brethren were not permitted to use the law to collect a debt; and later Annual Meeting statements of the 1800s continued to uphold the practice of not going to law. At least twice in these statements, verses from Matthew 5:38-48 are cited. The 1844 meeting reaffirmed the understanding that Brethren could not collect a debt by going to court and cited Matthew 5:38 and following. Then, in 1869, a query asking, "How is it considered by the brethren, for a brother to take the benefit of the bankrupt law?" was answered thus: "Considered, not according to the gospel. Matt. 5:40; Luke 16:9.10."[3]

In 1920, however, the Brethren officially changed their position on the use and practice of law. Early in the 1920 statement, Matthew 5:40-41, as well as Luke 6:30, is cited to show that Jesus taught that if the legal process cannot be avoided, then the Christian should do more than required by law. Later in the statement Brethren are given permission to go to law with three cautions. First, Christian principles, such as nonresistance, are not to be violated. Second, one member should not go to law with another member except by common consent. Third, always the counsel of the church should be sought before going to law.

A classic story of a Brethren's refusal to retaliate by going to law is that of George Miller (1722-1798), a Brethren minister living in Pennsylvania before the American Revolution. Miller had one of his oxen stolen. He knew who had taken his ox, but he refused to sue for the return of the ox for fear the offender would suffer the retaliation which British law prescribed for a thief in such cases, a whipping. His neighbors, however, knowing the situation, had the thief arrested. When Miller heard of the arrest, he walked twenty miles to intercede for the thief and offered to provide the thief with warm bedding since the weather was cold and the jail was lacking.[4]

Due to the lack of written records, it is difficult to document that the Brethren were pacifists from the beginning. By the time of the American Revolution, however, the Brethren peace position is well documented. The minutes of various Annual Meetings record the problems which the Brethren, as pacifists, faced in a land at war. In fact, they were still dealing with these problems after the Revolution, since the first in-depth statement of the peace position comes from the 1785 minutes. Included among the texts cited as biblical basis in this statement is this reference to Matthew 5:39: "Thus our Savior had said before, 'That ye resist not evil'; for so he believed and thus he spake, and thus he did."[5]

Moving into the 1800s the Brethren continued to affirm their refusal to muster (do military training) and go to war on the basis of their nonresistance principles. The 1840 minutes state: "Considered, that training or mustering is a preparation for war, and since we are inclined to peace and a defenseless state, it would in no wise be proper nor allowable for brethren to learn war."[6] Again in 1845 the minutes read:

> In regard to our being altogether defenseless, not to withstand the evil, but over come evil with good, Considered, that the nearer we follow the bright example of the Lamb of God, who willingly suffered the cross, and prayed for his enemies; who, though heir of all things, had on earth not where to lay his head—the more we shall fulfill our high calling and obtain grace to deny ourselves for

Christ's and his gospel's sake, even to the loss of our property, our liberty, and our lives.[7]

Finally, in 1859, a query came to Annual Meeting asking if it would not be better to muster occasionally rather than pay a heavy fine. In response the meeting said: "It would not, in as much as our Lord and Savior teaches nonresistance in the gospel throughout. And when we go to muster we there learn the art of war, and the most appropriate method of shedding our fellow creatures's blood."[8]

A good example of how a Brethren applied Matthew 5:38-48 during the Civil War is found in the actions of B. F. Moomaw (1814-1900) of Virginia when a Confederate regiment camped on his farm. The regiment was directed to the Moomaw farm by some of his neighbors who hoped to embarrass the pacifist. Moomaw, however, set out to win the friendship of the men of the regiment. In good Brethren fashion he invited the officers of the regiment to dinner. Then, when a serious epidemic of measles broke out in the camp, the Moomaw family cared for the sick in their home. These services were, of course, provided in the spirit of the Sermon on the Mount, even though some of Moomaw's enemies circulated the story that Moomaw charged the regiment for his aid.[9]

Throughout the twentieth century the Brethren have continued to speak out against war. Major statements were adopted in 1918, 1934, 1948, and 1970. All of these statements, except 1934, include references to Matthew 5:38-48 or its parallel in Luke 6:27-36. The 1918 statement was adopted at the Goshen Conference, a special Annual Meeting that was held on January 9, 1918, to deal with the problems created by World War I for conscientious objectors. Included in the "Goshen Statement" is a section quoting New Testament texts on which the Brethren base their understanding that "participation in war is wrong." Among the texts are Matthew 5:43-45; Luke 6:27-35; and Matthew 5:38-39. The officers of the Goshen Conference were later threatened with prosecution by the US government because the statement advised young men not to put on the uniform or to drill. As a result, the officers withdrew the statement.

In 1934 the Annual Conference passed a resolution which included the now famous words: "All war is sin." This resolution, which does not include biblical texts, was reformulated the following year and adopted as "A Restatement Concerning War and Peace." A 1948 statement was prompted, in part, by the government's proposal to create a permanent military conscription during peace time. This statement quotes Matthew 5:44 as one of the teachings of Christ on which the Brethren base their resolve that all war is sin. Finally, the 1970 statement, adopted during the Vietnam War, quotes Luke 6:27-28 as one of Christ's teachings to which Brethren pacifism is tied.

Even though the Brethren have continued officially in the twentieth century to reaffirm their historic peace position and its biblical basis, a 1985 survey conducted by sociologist Carl Bowman indicates that a majority of the Brethren do not support this position. Specifically, 61 percent of those surveyed said they would either take combatant or noncombatant service if faced with the military draft. Only 34 percent would seek alternative service, and a mere 1 percent would refuse to register.[10]

In spite of Bowman's findings, the Brethren remain a peace church. Denominational programs under the auspices of a peace consultant keep peacemaking issues before church members. The continuation of Brethren Volunteer Service, which began in 1948, and the On Earth Peace Assembly, which began in 1974, indicate Brethren commitment to their historic peace position. Furthermore, the Brethren remain well-known in ecumenical circles for their peace and service programs.

Notes

1. Peter Nead, *Primitive Christianity, or a Vindication of the Word of God* (Staunton, VA: Kenton Harper, Printer, 1834), 99.

2. Ibid., 104-105.

3. *Minutes of the Annual Meetings of the Church of the Brethren, 1778-1909* (Elgin, IL: Brethren Publishing House, 1909), 279.

4. J. E. Miller, *Stories from Brethren Life* (Elgin, IL: Brethren Publishing House, 1942), 36-37.

5. Minutes of the Annual Meetings, 10.

6. Ibid., 70.

7. Ibid., 85.

8. Ibid., 187.

9. Miller, 146-148.

10. Carl Bowman, *Profile of the Church of the Brethren* (Elgin, IL: Brethren Press, n.d.), 8-9.

The Text in Today's World

Unlike the passage on oath-taking, the passage on retaliation has not shifted in meaning. It has been ignored and rejected, but its meaning has remained fairly clear. It calls for conflict resolution. If a conflict is not to end in the destruction of one or the other of two opponents, someone must have the courage to risk trying another way. In a conflict the Christian is the one who has the freedom to rise above self-interest and competition. The Christian is the one who can ask if there is not another way to solve the quarrel. This is precisely the meaning of the apocalyptic origin of Christianity: The old has come to an end and now there is a new possibility. We Christians speak of this end of the old and beginning of the new as the death and resurrection of Jesus Christ. So these words on retaliation come from the very heart of the Christian faith.

Matthew 5:38-42 also hints at the *method* we are to use in dealing with conflict. Provocations result in hostilities when the injured party believes the act demands reparations or retaliation. If a Roman soldier asks a Palestinian to carry his pack and the Palestinian decides to make an issue out of the grievance, then there is an escalation of the conflict. But if the Palestinian refuses to treat the provocation at face value and goes yet a second mile with the soldier, then the conflict nature of the situation has been defused. In a similar fashion, if a "hotrodder" on a modern expressway tailgates a slower car, the situation becomes perilous only if the slower driver decides to make it a contest of wills. If the slower driver refuses to respond in such a manner, the relationship between the two drivers remains cool and there is no immediate escalation of expressway warfare. On the surface, the approach which Jesus recommends may appear to be acquiescence or milksoppishness. But it is not. It is an aggressive action by which one party seeks to resolve conflict rather than redress grievances. Carrying a pack is not an insufferable burden, a slap on the cheek is not an unbearable insult, losing a lawsuit is not the end of the world, being panhandled does not have to destroy faith in humanity. A Christian's faith does not destruct so easily.

Because Jesus' approach requires individual decisions, it has often been supposed that his words are directed primarily to individuals, not groups. But this is a matter of appearance only. In group conflicts, people are urged to take unilateral actions. The decision may finally be personal, but the result is social. And in fact, the admonition to "love your enemy" is directed toward the group. Groups, or people in groups, are asked to act toward other groups or people as they act toward each other in their own group. Christians are urged to love their own but to extend that love to others as well.

Here is the heart of the Brethren peace position and political philosophy. In regard to peace, love of one's own family need not imply hatred for others. In regard to political life, we can hold strongly to our own position without detracting from the positions of others. This is the genuine pluralism which so marks the free church life. Just as 1708 was a time when most people settled differences by resorting to violence, so today in America the first impulse is to destroy those who differ from us and our kind. The words of Jesus come directly across the years: Love those who do not belong to your group.

Case Study

On a cold Sunday morning in northern Ohio, a visitor to the local Church of the Brethren, driving a Chevrolet, started to slide in the church parking lot and eventually struck a church member's Ford. The Ford was parked on the adjacent street. The driver of the Chevrolet was very sorry and offered the services of his insurance. The owner of the Ford, however, was incensed and called the police. The visitor was given a moving violation ticket. As a result of this and two previous violations he also lost his license for six months. Needless to say the visitor did not return to that particular church.

1. Would you have acted the same way as the driver of the Ford?

2. Could calling the police ever result in reconciliation?

3. Was there any way justice and reconciliation could have been achieved without retaliation?

4. Would, or should, the driver of the Ford have acted differently if the driver of the Chevrolet had been a member of the church?

Session 4

On Living Simply

Matthew 6:25-34 (NRSV)

"Therefore I tell you, do not worry about your life, what you will eat or what you will drink, or about your body, what you will wear. Is not life more than food, and the body more than clothing? [26]Look at the birds of the air; they neither sow nor reap nor gather into barns, and yet your heavenly Father feeds them. Are you not of more value than they? [27]And can any of you by worrying add a single hour to your span of life? [28]And why do you worry about clothing? Consider the lilies of the field, how they grow; they neither toil nor spin, [29]yet I tell you, even Solomon in all his glory was not clothed like one of these. [30]But if God so clothes the grass of the field, which is alive today and tomorrow is thrown into the oven, will he not much more clothe you—you of little faith? [31]Therefore do not worry, saying, 'What will we eat?' or 'What will we drink?' or 'What will we wear?' [32]For it is the Gentiles who strive for all these things; and indeed your heavenly Father knows that you need all these things. [33]But strive first for the reign of God and his righteousness, and all these things will be given to you as well. [34]So do not worry about tomorrow, for tomorrow will bring worries of its own. Today's trouble is enough for today."

Matthew 6:25-34 (BNT)

"Therefore I want to say to you, do not let the question of what you will eat (or what you will drink) worry the life out of you, nor should you be overwrought about what you will wear. Is not 'who you are' more than food and your fellowship with others more than clothing? [26]Look up there at the birds; they neither sow nor reap, and they do not gather up into storehouses. And yet your heavenly Father feeds them. Are you not more valuable than they? [27]Which of you, by worrying, are able to add a half yard to your height? [28]And why are you concerned about clothing? Observe the lilies of the field, how they grow; they neither work nor spin. [29]Yet I tell you that not even Solomon in all his splendor was dressed like one of these. [30]So if God so clothes the grass of the field, which today is here and tomorrow is thrown into an oven, will God not clothe you even more so, O you of little faith? [31]Then do not be so worried and say, 'What shall we eat?' or 'What shall we drink?' or 'What shall we put on?' [32]For the unbelievers seek all these things. And your heavenly Father knows that you have need of all these things. [33]But seek first the reign (of God) and his style of setting things right, and all these things will be provided. [34]Do not be concerned about tomorrow, for tomorrow will have its own worries. The evil of today is enough in itself."

The Text in Its Biblical Setting

Chapter 5 of the Sermon on the Mount deals with the moral aspects of life together, much as does the Covenant Code of Exodus 21—23. Chapter 6 then shifts the emphasis to the *religious* life, much as the Exodus narrative shifts the emphasis when it introduces the Holiness Code in Exodus 34 (cf. Lev. 17—26). In 6:1-21 Jesus strongly attacks religious deeds done for ostentation and prayers said for display of word power. Then in verses 22-24 he turns to the topic of an appropriate style of religious life. First, Jesus insists on oneness of loyalty to God, on singleness in one's obedience (vv. 22-24). We cannot sway between loyalty to God and loyalty to things (mammon) in God's created order. Secondly, says Jesus, the things of this world will take care of themselves when we are loyal to God (vv. 25-34).

There are two levels at which we can become overly concerned about ourselves. We can become protective of our own person (*psyche* in Greek), and we can become anxious about how we appear to others (*soma* or body). In verse 25 Jesus states it most clearly. We are not to be overanxious about what we will eat, drink or wear. "Is not your *psyche* more than food and your *soma* more than clothing?" We frequently translate this: "Is not your life more than food and your body more than clothing?" But the intention of the saying goes far beyond simply external matters.

The Greek word *psyche* may mean purely physical life, as it does in Revelation 8:9 ("living creatures"). But more often than not it means life in its total sense. For this reason it is often translated "soul," or that part of a person that exists beyond purely physical life (Luke 12:16-21). But because the term "soul" has been associated with existence after death rather than with the total person in life, it has become necessary for translation purposes to search for other words. For example the Hebrew equivalent is translated "person" in Genesis 12:5. A similar translation is necessary in several important sayings of the New Testament. In John 15:13 we should read: "Greater love has no one than to share one's personhood for a friend." Likewise in Mark 8:35: "Those who wish to hang on to their personhood will lose it, but those who let loose of their personhood for my sake and the gospel's will save it." So here the meaning is not simply that there is more to life than just eating and drinking. Rather the meaning matches that of Matthew 10:39 and Mark 8:35 mentioned above: people who seek primarily their own gratification will destroy themselves, for personhood is much more than gratification, self-preservation, and self-fulfillment.

Just as *psyche* means more than life, so *soma* means more than a physical body. In some passages it refers to a collection of persons who are unified by a common conviction or fellowship (Rom. 12:5). Knowing it can have this corporate meaning, we see that even when used of a single person it means "a person as seen by others." 1 Corinthians 7:4 calls attention to the way in which we create each other's bodiness. In a covenant community we are constantly creating each other. *Soma* or body then is our corporate self-image, how we think others think of us. In Matthew 6:25 Jesus says that our self-image consists of much more than the clothes we wear. If our participation in the faith community depends on our physical appearance, then indeed we have lost the meaning of fellowship.

The section composed of verses 26-34 has an obvious intent to argue the case presented in verses 23-25. That argument proceeds as follows:

Verse 26:   God cares for his creation.
Verse 27:   Of what value is anxiety?.
Verses 28-30: God cares for his creation.
Verses 31-32: Of what value is anxiety?
Verse 33:   God will care for you, so live according to priorities.
Verse 34:   Of what value is anxiety?

In arguing from creation Jesus uses a very typical style of persuasion: *a minori ad maius*, or from the lesser case to the greater case. He frequently argues that if a parent would do so and so, then would not God do even more so (Matt. 7:11; Luke 11:13)? Here he argues that if God so wonderfully cares for birds, flowers and grass which have neither *psyche or soma*, how much more will he care for you who are conscious of your person and your identity?

Simultaneously Jesus argues that anxiety about your person and your identity will do little good. In verse 27 he argues that anxiety cannot increase your height. (The Greek actually says "life span," but the measurement "a half yard" forces the translation "height"). In verses 31-32 he argues that anxiety should be left to those of little faith, such as unbelievers. And in verse 34 he argues that stacking up future worries is a foolish procedure; we have enough problems as it is.

The key verse, however, is verse 33. There Jesus states what we *should* do. We are to seek first the reign of God. The word *first* is an indication of priority. Jesus does not say we are to be unaware of daily problems. But if we have the right priority, then God will care for our secondary concerns. This "care" can be taken two ways. Many of Jesus' hearers must have supposed from their Jewish background that God would indeed take care of the faithful (see Job 1:1-5). That may be part of what Jesus is saying, but it seems equally likely that Jesus means that the priority of the reign makes all secondary concerns pale by comparison. That is, when God is ultimate, then food, clothing, financial structures, political concerns, and even family life lose their ultimate value and have importance only as they serve our primary concern. This is probably why wealth was so frequently attacked by Jesus. His hearers supposed wealth to be a sign that one had been faithful. Jesus, however, would make everything in this life dispensable (see Matt. 19:16-30).

To seek the reign of God is to direct the total energy of our lives toward God's will (Matt. 7:7-8). Many of Matthew's parables stress that singleness of purpose (see Matt. 13:44-46). The reign of God will involve obedience to his rule; by seeking his reign we seek to extend that rule of God. Matthew's concern for righteousness in the Sermon on the Mount is also seen in Matthew 5:6, 10, 20; 6:1 ("piety"); 6:33 (note that the form of the latter saying found in Luke 12:31 has no "righteousness"). This could be an explanation of what it means to seek the reign, that is, to seek obedience to his will. But "righteousness" or "justification" often refers to the act of making things right. A major concern of Matthew is the action of the disciple to set things right, to reconcile persons who were enemies. Jesus is saying two things then in 6:33. Our priority in life should be the reign, and our function in life is to set persons right with God so that they can serve him and to set things right among persons so that they might enjoy the life God intended.

The Text in Brethren Life

Prior to the twentieth century, the *simple life* did not exist as a distinct Brethren doctrine. Emmert F. Bittinger, in an article titled "The Simple Life: A Chapter in the Evolution of a Doctrine," has traced its origins to the years between 1908 and 1920.[1] This does not mean, however, that the Brethren only began to practice plainness and simplicity in life during the twentieth century. For the first two hundred years of their existence, simplicity was included in the doctrine of *nonconformity to the world*. According to Peter Nead (1796-1877), nonconformity defines the people of God as a separate and distinct group who avoid the sinful customs and fashions of the world. Nead's biblical bases for this understanding include John 17:16 and Romans 12:1-2. It is the duty of all followers of Christ to observe plainness, and as proof Nead offers quotes from 1 Timothy 2:9 and 1 Peter 3:3.[2] (See chapter 15 for an in-depth discussion of nonconformity.)

To see how nonconformity led to simplicity, we need only turn to the minutes of the Annual Meetings. In 1804, ministers and bishops are advised against baptizing anyone who has not laid aside the fashions in vogue in the world. The minutes of the Annual Meeting of 1827 include a response to the question as to whether members of the church might have carpets in their homes. The response states that such things as carpets belong to the grandeur of the world and as such should not garnish the home of a follower of Jesus. In the minutes of 1846, church leaders are urged to "protest strongly against all manner of superfluity and vanity, such as building fine houses, having paintings, carpetings, and costly furniture, etc., together with the adorning of the body too much after the fashion of the world."[3] The minutes of 1864 advised Brethren against carrying gold watches since such items are likely to cause pride.

By the beginning of the twentieth century, the Brethren were embroiled in the dress question. In his book, *History and Doctrines of the Church of the Brethren* (1919), Otho Winger (1877-1946) presents a good summary of this question and how it was handled. Winger begins by pointing out that there was no established dress for members during the first hundred years of the church. But during the 1800s the Annual Meeting found it necessary to prescribe certain forms of dress. Even so, dress remained a troublesome question and, says Winger, was a major cause for the schisms among the Brethren in 1881 and 1883. After the schisms the question of dress still remained a problem. In 1911 Annual Meeting adopted a statement of the principles and practices of dress in the church. This statement lists Matthew 6:25-33 as one of the biblical passages in which Jesus condemned anxious concern over raiment and was, according to Winger, flexible enough to allow for differences in dress customs among the Brethren across the country.[4]

It was in the midst of the dress question debates that the simple life as an identifiable Brethren doctrine originated. According to Bittinger "the first full-fledged discussion of the simple life . . . is found in an address by Elder H. C. Early presented before Annual Conference."[5] In 1908 as part of the bicentennial celebrations, Early (1855-1941), an evangelist and seven-time moderator of Annual Conference, was asked to speak on Brethren doctrines. Since the dress question was the most controversial issue of the day, people anxiously awaited what he had to say. Early placed his comments on the question at the very end of his presentation and subsumed it under the heading *the simple life*. Concerning the simple life, Early says: "In opposition to parading the empty, carnal life of the worldly throng whose only aim is to make a 'fair show' before men, the strongest plea is made to live the simple life exemplified by Jesus and taught by the apostles."[6] While Early cites biblical texts to support the use of the veil among sisters and Brethren opposition to wearing gold and jewelry, he does not refer to a text concerning the simple life.

After discussing Early's initial presentation of the simple life, Bittinger describes its evolution into a doctrine among the Brethren. Unfortunately, most of the written sources noted by Bittinger as part of the evolution do not include specific biblical texts for the doctrine. A 1919 book titled *Studies in Doctrine and Devotion*, however, does provide texts. The publication of this book was authorized by the 1916 Annual Conference, which also approved a list of the doctrines to be included. In the book the simple life is paired with the topic of Christian adornment and presented in the section of ordinances by S. S. Blough (1868-1962). Blough, a minister and teacher, opens his discussion of the simple life with words which imply the recent development of the doctrine: "A great deal is being said about the simple life. It seems to be an important subject."[7] Among the texts cited by Blough is Matthew 6:25. In fact, he cites the verse twice, once while discussing Jesus as the example of the simple life and once in his discussion of dress.

According to the 1911 dress statement, the prescribed dress remained the ideal but was no longer a test of membership. As a result dress became less and less a concern, and Brethren began to dress more and more like the other members of American society. By the middle of the century, it was difficult to distinguish most Brethren from other Americans by either their dress or their lifestyle. In the 1970s, however, there was renewed interest among some Brethren in the simple life. During the decade three books and several articles were written by Brethren authors on the topic. The books include Vernard Eller's *The Simple Life* (1973); Art Gish's *Beyond the Rat Race* (1973); and Edward K. Ziegler's *Simple Living* (1974).

In their respective books, Eller and Gish agree that the statement "strive first for the kingdom God and his righteousness, and all these things will be given to you as well" (Matthew 6:33) is central to the concept of simple living. To strive first for the kingdom, says Eller, is "to let his [God's] will be done in one's life, to put oneself into appropriate relationship to him as a subject to his true and sovereign Lord."[8] For Gish, striving first for the kingdom "is to have singleness of purpose rather than trying to go in twelve directions at once."[9] To put the kingdom first, says Gish, enables us to distinguish the important from the unimportant, to live with centeredness and direction in our lives, and to be free from everything that would prevent our response to God. The major difference between Eller and Gish is at the point of advising the Christian on how to practice the simple life on a daily basis. Eller, while he cannot imagine anyone deciding to put first the kingdom without there being outward manifestations of that decision, is reluctant to specify what those manifestations will be. Gish, on the other hand, provides a number of concrete suggestions on how to live more simply in a complex world.

Not surprisingly the renewed interest in the simple life led to a 1980 Annual Conference statement on Christian lifestyle. In the opening of the statement, the simple life is reaffirmed and Matthew 6:33 is cited as the purpose of the simple life. The statement is very comprehensive and includes recommendations concerning solidarity with the powerless, wealth and possessions, taxation and militarism, and stewardship of natural resources.

In spite of the concern about the simple life during the 1970s and the 1980 statement on lifestyle, Carl Bowman's 1985 study indicates that the simple life makes little difference in the everyday lives of most Brethren today:

> Only 24 percent currently believe that Brethren should dress more simply than other Americans, and as few as 10 percent say their personal standards of simple living have ever affected their clothing purchases. Less than half of

today's Brethren (46 percent) believe that the typical American lives an undesirable, materialistic lifestyle.[10]

Bowman concludes: "Most Brethren have heard about the 'simple life,' but given the denomination's current commitment to the mainstream of American life, is it little more than a simple rumor?"[11]

Notes

1. Emmert F. Bittinger, "The Simple Life: A Chapter in the Evolution of a Doctrine," *Brethren Life and Thought* 23 (Spring 1978): 104-114.

2. Peter Nead, *Primitive Christianity, or a Vindication of the Word of God* (Staunton, VA: Kenton Harper, Printer, 1834), 110-112.

3. Minutes of the Annual Meetings of the Church of the Brethren, 1778-1909 (Elgin, IL: Brethren Publishing House, 1909), 90-91.

4. Otho Winger, *History and Doctrines of the Church of the Brethren* (Elgin, IL: Brethren Publishing House, 1919), 217-220.

5. Bittinger, 107.

6. H. C. Early, "What the Church Stands For: Her Doctrines," in *Two Centuries of the Church of the Brethren*, 2d ed. (Elgin, IL: Brethren Publishing House, 1909), 148.

7. S. S. Blough, "Studies in Ordinances," in *Studies in Doctrine and Devotion* (Elgin, IL: Brethren Publishing House, 1919), p. 174.

8. Vernard Eller, *The Simple Life* (Grand Rapids, MI: Eerdmans, 1973), 21.

9. Arthur G. Gish, *Beyond the Rat Race* (Scottdale, PA: Herald Press, 1973).

10. Carl Bowman, *Profile of the Church of the Brethren* (Elgin, IL: Brethren Press, n.d.), 20.

11. Ibid., 21.

The Text in Today's World

As we have seen in the section on the original meaning of the text, Matthew 6:25-34 focuses primarily on anxiety. Anxiety is inappropriate because God provides what we need. What is needed, however, ought not to be confused with material goods. What we need and what we want is a sense of personal worth and an acceptance in the human fellowship. Jesus insists that these are elements of life which we cannot obtain by being anxious about them. Indeed, they are gifts of God. Material goods and wealth are only mentioned because more often than not people use wealth to create a sense of worthiness and acceptance, therefore avoiding the issue.

Because the text does deal with anxiety, few passages of the New Testament are more pertinent for today than this one. The poet W. H. Auden has called our times "the age of anxiety." Psychologists (such as Rollo May), philosophers (including Kierkegaard and Sartre), dramatists (like Thomas Wolfe) and novelists (among them Camus, Kafka, and Hesse) share the same perception that modern people are more caught up in a sense of anxiety than any other condition. Their explanations for such anxiety differ considerably. Some, more existential types, see anxiety caused by the failure or deconstruction of the Christian world and a subsequent loss of any meaningful structure. Others see anxiety coming from an apprehension about life, vocation and significance. Emble, in Auden's *The Age of Anxiety* (Random House, 1947) says:

> It is getting late.
> Shall we ever be asked for? Are we simply
> Not wanted at all? (p. 42)

For some, such anxiety has created the cutting edge in our society, so that there has grown up, as one author puts it, a "love of anxiety." But Jesus' word points us in quite a different direction: Be not anxious. Being anxious can only lead to further anxiety. The life for which we are anxious can only be received as a gift.

If anxiety is a mark of this age, as it was at the time of Jesus, so the attempt to escape anxiety by building storehouses also marks our time. Again Auden speaks of

> . . . this stupid world where
> Gadgets are gods and we go on talking,
> Many about much, but remain alone,
> Alive but alone, belonging-where?
> Unattached as tumbleweed. Time flies. (p. 44)

Brethren interest in the simple life results from this awareness that people can hide their anxiety in a multiplicity of activities and a plethora of things. Vernard Eller reflects the meaning of this passage in *The Simple Life* when he says nonconformity is not the issue. The simple life is the subordination of possessions and activities to the single loyalty to God and his reign. Art Gish, in *Beyond the Rat Race*, may more nearly reflect Brethren history when he argues that living simply will reduce, if not destroy, our sense of anxiety. But whether we live with singleness of purpose or whether we greatly simplify our lives, the message remains much the same. We cannot gain meaning in life by adding on. Only reliance on God rather than ourselves can cure the age of anxiety. In these times of high anxiety and stress, Brethren will serve themselves and the world by emphasizing once more the simple life.

Case Study

An older woman in Germany tells how a struggle over inheritance has destroyed her family. When the woman's mother died she passed on several items to each of her three daughters. One of the items, an inexpensive bracelet often worn by the mother, was given to the elder sister. The younger sister objected. As a child she bought the bracelet for 15 Deutsche marks ($7.00) and gave it to her mother for her birthday. The older sister said her mother wanted her to have it. As a result of the conflict, the two sisters have not spoken to each other for five years.

1. Does simple living refer to standard of living?

2. Does simple living refer to conspicuous consumption?

3. Does simple living refer to excessive attachment to anything?

4. In what way do you deal with people who have an over-evaluation or over-attachment to "things"?

5. Do you own *anything* which, if damaged by someone, would also destroy your friendship?

Session 5

On Settling Differences

Matthew 18:15-20 (NRSV)

"If another member of the church sins against you, go and point out the fault when the two of you are alone. If the member listens to you, you have regained that one. [16]But if you are not listened to, take one or two others along with you, so that every word may be confirmed by the evidence of two or three witnesses. [17]If the member refuses to listen to them, tell it to the church; and if the offender refuses to listen even to the church, let such a one be to you as a Gentile and a tax collector. [18]Truly I tell you, whatever you bind on earth will be bound in heaven, and whatever you loose on earth will be loosed in heaven. [19]Again, truly I tell you, if two of you agree on earth about anything you ask, it will be done for you by my Father in heaven. [20]For where two or three are gathered in my name, I am there among them."

Matthew 18:15-20 (BNT)

If a person in your congregation sins, go speak to that person about the matter privately. If the person listens to you, then you have won back a member of the church family. [16]But if he or she does not listen, take two or three others with you, for every word should be established by the evidence of two or three witnesses. [17]But if the person does not listen to them either, report it to the church. And if he or she does not listen to the church, let that person be to you as an unbeliever or a tax collector.

[18]For I tell you for certain, that whatever decisions you make as a congregation will already have been made in heaven, and whatever decisions you set aside as a congregation will already have been set aside in heaven. [19]Again I say to you that if two of you on earth agree on what you would pray about, it will be done for them by my Father who is in heaven. [20]For where two or three come together in my name, I am there in their midst.

The Text in Its Biblical Setting

Many have assumed that the Gospel of Matthew has been so organized as to give the reader five books (as the Jewish Law consisted of five books, or the Pentateuch), each of which consisted of a narrative section and a discourse section. The five books would be:

Book I:	3:1—4:25	Narrative material
	5:1—7:27	The Sermon on the Mount
Book II:	8:1—9:35	Narrative material
	9:36—10:42	Discourse on mission and martyrdom
Book III:	11:2—12:50	Narrative and debate material
	13:1-52	Teaching on the kingdom of heaven
Book IV:	13:54—17:21	Narrative and debate material
	17:22—18:35	Discourse on church administration
Book V:	19:2—22:46	Narrative and debate material
	23:1—25:46	Discourse on final things

Each of the books closes with a formula: "And when Jesus had finished . . . ."

The passage 18:15-20 comes near the end of the discourse on church administration. In its present form and context, its purpose is to propose a method of handling conflict in the church community. As the earliest form of verse 15a indicates, however, the passage originally had a different focus. Its concern was not that of conflict between members but rather that of how to discipline wayward members of the church. The phrase "If a person . . . sins" could include conflict with a brother or sister in the congregation, but it is not limited to such an issue. And taking two or three persons along on the second visit has the purpose of establishing the truth, not achieving reconciliation.

The basic account reads very much like a similar section in the Manual of Discipline of the Qumran community (a sectarian group at the time of Jesus): A member should clear up any charges against another member immediately, for it is a sin to bear hatred. This should be done in front of two or three witnesses, before the matter is brought to the whole community (1QS 5:24—6:1). Similarly in 1 Corinthians 5:1-5 and 2 Corinthians 13:14, it is clear that members are disciplined by action of the total church community. The intent is not so much to reconcile a conflict as to redeem a sinner from a destructive situation. The person is, therefore, to be disfellowshiped until repentance has occurred. In Matthew 18:17 the mandate of the church is to return the impenitent member to the status of "Gentile and tax collector" (cf. Matt. 5:46-47 and 6:7).

Despite this original focus on disciplining the "sinning" church member, the sayings are now so arranged as to deal with conflict or differences between Christians. The purpose of the first conversation is to win back the alienated person (v. 15b). Though the two or three witnesses are present to protect the truth, as a matter of fact they obviously share in the attempt to reconcile (v. 16b). Taken this way, the passage sounds more like the conciliatory gesture of leaving the altar to make peace with a member of the church, described in Matthew 5:23-24. A similar style of reconciliation is set forth in Romans 14.

Apparently the words of Jesus about an impenitent brother or sister were used in the Gospel of Matthew as a pattern for handling conflicts in the church. To emphasize this function, the later church added the words "against you" to verse 15, so that it then read "If another member of the church sins against you." Early English translations, such as the King James Version and the German translation of Luther, included the addition "against you."

The sayings in verses 18-20 stress the incredible power of the local congregation. In line with the disciplinary structure of verses 15-17, Jesus says that the local group of disciples can make ultimate decisions and offer forgiveness when needed. Presumably this refers to the cases of conflict or impenitence which have come to the attention of the whole congregation. The "binding" and "loosing" then refer primarily to the discipline of excluding from fellowship or including in fellowship, but not to all decisions which the church might make.

Nevertheless, just as the Christ had ultimate authority, so his disciples also have such authority. The people of the end-time, the church, make decisions which are already ultimate, or heavenly. Verses 19-20 continue to stress this power. The prayer of two or more, that is a congregation, will be honored by God. This reflects the power of prayer so well attested in the New Testament (see Mark 11:23-24). Matthew 18:18-20 stresses the power of the congregation perhaps more than any other text in the New Testament. The phrase "two or more" excludes the individual from making binding decisions or offering grace. Only the congregation has the power of Christ. At the same time it is only the congregation in unity (see v. 19, "agree") which has that power. In Judaism the synagogue or congregation had a similar power. God would not despise or ignore the prayer of a congregation (which consisted of at least ten persons; see Berakoth 8a in the Talmud). This power is explained in Matthew 18:20. Christ is present where two or three are gathered together in his name. Again, Jewish perceptions have been shifted to Christian ones. In Aboth 3:2

in the Jewish Mishnah, a rabbi says: "But if two sit together and words of the Law (are spoken) between them, the Divine Presence rests between them." In the Christian congregation Christ is that divine presence.

The Text in Brethren Life

Matthew 18:15-17, or simply Matthew 18 as it is often called, is the text on which the Brethren of the past based the practice of *avoidance*. Other terms sometimes used for the practice were *disfellowship* and *ban*. It was a form of discipline whereby offenders were not allowed to participate in the functions of the church, such as the love feast and congregational business meetings, and were not permitted to give or receive the Holy Kiss. If the transgression was severe, no member of the congregation was allowed to associate with the offenders, even if the offender was a member of their own family. In general, people were placed in avoidance for not living according to New Testament principles as understood by the Brethren. Avoidance was seen as temporary since the purpose of the practice was to enable people to see that they were not living as Christians should. Once a person repented, he or she was restored to full membership in the community. Hannah, the daughter of Alexander Mack, Jr. (1712-1803), was disciplined so severely that her family was not permitted to eat with her. Even so, her father writes: "Most of the members said that they would be more willing to accept her again if she returned in repentance, in fact they would be more willing to accept her again than they were ready to expel her."[1]

It is clear that avoidance was practiced by the Brethren from the beginning, since Alexander Mack (1679-1735) quotes Matthew 18:15-17 twice in his *Rights and Ordinances* (1715). The first instance occurs in Mack's discussion of separation. Mack understands verses 15-17 as Jesus' ordination of separation as a means of church discipline for those who refuse to admit their wrongdoing when confronted by their brothers and sisters. According to Mack the separation occurs, not because of their sins but because their pride causes them to reject the good counsel of the other members of the church. Any member who refuses to acknowledge to the church that he or she has done wrong has indeed become evil and corrupt, says Mack, and must be separated from the church in order to prevent the contamination of other members with such corruption. The separated member can, however, be reinstated if purified by reformation and repentance.[2]

The second reference to verses 15-17 occurs in Mack's discussion of avoidance, or the ban. The question precipitating this discussion is that of how a member should relate to a spouse who has been placed in avoidance by the church. Mack says that those closest to a person under the ban must be first in avoiding the person. As biblical support for this stance, Mack quotes verses 15-17 as well as 1 Corinthians 5:11, which states that one is not to associate with, or even eat with, church members guilty of the immoralities named.[3]

That the Brethren found the practice of Matthew 18 complicated is revealed by Henry Kurtz's lengthy discussion of avoidance which precedes his even lengthier list of Annual Meeting statements concerning avoidance in his *Brethren's Encyclopedia* (1867). Kurtz (1796-1874), who is probably best known for initiating publication of the *Gospel Visitor*,[4] defines avoidance as "an institution of the Lord Jesus Christ for the preservation of the purity and unity of the church, and for the bringing to repentance and restoration of fallen members."[5] He then describes how the practice works. If a member commits a minor fault or private offense but refuses to acknowledge it and submit to the church, Matthew 18:17 must be practiced. This means that the church must *avoid in part* the offending member. To avoid in part is to refuse to admit such offenders to communion or church council and to refuse to salute them as members. However, continues Kurtz, in the case of heinous sins such as those listed in 1 Corinthians 5:11, acknowledgement of wrongdoing is not enough. Then *full avoidance* must be practiced as described in 1 Corinthians 5:11. This means that members must not associate with such offenders or eat with them.

Kurtz also notes that the Brethren are no longer "a unit on the subject" of avoidance. Specifically he says:

> For more than a century it was the universal belief among our brethren, that this was as much an institution of the Lord as baptism, or any other ordinance, and none could gainsay it. But times have changed; a whole generation of old and faithful and steadfast brethren has almost entirely passed away, and at least in some parts of our wide-spread fraternity a new generation has come up, "which knew not Joseph;" and of late, sad to tell, it has come openly to light, that we are no longer in such cordial union on this and some kindred subjects as our brethren once were. We love our dear brethren, even those who do

not see alike with us; indeed we thank them that they have come out openly and willing for discussion, and thus caused others to think and reflect on the subject more seriously than they ever did.[6]

Kurtz then indicates that the list of Annual Meeting actions concerning avoidance that follows is, in part, the result of his own investigation which was sparked by the dissenters.

Obviously the practice of avoidance, whether full or in part, was only as wise as the people who practiced it. It is only too easy to imagine avoidance being used by some church members as a club with which to threaten and beat other church members. Yet the practice, when wisely used, could be constructive. Consider the response of the Annual Meeting of 1863 to the question of what was to be done when a member preached that slavery was sanctioned by Scripture. First, the meeting stated that there was no doubt that slavery was contrary to Christian doctrine. Second, the meeting recommended that any member who remained obstinate after being admonished for justifying slavery be dealt with according to Matthew 18.

A second constructive application of avoidance is found in a story told by Harry H. Ziegler (1880-1971) to Dale W. Brown. Ziegler, an elder in Pennsylvania and Maryland, related the story of a young unmarried woman who became pregnant and was called before the church at a council meeting. The church voted to place her in avoidance, but after the woman admitted that her action was wrong before the church at the very same council meeting, she was reinstated. As part of her entrance back into the church community, each woman of the church gave her the kiss of peace; and all members were warned never to speak of the subject again lest they be disciplined also.

By the middle of the twentieth century, the practice of avoidance had disappeared among the Brethren. As a result, there remained very little discipline in the church, except that which took the unhealthy form of gossip. In the late 1960s and early 1970s, some voices were heard among the Brethren calling for church discipline. In an article titled "The Brethren and Church Discipline," Eugene Roop encourages the Brethren to reconsider church discipline, not by returning to the nineteenth century practice of avoidance, but by determining what values of the practice are still important and deciding how those values might be adopted to the present.[7] In another article Barry J. Weber ended with these words: "If we are to genuinely address the problem of discipline in this church era, we will need to face the fact that discipline currently is not practiced, we will need to discover biblically sound concepts of loving discipline, and then to consider how we can get discipline to actually be *practiced*."[8]

Today the closest the Church of the Brethren has come to an official position on church discipline is the "Discipleship and Reconciliation" paper adopted by the 1976 Annual Conference. This paper outlines the causes of brokenness in the church and recommends how to facilitate reconciliation. Matthew 18 is cited three times. First, failure to resolve differences according to Matthew 18 is listed as one of the causes of brokenness among members. Second, Matthew 18:15-22 is cited to indicate the understanding, trusting, and caring relationship which should exist so that members can approach each other when there is brokenness. Third, Matthew 18:17 is to be called into play only when all efforts at reconciliation have failed. Concerning Matthew 18:17 the paper states: "The biblical teaching of Matthew 18, traditionally practiced in the Church of the Brethren, can be misinterpreted. It can be insensitively and hastily employed. However, when verse seventeen . . . is understood within the context of the *total* chapter, it reflects the openness and unending compassion and forgiveness of Jesus. Gentiles and tax collectors . . . as well as other rejected persons were the focus of his compassion and forgiveness."[9]

Notes

1. "Mack-Preisz Correspondence," in *Brethren in Colonial America*, ed. Donald F. Durnbaugh (Elgin, IL: Brethren Press, 1967), 239.

2. Alexander Mack, *Rights and Ordinances*, in *European Origins of the Brethren*, comp. and trans. Donald F. Durnbaugh (Elgin, IL: Brethren Press, 1958), 365-370.

3. Ibid., 393-394.

4. Kurtz began publication of the *Gospel Visitor* in 1851 under the name *Monthly Gospel-Visiter*, but in December 1856 the spelling of *Visiter* was changed to *Visitor* and in February 1857 the word *Monthly* was dropped from the name. For the sake of simplicity, the name *Gospel Visitor* will consistently be used regardless of the publication date of the particular issue.

5. Henry Kurtz, *The Brethren's Encyclopedia* (Columbiana, OH: the author, 1867), 27.

6. Ibid., 26.

7. Eugene F. Roop, "The Brethren and Church Discipline (II)," *Brethren Life and Thought* 14 (Summer 1969), 178-182.

8. Barry J. Weber, "Let's Strive for a Loving Discipline," *Messenger*, November 1975, 27.

9. *Minutes of the Annual Conference of the Church of the Brethren, 1975-1979*, comp. Phyllis Kingery Ruff (Elgin, IL: Brethren Press, 1980), 202.

The Text in Today's World

As a study of Brethren history has indicated, Matthew 18 refers to two related practices: church discipline and conflict resolution. Church discipline has been practiced primarily to keep the church pure and holy, to maintain the unity of the church, or to create a redemptive situation for errant members. It would be difficult to imagine a church existing without any discipline. The New Testament indicates the church had the right and even the obligation to exercise discipline over its members.

Yet over the years the Church of the Brethren has not been able to maintain a balance among its reasons for discipline. Discipline was more often applied to questions of dress and household furnishings than to the essential elements of the Christian faith. As a consequence we lost much of the church discipline which so marked our earlier years. It must be admitted that the baby has been thrown out with the bath. By discarding one style of disciplining, we ought not to say that all church discipline is undesirable. Consequently many thoughtful leaders have been calling for a reconsideration of the issue.

The Church of the Brethren was a community of love and concern, as was the early church. Love in the church requires judgment, just as love in a family involves the exercise of decisiveness. But in the past that judgment became identified with marks of membership. Church discipline ought not to be confused with the rules for joining a club. Rather church discipline should deal with one's participation in a loving, caring, covenanting community of faith. When people join the church they should make a commitment to Christ and the assembled fellowship. Likewise the church should make a commitment to them. Violations of such a commitment would not be cause for losing membership in the "club" but would be cause for concern within a commitment relationship. Violations of such a covenant would be primarily failures to operate within a covenant understanding: the failure to minister to others; the failure to receive the ministry of the church; the rejection of Christ and his church. Even then violations would be treated with an objective of redeeming the offender rather than that of maintaining membership standards.

If such were the case, the primary meaning of this text would shift to conflict resolution. Though the church would have the "authority on earth" to make decisions of many sorts, its major object in discipline would be to renew a Christian life of commitment to each other. This involves dealing with conflict in a redemptive way within the covenant relationship. Historically, most of us have dealt with conflict by avoidance, containment, or psychological adjustment. Frequently, we handle conflict situations by avoiding the source of the problem. A family may not talk about financial matters; a grandparent and a grandchild may not talk politics; a pastor and the church may not talk about the music in worship. Avoidance may have value in creating an outer sense of unity, but it likely does nothing toward increasing the commitment of persons to one another. In some cases the Brethren ban or "avoidance" had that problem. Another way of handling conflict is to limit or contain the areas where it can occur. My parents would let my brother and me fight, but it always had to be outside the house. Limiting church conflicts to the athletic field, to social prestige, or to church elections helps keep the peace but saps the covenant nature of the community. A third method of dealing with conflict is to learn to live with it. By seeking psychological or spiritual help, some persons can adjust to constant irritation. Again this can be helpful, but it fails to reckon with the real problem of a broken community.

Matthew 18 advocates personal encounter. The sense of covenant in the church should allow Christians to approach personally anyone with whom they have a conflict. If the commitment is strong there can be no loss, and there is much to be gained in the way of renewal. But when personal encounter fails to bring about a solution, then Matthew 18 calls for third-party intervention. That is, the church acts as a third party to settle the problem and bring about reconciliation. If even this fails, then, as the early Brethren noted, some party has failed to sense the nature of the covenant. At that point a critical decision involving covenant participation would have to be made.

If the church is to serve its Lord and the community of faith, it will need once more to consider the discipline of conflict management found in this passage.

Case Study

The board chairperson of a church in Kansas recently lost her husband in a fatal accident. Members of the church rallied around her. She decided to remodel her upstairs so she could rent it out to a university student. The chair of stewards, professionally a plumber, agreed to remodel the bathroom. They signed a contract for an amount quite advantageous to the board chairperson. During the time of construction, the board chairperson asked if the bathtub could be installed in the opposite corner. The plumber agreed. When he presented the final bill it was $500 more than the contract. The owner protested. The plumber said alterations in the plan were not included in the original contract. The board chairperson refused to pay the extra. The plumber put it in the hands of his bill collector.

At the next board meeting the board chairperson made several good suggestions but was opposed each time by the chair of stewards. No one, including the pastor, knew why.

1. Should the church "keep its hands out of" this conflict?

2. If the church were to become involved, would it attempt to resolve the contract conflict or only deal with what happens at church board meetings?

3. In your church who deals with conflict resolution?

4. What do you see as the goal of conflict resolution? Justice? Reconciliation? Forgiveness? Repentance?

Session 6

On Church and State

Matthew 22:15-22 (NRSV)

Then the Pharisees went and plotted to entrap him in what he said. [16]So they sent their disciples to him, along with the Herodians, saying, "Teacher, we know that you are sincere, and teach the way of God in accordance with truth, and show deference to no one; for you do not regard people with partiality. [17]Tell us, then, what you think. Is it lawful to pay taxes to the emperor, or not?" [18]But Jesus, aware of their malice, said, "Why are you putting me to the test, you hypocrites? [19]Show me the coin used for the tax." And they brought him a denarius. [20]Then he said to them, "Whose head is this, and whose title?" [21]They answered, "The emperor's." Then he said to them, "Give therefore to the emperor the things that are the emperor's, and to God the things that are God's." [22]When they heard this, they were amazed; and they left him and went away.

Matthew 22:15-22 (BNT)

Then the Pharisees went to consider how they might trap him in his speaking. [16]So they sent to him their disciples, along with the Herodians, saying, "Teacher, we know you are consistent, and you teach the way of God truthfully, and you do not care what people think of you, because you are not impressed by the position of others. [17]Tell us then what you think. Is it right to pay taxes to Caesar or not?" [18]But Jesus, knowing of their malicious intent, said, "You hypocrites, why do you test me? [19]Show me the coin used for the tax." And they brought him a denarius. [20]And he said to them, "Whose image is this and whose inscription?" [21]And they said to him, "Caesar's." Then he said to them, "Give to Caesar, then, the things that belong to Caesar, and to God the things of God." [22]And when they heard this they were amazed. And they left him and went away.

The Text in Its Biblical Setting

In the Synoptic Gospels there are several stories in which the opponents of Jesus try to trap him. Some of these have been collected in Matthew 22. In 22:23-33 we find the Sadducees trying to trap Jesus between the ancient law of levirate marriage and the Pharisees' doctrine of the resurrection. According to ancient Jewish custom, a man is responsible to his family and his brother's wife to conceive a child with her if his brother dies before their child is conceived. The Sadducees, who did not believe in the resurrection, asked Jesus, who did, whose wife she would be at the end time.

Another occurs in the question about the greatest commandment (22:34-40). The Pharisees intend to catch him denying some part of the decalogue, but they fail. A similar question by a lawyer triggers the famous story of the Good Samaritan (Luke 10:25-37). There are several other stories in the same style where Jesus perceives their question before they ask it. In the healing of the paralytic, the crowd suspects it was blasphemous of Jesus to forgive sins (Mark 2:1-12). In the story of the man with the withered hand, the crowd watches to see if he breaks the Sabbath (Mark 3:1-6).

In all these stories the opponents attempt to trap Jesus in such a way that either defies tradition and law or alienates him from his followers. Normally Jesus answers with a question which puts the shoe on the other foot. He asks them, "Is it lawful to do good on the Sabbath?" Or, "Is it easier to forgive sins or heal a paralytic?" Or, "How do you read the Jewish law?" If his adversaries answer his question, it is they who may either break with tradition or bring down on themselves the disapproval of the crowd. At other times, such as with the question about resurrection or the decalogue, Jesus answers with such insight that his adversaries dare not ask a counter-question or make an accusation.

The question about the Roman coin follows the same pattern. The Pharisees plan to entrap Jesus (v. 15). In contrast to the Sadducees, the Pharisees did not cooperate with the Romans who occupied Palestine. Though not rabid opponents of Rome, like the Zealots, they did keep the Roman empire in a clear tension. For their part the Romans feared a Jewish-led uprising. It is estimated about 10% of the population of the Roman Empire was Jewish, spread primarily throughout the eastern provinces, such as Syria and Asia Minor. But some large cities, like Alexandria and Rome had very large Jewish populations. When the Jews did revolt in 66 A.D., the Romans sent their best legion to quell it. But for their part the Romans of the first century were fairly tolerant of diverse religious expressions. While wanting a firm hand on the political situation in Palestine, they nevertheless allowed the Jews considerable latitude. As is well known, the Jews had a temple tax which was assessed every adult male. With Roman permission, this tax could cross provincial lines duty free. These large sums were collected in the Jerusalem temple (see Mark 11:15; 12:41). Some have even suggested the size of the Jerusalem bank was second only to that of the Capitoline in Rome.

While the Jews collected taxes for the temple, the Romans collected taxes for the administration of the empire. The job of collecting taxes was given on contract to local citizens. They received a percentage of what they could collect. Tax collectors were often unscrupulous and certainly disliked (Luke 19:1-10).

So the question by the Pharisees was a serious trap (v. 18). If Jesus answered that they should pay the tax, he surely would arouse the antagonism of the crowd and many of the religious leaders. If he answered that they shouldn't pay the tax, then he faced eventual, if not immediate, conflict with the Roman administration. As we have seen in other stories, Jesus did not answer "Yes" or "No," but came back with a counter question. He asked them to show him the money for the tax. Now the Jews also had their own monetary system. But the Roman tax would have been payable with Roman coins. So his adversaries produced a Roman coin (v. 19). With that they condemned themselves. By possessing a Roman coin, they signalled to everyone their complicity with the Roman empire. Actually there was nothing more to be said.

But there is more to the passage. By asking whose likeness was on the coin, Jesus actually rubs their noses in the dirt (v. 20). The Jews were not to countenance any human likeness (Deut. 5:8-10), much less the likeness of a Roman emperor who might claim divinity (Dan. 3:8-12; 11:31; 1 Macc. 1:54). There were no human images on Jewish coins, but every Roman coin would have borne the image (head) of an emperor. As they stood holding a coin with the image of Caesar on it, Jesus, in essence, said, "Since you have in your hand a coin of Caesar, you owe him a tax. Those who have no Roman coin belong to God."

The Text in Brethren Life

Among the biblical texts most often cited by the Brethren as providing guidance on the relationship of church and state are Matthew 22:15-22 and its parallels in Mark 12:13-17 and Luke 20:20-26. Other texts cited on the topic are Acts 5:27-32; Romans 13:1-7; 1 Timothy 2:1-2; and 1 Peter 2:13-17. The position of the Brethren on the relationship of church and state was initially stated by Alexander Mack (1679-1735) himself. In 1715 he wrote: "They [the faithful] should give the government taxes, imposts, honor, and respect, for all authorities are ordained of God to punish the evil, and to help protect the good, provided that they desire to carry out their offices in accordance with the will of God."[1] Over a century later Peter Nead (1796-1877) wrote similarly: "I believe that it is the duty of the church of Christ to obey the law, in all such cases as do not come in contact with the precepts of the Gospel."[2] A few sentences later Nead quotes Matthew 22:21 to show that Christ did not refuse to give tribute to the civil authorities.

Since the Brethren of the eighteenth and nineteenth centuries combined the desire to obey the state with the understanding that gospel precepts come before civil authorities, they could not obey every law and sometimes experienced persecution. Two notable examples of such persecution occurred while the Brethren were still in Europe. Christian Liebe was sentenced to life as a galley slave for giving aid and comfort to Anabaptists, and six Solingen Brethren were imprisoned for practicing adult baptism. A more detailed description of their suffering is found in chapter 10, "On Counting the Cost."

After coming to America, in part to escape persecution, the Brethren still sometimes came in conflict with the state. Problems with the state were particularly acute during the Revolution. In 1775 the Pennsylvania Assembly "asked that all able-bodied white male inhabitants 'associate' for the common defense."[3] Members of pacifist groups in the state, such as the Brethren, Mennonites, and Quakers, were unable to comply with this call and became known as *nonassociators*. While the assembly exempted the nonassociators from bearing arms, much criticism against them developed. Therefore, the Quakers, in October 1775, and the Brethren and Mennonites, in November 1775, petitioned the Assembly for the preservation of their pacifist stand. Matthew 22:21 is quoted in the petition presented by the Brethren and Mennonites as the biblical basis for their willingness to pay taxes while refusing to bear arms. In general Brethren were willing to be taxed during the Revolution, although the Annual

Meeting of 1781 admonished members not to pay money voluntarily in order to buy themselves out of being drafted.

The most documented instance of the persecution of a Dunker during the Revolution is the case of Christopher Sauer, Jr. (1721-1784), who headed the influential Sauer printing business after the death of his father and served as an elder in the Germantown congregation. In the short span of two years (1777-1778), Sauer lost his money, his property, and even his clothing. Like most Brethren at the outbreak of the Revolution, Sauer did not know which side to support because God's will was unclear. In fact, the Annual Meeting of 1779 stated: "we can not know whether God has rejected the king and chosen the state . . . therefore we could not, with good conscience, repudiate the king and give allegiance to the state."[4] As a result of such a position, Brethren were considered Loyalists and sometimes accused of being traitors. In such a climate it is not surprising that Sauer elected to go to Philadelphia, which was under British control, in October 1777 to be with three of his children. His mistake, however, was returning to Germantown in May 1778. There he was seized by American soldiers. Sauer later described the events which followed thus:

> They led me through the Indian corn fields. When I could not come along as fast as they wanted me to go they frequently stuck me in the back with their bayonets. They brought me to Bastian Miller's barn where they kept me til next morning. Then they stripped me naked to the skin and gave me an old shirt and breeches so much torn that I could barely cover my nakedness. Then [they] cut my beard and hair and painted me with oil colors, red and black, and so led me along barefooted and bareheaded in a very hot sunshining day.[5]

Later Sauer was held captive at a Continental camp until someone intervened on his behalf with General Washington. Even then, however, he was not permitted to return to Germantown until June 23. Since Sauer had been declared a traitor while he was being held captive by the soldiers, approximately a month after his return to Germantown he was evicted from his home and his property was sold. As during the Revolution, the Brethren suffered during the Civil War because of their understanding of church and state. Persecution was particularly harsh in the South where at least three Brethren leaders—John Kline (1797-1864), John Bowman (1813-1863), and Henry Bowman (dates unknown)—were killed. Not unexpectedly many questions arose among the Brethren concerning the church-state relationship. The Annual Meeting minutes of 1864 have several items related to the topic. Included is a reference to Matthew 22:21. The verse is cited as support for this statement: "We think it more in accordance with our principles, that instead of paying bounty-money, and especially in taking an active part in raising bounty-money, to await the demands of the government, whether general, state, or local, and pay the fines and taxes required of us, as the gospel permits, and, indeed, requires."[6]

Included also in the minutes of 1864 is this statement: "We have been led to think that at all times it would be best and most consistent with our profession, and especially most proper and safe in the present critical state of things, to have nothing at all to do with politics, and entirely abstain from voting."[7] Such an attitude toward voting was not entirely due to problems which the Brethren faced during the Civil War. As early as 1813, and several times thereafter, the Annual Meeting took a negative stand on the question of voting. Sometimes in conjunction with this negative stance, the Brethren were called to pray for the government and its elections. At the 1865 Annual Meeting, voting was made a test of fellowship by stating that those who continued to vote were to be treated according to Matthew 18. The next year, however, the test was revoked, and those who did not vote (the majority) were advised to act with forbearance toward the members who chose to vote. By the beginning of World War I, most Brethren were voting, according to Rufus Bowman (1899-1952),[8] and a few had been elected to positions in the government. The most notable example of a Brethren in an elected position was Martin G. Brumbaugh (1862-1930), who was governor of Pennsylvania from 1915 to 1919.

This change in voting practices reflected a larger change in the attitude among the Brethren concerning the relationship of church and state. Among the resolution passed at the 1917 Annual Conference, just two months after the US entry into World War I, was a commitment "to a constructive patriotism and loyal citizenship of real service."[9] Now the Brethren were willing to promote positive institutions such as church, school, and home, as well as ideals such as humanity and liberty, while remaining true to their pacifist beliefs in wartime. This new understanding was further elaborated upon by H. C. Early (1855-1941) in a *Gospel Messenger* article titled "Our Relation to War" (13 October 1917). Early ended his article by quoting Matthew 22:21.

Even though it was difficult for the Brethren to be both pacifists and constructive citizens during World War I, they retained this approach after the war. Two pamphlets—"The Church and State (1936) by D. W. Kurtz (1879-1949) and "Creative Citizenship (1940) by Paul H. Bowman (1887-1964)—express the Brethren desire to be both good Christians and good citizens. Kurtz, who served as president of both McPherson College and Bethany Biblical Seminary during his lifetime, opens his pamphlet by quoting Matthew 22:21 to show that Jesus recognized the Christian's obligation to the state. He then presents the view that while the Christian's ultimate responsibility is to God, the Christian also has the responsibility to help improve the social order by participating in the democratic process. Bowman, the president of Bridgewater College who presented the contents of his pamphlet before the Committee on Military Affairs of the House of Representatives, describes creative citizenship as participating in voting and holding office as long as Christian principles are not violated.

During World War II, the Brethren did not experience as much conflict with the US government over their pacifist position as they did in previous wars. This was due, in part, because they had begun to articulate their understanding of the church-state relationship. Since World War II the articulation of this relationship has continued. Two major statements on church and state have been adopted by the Annual Conference—one in 1967 and one in 1989. In addition, two major statements on the use of taxes for military expenditures have been adopted—1973 and 1983. Three of these four statements quote Matthew 22:21 or one of its parallels. The 1967 statement says that the text "must never be taken to mean that God does not care what Caesar does or leaves undone."[10] The 1973 statement says that the "implication would seem to be that what belongs to God is much more inclusive and in every way prior to what belongs to Caesar."[11] Finally, according to the 1989 statement: "The first part of the saying must not be taken as something to be understood by itself or interpreted in terms of an autonomous sphere alongside that of God. Jesus was expressing the central imperative of the Torah: You, made by God in God's image, are to give yourselves fully to God and, in your doing that, you will be enabled to discern what you can properly give to the state."[12] Thus while the Brethren of the late twentieth century seek to participate in the democratic government of the United States instead of avoiding it, they still place gospel precepts ahead of civil authorities.

Notes

1. Alexander Mack, *Rights and Ordinances*, in *European Origins of the Brethren*, comp. and trans. Donald F. Durnbaugh (Elgin, IL: Brethren Press, 1958), 376.

2. Peter Nead, *Primitive Christianity, or a Vindication of the Word of God* (Staunton, VA: Kenton Harper, Printer, 1834), 106.

3. Rufus D. Bowman, *The Church of the Brethren and War* (Elgin, IL: Brethren Publishing House, 1944), 78.

4. *Minutes of the Annual Meetings of the Church of the Brethren, 1778-1909* (Elgin, IL: Brethren Publishing House, 1909), 6.

5. Christopher Sauer II in *Brethren in Colonial America*, ed. Donald F. Durnbaugh (Elgin, IL: Brethren Press, 1967), 401-02.

6. *Minutes of the Annual Meetings of the Church of the Brethren, 1778-1909*, 232.

7. Ibid., 225.

8. Bowman, 164.

9. *Minutes of the Annual Conference of the Church of the Brethren*, held at Wichita, KS, 12-13 June 1917, p. 16.

10. *Minutes of the Annual Conference of the Church of the Brethren, 1965-1970*, comp. and ed. William R. Eberly (Elgin, IL: Brethren Press, 1970), 250.

11. *Minutes of the Annual Conferences of the Church of the Brethren, 1970-1974*, comp. and ed. William R. Eberly (Elgin, IL: Brethren Press, 1975), 348.

12. *Minutes of the Annual Conference of the Church of the Brethren, 1985-1989*, comp. Annual Conference Office (Elgin, IL: Brethren Press, 1990), 823.

The Text in Today's World

The "give unto Caesar" text has puzzled Christians over the centuries as much as it confounded the Pharisees who first heard it. Most Christians have read it as a form of dual citizenship. We live in the realm of state and also in the realm of divine Lordship. In our earthly, political life we owe allegiance to the state (Caesar), while in the religious or spiritual life we owe allegiance to God. Many Christians have not been satisfied with the complexity of trying to determine when we owe allegiance to state and when we owe allegiance to God. Some Christians have decided one can belong to the realm of the state or the realm of God, but not both. Some Mennonites, particularly, believe committed Christians belong to the realm of God, while all others belong to the realm of the state. Both have legitimate functions. The faith community expresses divine love in the world. The state keeps order and strives for universal justice.

It could be that the complex saying about Caesar and God will always remain an insoluble problem. But if we follow the form of controversy stories, the climax really comes when the antagonists can produce a Roman coin. In so far as the Jews carried Roman coins, they owed something to the state which produced that monetary system. It would indeed be impossible to isolate oneself totally from the state. It would also be impossible to build the church as a realm parallel to the state. The Christian must be responsible to both. But Christians could refrain from over-involvement in or over-responsibility for the state.

Through the period of the Roman Empire, the Reformation, and even to our day, mainline churches have either been coextensive with the state or have felt responsible for public policy and corporate morality. Now the churches of the United States are experiencing a forced deconstruction of that earlier time when church and state were responsible for each other. If the mainline churches do not learn how to act as non-dominant organizations, then much of American Christianity is doomed. Non-dominant churches would call all persons to discipleship; understand itself to be composed primarily of persons without power or resources; and live a community life which places parabolic tension on society as a whole.

Such a sense of discipleship does not come easy. Most Christians think first of what the state should do or what is appropriate Christian citizenship. The Free Church tends to produce persons who think first of what it means to be a follower of Jesus. It is a way of thinking that is not easy to attain. Since that sense of discipleship so marks the Church of the Brethren, it is essential that we continue in local churches, in camps, and in colleges to nurture that kind of formation which places the things of God first.

Case Study

With the entry of the United States into World War I (April 1917) neither the United States government nor the Church of the Brethren were prepared to deal with conscientious objection. At a special conference in Goshen, Indiana, the Church of the Brethren reaffirmed its historic opposition to war and urged Brethren young men not to enlist in or accept assignment to any service which compromised the church's peace position. Several months later the officers of the Goshen Conference were called to Washington by the Secretary of War. They were threatened with charges of treasonable intent for obstructing the operation of the draft. As a result, the leaders of the church withdrew the statement and allowed Brethren young men to decide for themselves what form of service they would accept in light of the church's pacifist belief.

1. Does the church have the right to refuse participation in what the state considers an action for the common good?

2. When does the church, in obedience to its Lord, have the obligation to oppose the state?

3. Do individual members of the church have the right to decide "what is God's" for themselves, or should the church (at Annual Conference, for example) determine when something is owed to Caesar?

4. Can an action be legal and yet immoral? Give examples, and explain what you do in such instances.

Session 7

On Pure Service

Matthew 25:31-46 (NRSV)

"When the Son of Man comes in his glory, and all the angels with him, then he will sit on the throne of his glory. [32]All the nations will be gathered before him, and he will separate people one from another as a shepherd separates the sheep from the goats, [33]and he will put the sheep at his right hand and the goats at the left. [34]Then the king will say to those at his right hand, 'Come, you that are blessed by my Father, inherit the kingdom prepared for you from the foundation of the world; [35]for I was hungry and you gave me food, I was thirsty and you gave me something to drink, I was a stranger and you welcomed me, [36]I was naked and you gave me clothing, I was sick and you took care of me, I was in prison and you visited me.' [37]Then the righteous will answer him, 'Lord, when was it that we saw you hungry and gave you food, or thirsty and gave you something to drink? [38]And when was it that we saw you a stranger and welcomed you, or naked and gave you clothing? [39]And when was it that we saw you sick or in prison and visited you?' [40]And the king will answer them, 'Truly I tell you, just as you did it to one of the least of these who are members of my family, you did it to me.' [41]Then he will say to those at his left hand, 'You that are accursed, depart from me into the eternal fire prepared for the devil and his angels; [42]for I was hungry and you gave me no food, I was thirsty and you gave me nothing to drink, [43]I was a stranger and you did not welcome me, naked and you did not give me clothing, sick and in prison and you did not visit me.' [44]Then they also will answer, 'Lord, when was it that we saw you hungry or thirsty or a stranger or naked or sick or in prison, and did not take care of you?' [45]Then he will answer them, 'Truly I tell you, just as you did not do it to one of the least of these, you did not do it to me.' [46]And these will go away into eternal punishment, but the righteous into eternal life."

Matthew 25:31-46 (BNT)

"When the Son of Man, and all the angels with him, comes in his glory, then he will take his seat upon that throne which signifies his authority. [32]And all the nations (Gentiles) will be assembled before him, and he will make a division between them, much like a shepherd separates the sheep from the goats. [33]And he will place the sheep on his right hand and the goats on his left.

[34]"Then the ruler will say to those on his right, 'You are the ones who will receive my Father's blessing. Come, take rightful possession of that reign which was prepared for you from the creation of the world. [35]For I was hungry and you gave me something to eat, I was thirsty and you gave me something to drink, I was an outsider and you befriended me, [36]I was poorly dressed and you clothed me, I was sick and you took care of me, I was in prison and you visited me.'

[37]"Then those approved will answer him saying, 'Lord, when did we see you hungry and feed you, or thirsty and give you something to drink? [38]When did we notice you were an outsider and befriend you, or poorly dressed and clothe you? [39]When did we find out you were sick or in prison and visit you?' [40]And in reply the ruler will say to them, 'I tell you as a matter of fact, that whatever you do for the least member of my family, you have done for me.' [41]Then the ruler will say to those on the left, 'You are accursed. Depart from me to that everlasting fire prepared for the devil and his angels. [42]For I was hungry and you did not give me anything to eat, I was thirsty and you did not give me anything to drink, [43]I was an outsider and you did not befriend me, I was poorly dressed and you did not clothe me, sick and in prison and you did not care for me.' [44]Then they will say in reply, 'Lord, when did we see you hungry or thirsty or an outsider or poorly dressed or sick or in prison and not serve you?' [45]And in answer he will say to them, 'I tell you for a fact, that whatever you failed to do for the least of these, you failed to do it for me.' [46]So they will depart for everlasting punishment, but those approved receive that life which knows no death."

The Text in Its Biblical Setting

In the structure of Matthew's Gospel, 25:31–46 is the last item in the discourse on last things (see session 4). It is preceded in chapter 25 by two parables, those of the Ten Maidens and the Talents. Verses 31-46, however, are not a parable but an apocalyptic vision. Such visions were common in Jewish literature at the time of the New Testament. They normally dealt with a disclosure of final events (the word *apocalyptic* means "revealing") via a dream or vision (see Rev. 1:1, 9-10). The function of these visions was either to encourage repentance or moral action by stressing the immediacy of the end, or, on the other hand, patience and endurance by stressing the certainty of God's judgment. Matthew's vision of the last judgment does not stress so much the sense of immediacy as that of certainty. Its intent is to bolster a certain community of believers in its lifestyle. Similar last judgment passages can be found in Revelation 4—9 and Daniel 7:9-10. They, too, had the purpose of encouraging the faithful in moments of persecution or difficulty.

This vision of the last judgment starts out much like the account in Daniel. The Son of Man (a technical term in some apocalyptic literature) comes and assumes a royal role. One would have expected God to be the ruler (as in Rev. 4:8-11) and the Christ-figure to be a mediator (such as the Lamb in Revelation). But as Daniel speaks of the Son of Man receiving everlasting sovereignty from God (7:14), so in Matthew the Son of Man takes over the function of the great ruler. Nevertheless, we are constantly aware that the ultimate power is not sitting on the throne, but that Christ has been given the power he exercises by the Father (see v. 34).

The division of the righteous and the unrighteous is compared to a pastoral separation of sheep and goats. The simile should not be taken too seriously. The readers were probably aware that shepherds often did make such a separation, but there is nothing particular about sheep that makes them an apt image for good Christians. The imagery probably goes back to Ezekiel 34, where the leaders of the Jews are called shepherds and are admonished for failing to perform their functions. God then resolves to be the shepherd, as is the case in Matthew 25:31-46. In Ezekiel 34 the goats are scolded for trampling the grass (34:18-19). Goats then are members of the flock who stir up trouble, i.e., do not submit to the leadership of the shepherd.

The reason for the division has little to do with "faith" as we find it elsewhere in the New Testament. In fact, the entire list of good deeds can be found in Jewish material. The following quote from the Sotah (14a), a section of the Talmud, indicates the similarity. A rabbi has asked what it means to walk after the Lord your God (Deut. 13:5). The reply is:

> But the meaning is to walk after the attributes of the Holy One, blessed be He. As He clothes the naked, for it is written, "And the Lord God made for Adam and for his wife coats of skin and clothed them" (Gen. 3:21 RSV), so do thou also clothe the naked. The Holy One, blessed be He, visited the sick, for it is written, "And the Lord appeared to him by the oaks of Mamre" (Gen. 18:1 RSV; note 17:27), so do thou also visit the sick.

The striking part of the vision is the surprise registered by both the righteous and the unrighteous. It would be tempting to suppose that the righteous were surprised because their kindness was so genuine that they were unconscious of their good deeds. This would relate to the childlike quality of becoming a Christian, of which Matthew speaks in 18:14. But the text probably does not have that meaning. It would appear that the righteous and unrighteous are not surprised about the good deeds, or lack thereof, but that the good deeds were done, or not done, to the great ruler himself. The teaching underscored by the vision of the last judgment is that deeds of kindness done to God's family are done to God.

This teaching is directed particularly to the Gentiles (see the alternate translation for "nations" in v. 32). God's judgment against the Jews was described in an earlier apocalyptic section, 24:1-44. The Jews are judged for failing to repent in the face of the end-time (24:45-51). The Gentile judgment is quite different. Gentiles did not share the deep sense of religious unity which characterized the Jews. Their relationship to God was much more individualistic. To them true service was viewed as appropriate supplication of the gods. Matthew 25:31-46 attempts to define for the Gentile world the true nature of serving God. It impresses upon the nations (non-Jews) that true service to God is nothing less than service to the *family* of God. In verse 44 the very term "serve" (Greek: *diakoneo*) carries with it the implication of service to God, or ministry on the part of the church (see Acts 6:2).

For those who failed to serve God in this way, the result was ultimate separation from God and his glory (v. 46). For those who did so serve, the result was life with God. The Greek word used here and elsewhere to describe this life is *aionios*. In early translations into

English, the term used to convey its meaning was "eternal." In this century we have come to see that the English word "eternal" belongs more to Western philosophy than the Bible. Therefore the English word "everlasting" became popular. However this still places emphasis on the *length* of life as the reward. This is false. The reward consists not of the length of the afterlife, but of the joy of life which knows no separation from God.

The Text in Brethren Life

In his discussion of Brethren relief and service work in *Church of the Brethren: Yesterday and Today* (1986), David B. Eller states that "the biblical foundation for this ministry was the teaching of Jesus" in Matthew 25:34-40. "For many Brethren in the 20th century, 'service'... became the most important priority of the denominatior.."[1] Likewise, in the book *To Serve the Present Age* (1971), L. W. Shultz says: "Brethren Service has its origins in the words of our Lord" and then quotes Matthew 25:35-36. In the same book, M. R. Zigler states: "The Church of the Brethren . . . awakened after the Second World War to a sense of mission, based upon the message of the Good Samaritan and the vision of Matthew 25, upon the principle that these two New Testament directives had to be lifted from the traditional aspects of individual obedience to the teachings of Jesus to the obedience of a church as a body."[3] Thus, there is abundant testimony to the fact that the Great Judgment described in Matthew 25 has been understood by Brethren of the twentieth century as a command to serve the needs of others on a worldwide basis.

The Matthew 25 text, however, was also the basis of Brethren service on the individual and local levels during the eighteenth and nineteenth centuries. Peter Nead (1796-1877), writing about hospitality and almsgiving in his *Primitive Christianity* (1834), quotes verses 34-40 of the judgment scene. Commenting upon the quote, Nead says: "We may conclude, that the righteous who, in this life, performed charitable deeds toward the children of God, have done them out of love to them, and because they were the Lord's disciples; and that they did not perform these good acts with an expectation of meriting or purchasing the kingdom of heaven."[4] Two tracts on the topic of Christian giving written by I. J. Rosenberger (1842-1923) in the latter part of the nineteenth century mention Matthew 25:40.[5] One of the tracts (No. 274) presents the design for giving in terms of God constantly repeating "his humiliation by coming in the person of the poor."[6] With this confrontation goes the assurance that any charitable deed done for the poor is rewarded as a deed done for God.

During the first two hundred years of the Church of the Brethren, the precepts of service described by Matthew's vision of the Great Judgment were practiced either by individuals in one-to-one relationships or by local congregations responding to the needs of their own members or the needs in their local communities. It is said that Alexander Mack (1679-1735) himself used much of the money he received from the sale of his mill and vineyards to pay the fines of those arrested for practicing Pietism and to aid those fleeing to Schwarzenau to escape religious persecution.[7] Christopher Sauer, Jr., (1712-1784) was also noted for his charity. His "greatest philanthropic gesture on record was his *Geistliches Magazien* (Spiritual Magazine), a religious publication distributed *gratis* by Sauer."[8]

The minutes of Annual Meetings indicate that congregations regularly met the needs of their poor members. For example, the minutes of 1793 delineate a method for helping the needy. This method was established because the former method of allowing any needy member to go from one congregation to another seeking aid proved too flexible, for it allowed unscrupulous people, who pretended to be poor Brethren, to deceive local congregations. The new method prevented the possibility of deceit by stating that members in need could only approach their own local congregation for aid. If the local congregation could not meet the need, then the congregation would request help from a neighboring congregation by letter. The needy individuals, however, were not permitted to approach a neighboring church on their own. It is interesting to note that appended to the description of this new method of looking after the needy is a sentence warning Brethren that this discussion of how members may seek aid is not to be understood as meaning that the Brethren are only to meet the needs of their own poor members. To the contrary, it is necessary for them to do good for the poor outside the church also.

Another well-known example of Brethren aiding their fellow Brethren is the story of Barbara Kindig (1829-1915) and James Rufus Gish (1826-1896). The Gishes, while based in Illinois, traveled about, particularly in Tennessee and Arkansas, spreading the gospel. Even with all the travel, they managed to amass a sizable estate, for, it was said, Rufus was a good businessman. They used some of this estate to locate Brethren ministers in new communities. The Gishes would purchase a farm in a community needing a minister. Then they would sell the farm to a minister looking for a new home and allow the minister to pay for the farm as his means permitted. Upon the death of Rufus, Barbara used the estate, about fifty thousand dollars, to establish the Gish Fund, which provided money for the publication of books for Brethren ministers and, for many years, enabled Brethren ministers to purchase books at a reduced rate.[9]

A typical twentieth-century Brethren understanding of Matthew 25:31-46 is found in Edward Frantz's *Basic Belief* (1943). Writing about the Great Judgment scene, Frantz (1868-1962), editor of the *Gospel Messenger* for twenty-seven years, asks why the Son of man judges men and women by what they have done and not done, without ever asking about their beliefs. Does this mean that what they believe is unimportant? No, says Frantz, but it does mean "that the value of what a man believes concerning any fundamental doctrine of Christian faith is shown not by what he says about it but by what he does about it."[10]

Frantz was writing just as the worldwide work of the Brethren Service Commission (BSC) was beginning to flower. Created in 1939, under the name Brethren Service Committee, BSC helped administer Civilian Public Service (CPS) during World War II. CPS, a cooperative program of the historic peace churches, provided conscientious objectors during the war with opportunities to serve in nonmilitary positions as conservationists, fire fighters, hospital attendants, control patients, etc. After the war the work of BSC went worldwide with relief and reconstruction work in Europe, China, India, Nigeria, and Ecuador. Particularly notable BSC programs were the resettlement of Japanese-Americans, Heifer Project, the Kaltenstein Project, Brethren Volunteer Service (BVS), and the high school student exchange program. BSC also cooperated with other groups in such programs as CROP (Christian Rural Overseas Program), NSBRO (National Service Board for Religious Objectors), and UNRRA (United Nations Relief and Reconstruction Administration). Heifer Project eventually developed into an interdenominational independent program, in which the Brethren now participate as a partner with other Christian groups.

Writing about the work of BSC in his introduction to *To Serve the Present Age*, Donald F. Durnbaugh says:

> The relief and rehabilitation work of the Brethren Service Commission (BSC) had a dual focus: the first was to send material aid—food, clothes, medicine—to those in dire need, even to those former enemies such as the Germans. The second, made necessary by the first, was to appeal to the conscience of the membership of the Church of the Brethren. For the most part, Brethren had not been

directly touched by the impact of the war and its after-
math. The response was impressive. During the fiscal year
ending February 28, 1947, the value of materials administered and distributed reached $7,189,000, although not all
of this was contributed directly by Brethren. The administrative cost was less than two percent. The work done at
that time earned for the Brethren a reputation for concern
and effectiveness.[11]

In 1968, due to reorganization, the work of BSC was transferred to
the World Ministries Commission, which combines service, overseas
missions, and concern for peace and justice.

Notes

1. David B. Eller, "Social Outreach," in *Church of the Brethren: Yesterday and Today,*
   ed. Donald F. Durnbaugh (Elgin, IL: Brethren Press, 1986), 130.

2. L. W. Shultz, "The Formation of the Brethren Service Committee," in *To Serve the
   Present Age,* ed. Donald F. Durnbaugh (Elgin, IL: Brethren Press, 1975), 111.

3. M. R. Zigler, "A Personal Testimony," in *To Serve the Present Age,* 67.

4. Peter Nead, *Primitive Christianity, or a Vindication of the Word of God* (Staunton,
   VA: Kenton Harper, Printer, 1834), 150.

5. Both tracts are titled "Christian Giving" and are found in *The Brethren's Tracts
   and Pamphlets* (Elgin, IL: Brethren Publishing House, 1900). The tracts are Nos.
   274 and 313.

6. Ibid., Tract No. 274.

7. D. L. Miller and Galen B. Royer, *Some Who Led* (Elgin, IL: Brethren Publishing
   House, 1912), 11.

8. Stephen L. Longenecker, *The Christopher Sauers* (Elgin, IL: Brethren Press, 1981),
   121.

9. J. Ezra Miller, "The Gish Fund and the Care of Superannuated Ministers and
   Missionaries," in *Two Centuries of the Church of the Brethren* (Elgin, IL: Brethren
   Publishing House, 1908), 371-378.

10. Edward Frantz, *Basic Belief* (Elgin, IL: Brethren Publishing House, 1943), 92.

11. Donald F. Durnbaugh, "Introduction," in *To Serve the Present Age,* 10.

The Text in Today's World

A criticism which has constantly plagued Brethren Service and
other church service groups has been the lack of any "good news" for
the recipients of our giving. As can be seen from the history of our use
of the passage, advocates of Brethren service-type projects did use

Matthew 25:31-46 to support activities which expected no response from the recipients. There is much to be said for service which does not expect return, does not force the recipient to do a particular action, and does not have even psychological strings attached to it. Though the giver has a right to expect responsible use of the gift, it is the desire for reciprocity on the part of the giver which so often destroys a gift. By this means whites have kept minorities in debt, the wealthy have made demands the poor could not meet, and the First World has dictated what form Third World Christianity would take.

Because Jesus so frequently equates goodness with intentionality rather than specific actions (see, for example, Jesus' comments on murder and adultery in Matt. 5:21-30), one could reasonably suppose that true followers of Jesus might not know when they are doing acts of charity and kindness. Their ethical actions are not based on rational decision but on living out the stories (narratives) and examples of the faith community. If the truest act of worship is to step outside one's own self-interest and place God totally in the center, without thought of gain (Matt. 6:1-21), then the truest act of love is to think of another person and act on that person's behalf without concern for self. Some theologians place *agape*, that love of God which requires no return, at the very center of Christianity. We ought not lose this dimension of the text.

As indicated, however, in our earlier comments on the text, the passage stresses more the doing to Christ than the selfless service. And it makes clear that the point at which we serve Christ is in our acts of ministry to those who make up God's family, a family that includes all of humanity, all of God's children. Matthew 25 tells us that the outsider in the community, the person without sufficient clothes, the person caught in jail without bail money, the person without a home, are all members of the body of Christ.

Such a message flies in the face of popular notions of what it means to be religious in America. Religion has become one's private piety and personal experience. It has become an interior sense of sin and guilt, followed by repentance and the reception of God's grace. For many there is no gospel unless souls are being saved. Ethics becomes then a matter of personal rectitude. Little wonder then that many do not see in this passage the kind of gospel they would like to hear. Over and against this kind of approach to faith and morality, our text calls us to see life in terms of care for the human community and to see faith in terms of sensitivity to the Christ of the poor and outcast. It is in this way that we really "come to Christ" and worship him.

Put this way, we see that the common distinction between service and the gospel is rather questionable. Acts of service to our partners in humanity are not just acts of service but a ministry to Christ in our brothers and sisters. When we serve humanity, we are serving the body of Christ at the same time.

Case Study

A Church of the Brethren located in an eastern metropolitan area recently became aware that its totally white appearance made it a "dying congregation." The church, eager to face its own destiny, called the Church of the Brethren offices in Elgin, Illinois. Eventually, the congregation was visited by a staff member experienced in multi-racial churches. The staff member suggested a consciousness-raising retreat for the congregation. With excellent outside help, the inner city congregation learned about African-American music; about particular patterns of leadership which differ from the historic Brethren way; about the need for mutuality rather than patronizing; about "we" and "they" language which might be offensive.

The local church took these lessons to heart and did indeed change the worship, became involved in cooperative projects with community people, and eliminated offensive language and customs. The church grew. It recommended to other inner-city churches the program of consciousness raising.

1. Is ethical service best done naturally or with conscious aware-ness?

2. Did this Brethren congregation need consciousness raising? Why didn't it know what to do naturally?

3. Where does "natural service" come from?

4. Does your congregation serve the community as a matter of course, or do you need to think about it?

Session 8

On Making Disciples

Matthew 28:16-20 (NRSV)

Now the eleven disciples went to Galilee, to the mountain to which Jesus had directed them. [17]When they saw him, they worshiped him; but some doubted. [18]And Jesus came and said to them, "All authority in heaven and on earth has been given to me. [19]Go therefore and make disciples of all nations, baptizing them in the name of the Father and of the Son and of the Holy Spirit, [20]and teaching them to obey everything that I have commanded you. And remember, I am with you always, to the end of the age."

Matthew 28:16-20 (BNT)

The eleven disciples went into Galilee, to the mountain where he had directed them. [17]And when they saw him they worshiped, though some doubted. [18]And Jesus came and spoke to them with these words: "All the power in heaven and on earth has been given to me. [19]So go and make disciples of all the nations. Baptize them in the name of the Father, and in the name of the Son, and in the name of the Holy Spirit. [20]Teach them to keep the commandments which I have given you. And, look, I will be with you every day until this age is finished."

The Text in Its Biblical Setting

According to Matthew and Mark, the risen Jesus was to appear to his disciples in Galilee (Matt. 28:7, 9; Mark 16:7). Since the earliest texts of the Gospel of Mark end at 16:8, we do not have stories of resurrection appearances in Mark's gospel. In fact, the author of Mark may have wished to stress the suffering death of Jesus on the cross rather than the resurrection. But in Matthew the disciples do, indeed, go to Galilee, where Jesus appears to them on a mountain. These earliest accounts show a "prejudice" against Jerusalem not present in later accounts. Jerusalem was the blue-blooded capital of Palestinian Judaism. Galilee, on the other hand, was the epitome of racial mixture, impurity, radicalism, and localism (see Isa. 9:1-2). Nothing good could come from Galilee (John 1:46). The Gospels of Matthew and Mark have, in a sense, reversed this. It was Jerusalem which crucified Jesus—an act which covered it with shame and darkness (see Matt. 27:45 and parallels). But it was in Galilee that the resurrection was made known. (Only in Luke and John do we find reports of resurrection appearances which occurred in Jerusalem; see Luke 24:13-53 and John 20:11-29.)

So, just as the Sermon on the Mount was given on a hill in Galilee, so are Jesus' final instructions to the disciples. These events place the Christian revelation through Jesus in sharp contrast with the revelation of the priests and rabbis of Jerusalem (Mount Zion). In order to shift the revelation from Jerusalem to Galilee, it was necessary to reinterpret the Old Testament (see for example, Luke 24:25-27), much as Jesus reinterpreted the law in Matthew 5. As a result, some of the disciples did perceive that the resurrection of Jesus was the fulfillment of their expectations regarding the Messiah. Still others doubted (Matt. 28:17). Their doubt, however, does not disqualify them from participating in the mission.

The call to mission was based on the supreme authority of the resurrected Lord. In the ancient world people believed in tribal and geographically limited gods. As people traveled from one area to another, they might need to deal with the god of the new area (see Gen. 32:22-24). Or persons would attempt to flee from their god by leaving the god's territory (see Jon. 1:3). Pre-Christian Jews were fully aware that there was only one God over all (see Deut. 6:4), but their specific knowledge of that one God was through the Jewish Jahweh (Lord). The dramatic and powerful affirmation of Christianity is that the specific Lord of Israel also is the Lord of all—and that Lord is the resurrected Jesus. Put another way, verse 18 claims that Christianity is the true faith for the world. Therefore, disciples of Jesus will actively make disciples of others, even among the Gentiles. (The reference to "nations" likely has that meaning.)

In Greek the content of the great commission consists of three Greek participles and an imperative, all of which we treat as commands: Go, make disciples, baptize, and teach. The "go" refers to an aggressive effort to preach the gospel among the Gentiles. However, we do not possess a Matthean account of the implementation of this mission as we find in Luke—Acts. We do suspect the Gospel of Matthew was written in Antioch, and Antioch was known in early Christianity as the place where the Gentile mission began (Acts

11:19-26). This might account for the strong commission to go to the Gentiles in a gospel which elsewhere has a strongly Jewish flavor.

The Greek term translated "make disciples" ordinarily means "to *be* a pupil of" (as in Matt. 27:57), but here in Matthew 13:52 and in Acts 14:21, it means to *make* other persons pupils or disciples of Jesus. A disciple is simply a person who submits to the process of learning from a master. In responding to the mission of Jesus' followers, then, the first step for the Gentile was to submit to the authority of Jesus as Lord.

Baptizing was an act of immersion in water, common among many religious groups of the time. At the time of Jesus, it was not customary to baptize Gentiles into Judaism. That was still done by circumcision. The baptism of John the Baptist was not for conversion but for repentance (Matt. 3:11). If Christian baptism derives from the baptism of John, it has been altered considerably in the process, for the term *baptism* in Matthew 28:19 refers to conversion from paganism to Christianity (see Acts 16:33; 1 Cor. 1:14-17). It implies not only a change of religious loyalty but also participation in a fellowship of persons who also have made a commitment to the Christian way. This is indicated by the baptismal formula: "in the name of the Father, and of the Son, and of the Holy Spirit." To be baptized in the name of someone is to join a fellowship established in the name of that person. In 1 Corinthians 10:2, Paul says the Jews were baptized "into Moses," which means essentially the same thing as "in the name of Moses." To be baptized into Moses is to become a part of that corporate group or family who identifies with Moses. Likewise, to be baptized in the name of Jesus (Acts 8:16; 19:5; compare Gal. 3:27) is to express one's participation in that fellowship who identifies with Jesus.

To be baptized in the name of God (the Father) *and* in the name of Jesus (the Son) *and* in the name of the Holy Spirit adds considerably to the meaning of baptism. We should note that the word *name* occurs only once in the Greek text, but its use is surely distributive. That is, *name* was intended to precede each of the members of the trinity. This is the only trinitarian baptismal formula in the New Testament. In fact, this and the benediction of 2 Corinthians 13:14 are the only *explicit* trinitarian formulae we can find in the New Testament. There are other expressions that imply a trinitarian faith, however. Very helpful is the passage in 1 Corinthians 12:4-6 where the Spirit gives gifts, the Son does service, and the Father effects works. Trinitarian thinking is also reflected in Ephesians 4:4-6; Acts 2:32-33; and 1 Peter 1:2.

If we put together the New Testament references to the trinity, we would come up with definitions something like this: God (the *Father*) is the power of divinity. God gives form to creation and also to what is yet to come. God's power pushes us from behind (because we know what we once were) and pulls us from ahead (because we yearn for what we are to be, Rom. 8:23). Jesus (the *Son*) gives specific form to the Christian community, much as Moses gave specific form to the Jewish community. In the community of the Son, one serves God and other persons (1 Cor. 12:5). The function of the *Spirit* is to enable us to reach beyond the limitations of our given form of serving God, to move toward the end-time vision, to fulfill the promises of God. For this purpose the Spirit equips us with the gifts of freedom, preaching, administration, and many more. In its many varied expressions, all of them Christian, the church in its present pilgrimage is the community of the Holy Spirit.

Baptism in all three names is the normative expectation: The Christian becomes a part of the total and universal family of God the Father. The Christian takes up the specific form of a worshiping family which goes back to Jesus of Nazareth, the Son. The Christian also participates in local groups of believers who receive gifts of the Spirit to enable them to reach toward the vision revealed to them in the Bible.

The fourth command is to "teach." As noted previously, the Gospel of Matthew was organized as an authoritative teaching Gospel, a kind of early church curriculum. Its systematic units would indicate this. Jesus teaches about the meaning of the law, the mission of his disciples, the nature of the kingdom, the function of the church, and the nature of the last times which call disciples to watchfulness. After baptism into the fellowship of believers, the new Christian is to learn from these assembled teachings.

The Text in Brethren Life

Merle Crouse opens the discussion of missions in *Church of the Brethren: Yesterday and Today* (1986) with the observation that Brethren "have used the Great Commission text (Matt. 28:19-20) more for justifying the practice of trine immersion baptism than for sending God's people into the world."[1] Crouse is indeed correct in his analysis of the Brethren use of Matthew 28:19-20. Until the late nineteenth century, Brethren valued the Great Commission more as a statement about baptism than as a call to mission or evangelistic work.

The words of Matthew 28:19-20 have provided the Brethren with answers to several questions about baptism. For Alexander Mack (1679-1735), it proved that Christ intended water baptism for all believers and that such water baptism is to continue until the return of Christ to earth.[2] Furthermore, Mack understood the word *baptize* to mean "immerse." Thus, he believed that the words of verse 19 command that the whole person should be immersed in water. Says Mack: "The Lord Jesus did indeed not say to baptize the head or some other part of the body of the person, or sprinkle the person a little with water in His name. No, the Lord Jesus did not command this, but rather that the whole person should be immersed in water."[3]

For Peter Nead (1796-1877), verse 19, along with John 3:5 and Mark 16:15-16, proved that baptism is both a commandment and essential for salvation and provided information on the form and mode of baptism. The proper form for baptism, says Nead, is with the words "in the name of the Father and of the Son and of the Holy Spirit," as stated in verse 19. This form, according to Nead, is preferred by the New Testament over the words used in Acts 8:16 and Acts 10:48. The proper mode of baptism is trine immersion, that is, three immersions in water, one immersion for each of the names of the trinity. Nead's biblical basis for trine immersion is the fact that verse 19 reads "in the name of" not "in the names of."[4]

It was also to Matthew 28:19 that R. H. Miller (1825-1892), best known for his debates, turned for his first argument of support for trine immersion in his book *Doctrine of the Brethren Defended* (1876). According to Miller's argument, trine immersion "is founded on the plurality of the Deity,"[5] as expressed in verse 19. To counter the argument that single immersion should be practiced since the Deity is one as well as three, Miller says: "If Christ wished his disciples to baptize into the Deity in the sense in which he is one being, we would expect to find it so commanded . . . but he did not give that in the formula of baptism."[6] What he did give in the commission, says Miller, is a formula for trine immersion.

Several Brethren tracts on baptism, published in the late nineteenth century, also cite the Great Commission in Matthew 28. Generally, such references are quoted as evidence for trine immersion, and the logic is similar to that of R. H. Miller. In one tract by B. F. Moomaw (1814-1900), however, Matthew 28:19 is also used as evidence in the case against infant baptism. According to Moomaw, the words "teach all nations" (KJV) indicate that the risen Lord had adult baptism in mind. Since teaching precedes baptism, argues Moomaw, "it is necessary, therefore, that the mind be sufficiently developed so as to be capable of being taught, and this will exclude infants."[7]

The first occurrence of concern for missions in the minutes of Annual Meeting, according to Henry Kurtz's *Brethren's Encyclopedia* (1867) was in 1852.[8] In that year the question was raised as to whether the Great Commission, in Matthew 28:19-20, and its parallel, in Mark 16:15, did not require the church to provide preachers for those who do not know the gospel. In response the Annual Meeting acknowledged the concern and urged all members to fulfill the commission. The concern continued to be raised throughout the 1850s, and in 1860 the Annual Meeting appointed a board to work with the Brethren in California and Oregon, who had requested that a delegation be sent to aid them in the organization of churches and to preach to those who did not know the gospel.

In 1876 Christian Hope (1844-1899) became the first Brethren missionary to be sent to a foreign country. Hope was sent to Denmark, the land of his birth, by the Northern Illinois District, in response to his request for Brethren missionaries for Denmark. From this beginning the Brethren developed overseas missionary programs in Turkey, Switzerland, France, India, China, Nigeria, and Ecuador. According to Floyd Mallott (1897-1971), missionary and professor of church history, "from 1884 to the outbreak of World War II (1939) most Brethren would have held missions, to be the primary work of the church."[9] Good summaries of Brethren foreign missions, as well as home missions, are found in the *Brethren Encyclopedia*[10] and *Church of the Brethren: Yesterday and Today*.[11]

In 1955 the Annual Conference adopted a new foreign missions policy. Whereas the Brethren had been following traditional patterns whereby the US Brethren tended to relate to new churches in other countries as a parent relates to a child, the new policy favored *indigenization*. This new approach encouraged the development of national leadership in the new churches and sought to place control in their hands.

The Brethren moved to a newer understanding of missions in 1981 with the adoption of the "World Mission Philosophy and Program Statement" by Annual Conference. Early in this statement is the biblical mandate for missions which includes six themes based on Scripture texts. One of the texts is Matthew 28:19-20. Later in the statement, the Great Commission is again cited, this time as God's summons to all Christians to be in mission. "In today's world the terms *home* and *foreign* missions are no longer appropriate. Christians are to be in mission wherever they are. The field is the world. We are to witness to our next door neighbor, to any of the 80-100 million non-Christians in the United States, to persons elsewhere in the world where Christ is not known or obeyed."[12] In addition to this new emphasis on the need for missions in the United States itself, the statement also calls for a new approach to succeed indigenization—*mutuality in missions*. This approach, based on 2 Corinthians 8:14, stresses the interdependence of all Christians throughout the world. "Mission should now be a two-way process . . . . The future of humankind can best be guided toward the fulfillment of God's purpose if God's people, East, West, North, and South, will carry forward a unified ministry in the spirit of partnership and mutual caring."[13]

As a result of the 1981 statement, Brethren began to place more emphasis on evangelism, particularly in the United States; and programs were developed to plant new churches and train people in evangelism. Some people, however, felt that due to the new statement, there was less emphasis on aggressive world missions. Furthermore, the statement did not indicate how already existing Christian groups in both the US and other countries could join the Church of the Brethren. Given these problems, a new version of the statement was adopted in 1989. In many ways the 1989 version is the same as the 1981. Both Matthew 28:19-20 and 2 Corinthians 8:14 are still major biblical bases for the theology of mission. Also the principles of indigenization, mutuality, and interdependence are affirmed. The 1989 statement, however, does call for aggressive new mission programs. Furthermore, the authority to determine when an existing Christian group in the US becomes Brethren is placed with the districts; and the authority to determine the same for groups in other countries is placed with Annual Conference.

Notes

1. B. Merle Crouse and Karen Spohr Carter, "Mission," in *Church of the Brethren: Yesterday and Today*, ed. Donald F. Durnbaugh (Elgin, IL: Brethren Press, 1986), 135.

2. Alexander Mack, *Rights and Ordinances*, in *European Origins of the Brethren*, comp. and trans. Donald F. Durnbaugh (Elgin, IL: Brethren Press, 1958), 356-357.

3. Ibid., 361.

4. Peter Nead, *Primitive Christianity, or a Vindication of the Word of God* (Staunton, VA: Kenton Harper, Printer, 1834), 55-78.

5. R. H. Miller, *Doctrine of the Brethren Defended* (Indianapolis: Printing and Publishing House Print, 1876), 141.

6. Ibid., 147.

7. B. F. Moomaw, "Christian Baptism," in *The Brethren's Tracts and Pamphlets* (Elgin, IL: Brethren Publishing House, 1900), 3.

8. Henry Kurtz, *The Brethren's Encyclopedia* (Columbiana, OH: the author, 1867), 151.

9. Floyd E. Mallott, *Studies in Brethren History* (Elgin, IL: Brethren Publishing House, 1954), 233.

10. Donald E. Durnbaugh and Dennis D. Martin, eds. *Brethren Encyclopedia* (Philadelphia: The Brethren Encyclopedia, Inc., 1983), s.v. "Evangelism," by Edward K. Ziegler, and "Missions," by S. Wayne Weaver and Dennis D. Martin.

11. Crouse and Carter, 135-159.

12. *Minutes of the Annual Conference of the Church of the Brethren, 1980-1984*, comp. Phyllis Kingery Ruff (Elgin, IL: Brethren Press, 1985), 206.

13. Ibid., 209.

The Text in Today's World

Historically the Brethren have been "Anabaptists." The term refers to those who rebaptize adults who were baptized as infants. In eighteenth-century Germany, where everyone was automatically baptized at infancy by the state church, rebaptism of state church Christians was the one and only way for a new group like the Brethren to grow. Evangelism as we know it, as a mission to outsiders, was of course impossible in that setting.

Apparently the emigration to America did little to modify the non-evangelistic stance of the Brethren, even though church and state were no longer officially united in this country. At first, Brethren resisted the coming of a revivalism in America, a movement which led to a membership explosion in many denominations. Extended meetings, with altar calls designed to bring about large numbers of individual conversions, were adamantly rejected. Gradually, however, Brethren joined the bandwagon. And we, too, grew into a church of nearly 200,000 members.

The religious world of today differs vastly from previous years. The idea of Western culture as a Christian civilization has disappeared in America as well as Europe. Living as we do in a world which has rejected the gospel, we undoubtedly have an evangelistic task to perform. Matthew 28:16-20 is as pertinent for our day as it was at any time in Brethren history. For Brethren, however, evangelism will mean more than revivalism. Matthew calls us to *make disciples*. The development of discipleship is a slow process that occurs in the company of others who also are sitting at the feet of the Master.

Since rebaptizing persons who once belonged to a state church is no longer a current issue, one can predict that *the form* of baptism will not be as important for Brethren today as it was for our forerunners. However, Brethren will surely want to emphasize the seriousness of casting one's lot with those who would be disciples. Being disciples is not a function of the natural community or the family unit. It is a voluntary decision to accept and be accepted by a new family of God. That decision must be marked by some sign of death to the old and of new life in the faith community. Baptism is such a sign.

The trine immersion of former years pointed to the trinitarian faith of the Brethren. If the evangelistic fervor of Brethren in the coming years is to focus on the formation of communities of faith and persons in such communities, then the trinitarian faith will be as important, or even more so, than in previous generations. Baptizing in the name of God, Christ, and the Holy Spirit means more than just theological formula. It means joining a community which expresses in the world the power of God, lives by the forgiving reconciliation of Jesus Christ, and forms a faith community led by the Holy Spirit. Brethren are reluctant to drop this "baptism." Consequently, evangelism takes on a different form than for those who stress simply salvation of souls or winning people for Christ; or a rational faith in God; or a personal, charismatic experience of the Spirit. For Brethren, new Christians must also find an environment in which to grow. Lifelong development and formation are essential for the kind of Christian life we envision. Some today call this hospitality evangelism. It is a kind of faith we should not hesitate to share in this country or around the world.

A triune understanding of God in itself affirms the communal nature of reality. Our mission to the modern world is not only to invite them to turn to Jesus Christ but to insist that such turning is a process of discipleship which involves a faith commitment to other Christians. This is the nature of *our* life, just as it is the nature of divine reality.

Case Study

The last half of the twentieth century has seen several radical shifts in mission philosophy. Most everyone saw the dangers of earlier missions where European and American Christians not only tried to convert masses of non-Christians but also, often consciously, exported the Western way of life. By the middle of this century, Western Christians realized fast-growing churches in Africa and the Pacific should manage their own mission strategy. They should relate to local religious beliefs in their own way, not the Western way. Yet indigenization seemed to leave the mission churches without any support. Many then suggested the American and European churches should form alliances with mission churches but not determine their strategy.

The conflict in mission strategy came to a head at the 1990 Annual Conference of the Church of the Brethren. Some Brethren believed the church should join with like-minded Korean Christians to promote a Free Church mission in the Pacific Basin. Others felt the Brethren should work with US Brethren from Korea to establish specifically Brethren churches in Korea. After considerable warm debate the Annual Conference voted, in essence, to do both.

1. Which is more important to you: that the Christian faith spread in the Pacific Rim, or that the Church of the Brethren grow (with its vision) in these areas of the world?

2. How do you make disciples for Christ without making, at the same time, disciples for Western social values and economic structure?

3. Can you, as a member of the Church of the Brethren, tell people about your faith *without* telling them about your particular church? Have you tried?

Session 9

On Gambling

Luke 6:27-36 (NRSV)

"But I say to you that listen, Love your enemies, do good to those who hate you, [28]bless those who curse you, pray for those who abuse you. [29]If anyone strikes you on the cheek, offer the other also; and from anyone who takes away your coat do not withhold even your shirt. [30]Give to everyone who begs from you; and if anyone takes away your goods, do not ask for them again. [31]Do to others as you would have them do to you. [32]If you love those who love you, what credit is that to you? For even sinners love those who love them. [33]If you do good to those who do good to you, what credit is that to you? For even sinners do the same. [34]If you lend to those from whom you hope to receive, what credit is that to you? Even sinners lend to sinners, to receive as much again. [35]But love your enemies, do good, and lend, expecting nothing in return. Your reward will be great, and you will be children of the Most High; for he is kind to the ungrateful and wicked. [36]Be merciful, just as your Father is merciful."

Luke 6:27-36 (BNT)

But I say to you who are listening, Love your enemies, do good to those who hate you, [28]bless those who curse you, pray for those who mistreat you. [29]To the one who strikes you on the cheek, offer also the other; and from the one who takes your cloak do not withhold your tunic. [30]Give to anyone who asks of you, and do not demand back whatever someone takes that belongs to you. [31]And as you wish others would do to you, do likewise to them.

[32]And if you love those who love you, of what benefit is that for you? Even sinners love those who love them. [33]And if you do good to those who do good to you, of what benefit is it to you? Even sinners do the same. [34]And if you lend to someone from whom you hope to receive, of what benefit is that to you? Even sinners lend to sinners in order that they might receive the same privilege. [35]So love your enemies, and do good, and lend

without expecting anything in return. Then your reward will be great, and you will be children of the Most High, because that one (too) is kind to the selfish and evil. [36]Therefore be merciful even as your Father is merciful.

The Text in Its Biblical Setting

The Gospel of Luke was put together by someone who wished to present the gospel about Jesus and the story of the early church to an otherwise unknown patron named Theophilus (Luke 1:1-4). According to tradition and the story itself, the author was a companion of Paul (note the "we" passages as in Acts 16:11) and may have been Luke the physician (Col. 4:14). The entire Luke-Acts corpus tells how the new faith reversed the particularism of Judaism and established itself as a universal religion accepted finally in the capitol of the world, Rome.

The Gospel of Luke takes the book of Mark and incorporates many sayings of Jesus from a collection we no longer possess, much like the noncanonical Gospel of Thomas (a first-century gnostic gospel). This particular passage, taken from that sayings source, occurs in Luke's Sermon on the Plain, a section parallel to Matthew's Sermon on the Mount (5:38-48). However, in Matthew the Golden rule occurs in quite another group of sayings, just after the Lord's prayer (Matthew 7:12). The passage in Luke contains the two most important ethical guides in the New Testament: "Love your enemies, do good to those who hate you," and "Do to others as you would have them do to you." It will be necessary to ponder the relationship between these two, but our concern now is for the famous Golden Rule in 6:31.

The Golden Rule is a positive statement by Jesus of the well-known negative rule attributed to the great Rabbi Hillel: "Don't do to your neighbor what you would hate done to you. This is the entire Law, the rest is mere commentary." The Jewish Law to which Hillel refers is primarily a reciprocal law. It is based on mutual relationships within the tribal structure. Laws like the Ten Commandments describe the boundaries of community relationships. They are not simply to be understood as arbitrary divine rules. Hillel then summarizes the nature of peaceful community as one in which no one acts toward another in such a way that the reciprocal action would be painful or undesired. Jesus made it more powerful by saying that you should act toward another in such a way that you would want the reciprocal action to be done to you.

Attempts have been made to reduce the Christian ethic to one or more basic rules, mandates, or commands. When the ethic is placed in the will or self-discipline of an individual, then "right" is defined by what we perceive to be "right." One later Christian thinker, Immanuel Kant, said we should act in such a way that, if everyone acted as we did, the world would be good. Such rules, while very important, tend to place all the emphasis on what we consider the right thing to do. What matters is that the individual (the actor) do the right thing. What others do or think is not relevant.

But the Golden Rule puts it another way. The basis for action depends on how it affects the other and what the other will do in return. This makes it necessary for us to consider how the other person feels, how she/he thinks, how our action affects her/him, how the other feels about you, and what action will result. Most ethical concerns would be covered by the Golden Rule. We would not kill someone because we would not want them to kill us. We would not steal from someone because we would not want them to steal from us. We would not betray someone because we would not want them to betray us. Or, putting it as Jesus did, we would care for others because we would want others to care for us. Or we would share with others because we wanted others to share with us.

Because the Golden Rule covers nearly everything, in Matthew 7:12 Jesus says, as did Hillel, that the maxim covers the entire Law (Torah) and Prophets (historical and prophetical writings of the Hebrew Scriptures). But it surely covers more than simply ethical and religious mandates. The Golden Rule serves in almost any situation. For example, speak to the children of your neighbor as you would like the neighbor to speak to yours. Or, make no more noise at a concert than what you would like for the one sitting next to you to make.

In that sense Luke had a right to omit the reference to the Law and Prophets. Writing to Greeks who may not have known the Hebrew Scriptures, Luke is simply saying that the Golden Rule is a valid approach to all of life. However, Luke also recognizes that not all relationships are reciprocal. The Golden Rule fails precisely when the other person has no reason to respond or would have responded negatively in any case. So Luke connects the Golden Rule with yet another maxim: Love your enemies, do good to those who hate you. In so doing Luke raises the Christian ethic to the highest level.

We might suppose that when there is no reciprocity, no use for the Golden Rule, then we might do as we please. That is not true. When there is no reciprocity, Jesus counsels us to love the other, nevertheless. Unlike the sinners (persons who have no sense of community), followers of Jesus will love without being loved, do good without return, and lend to others without expecting the same privilege (vv. 32-34). Like Matthew (5:45-48), Luke places the motivation for unrequited love in our relationship to God. God loves the just and the unjust, the sinner and the righteous. God's love is mature (this is a better translation of *teleios* which in Matthew 5:48 is often translated as "perfect") rather than unpredictable or arbitrary.

The Text in Brethren Life

The most recent Brethren statement on gambling is a report adopted by Annual Conference in 1986. This report came as a result of a query which raised questions about the proliferation of legalized gambling in the United States, especially the popular new state lotteries. A major section of the report deals with biblical guidelines concerning gambling. This section begins by acknowledging that there is no direct commandment against gambling in the Bible. The report then cites three sets of biblical texts which provide the Christian with a proper understanding of the nature of gambling. First, there are the texts which call the Christian to be a good steward of God's gifts, such as 1 Chronicles 29:14-18; Luke 16:1-13; and 1 Corinthians 6:19-20. Second are the commandments against greed and coveting, such as Exodus 20:17 and Deuteronomy 5:21. Finally, there are the Golden Rule texts—Luke 6:31 and Matthew 7:12.

Concerning the relationship of the Golden Rule to gambling, the report says: "Gambling tends to destroy the concern for others taught in the 'Golden Rule.' " As a result people are encouraged to obtain wealth "at the cost of another person's loss" and thus gambling is "a concession to greed and self-interest." Furthermore, "dependence on lottery revenue has led many states to become exploiters of their own citizens." Obviously the report concludes by calling Brethren to "oppose the legalization of and participation in any form of gambling."[1]

The year 1986 was not the first time Brethren have taken a stand against gambling and, particularly, lotteries. As early as 1804, the Annual Meeting made the following statement about the purchasing of lottery tickets: "It was unanimously concluded that such can not be approved in members, and parents should by all means prevent their children from it, because it can not be viewed any better than any other form of gambling for gain."[2] Similar statements against lotteries were made in 1841, 1850, and 1853. The 1841 statement included an explanation as to why the purchase of lottery tickets was wrong: "Considered, that as a species of gambling for gain's sake, whereby others must necessarily lose, it is wrong."[3] While this explanation does not cite the Golden Rule, it does recall the concern for others expressed in Luke 6:27-31.

After 1853 the issue of lotteries did not come before Annual Conference until the 1980s. However, another form of gambling did become an issue among the Brethren, card playing. In 1892 a query came to Annual Meeting asking about the rightness of games such as cards, croquet, and checkers. In response Annual Meeting stated: "We decide that card playing and like games are unquestionably wrong, and should not be indulged in by members or allowed in their homes."[4] Unfortunately no reason is given as to why card playing is unquestionably wrong. In 1906 Annual Meeting prohibited members from selling articles such as playing cards, dominoes, and dice. This time several texts were cited for the prohibition: Romans 12:1; 14:13; 1 Peter 3:4; and 1 Timothy 2:9. Since these texts tend to be ones used by Brethren to condemn worldly practices, perhaps it was the worldliness of card playing which most offended the Brethren of the early twentieth century.

This theory is supported by the fact that J. H. Moore's condemnation of card playing is found in the section titled "Worldly Amusements" from his book on New Testament doctrines. Moore (1846-1935), a noted Brethren author and editor, says: "This is a pleasure-loving age, and millions are more concerned about the life of pleasure than they are about the life beyond .... They think more about the theater than they think about the house of God. Not a few are more interested in the card table than the Lord's table, and are more gifted in shuffling cards than in turning the leaves of the Sacred Volume."[5] Interestingly, only a few pages later Moore discusses the Golden Rule. His understanding of it includes this statement: "It means honesty all around, and also means a fair chance for everybody, and a square deal for each person, whether rich or poor, great or small."[6] While Moore does not directly connect card playing with the Golden Rule, he does understand the Golden Rule as a command against exploitation.

In 1923 Annual Conference approved the use of the *Brethren's Card*. This short statement of Brethren beliefs, which was never understood as a creed, included a phrase in opposition to "games of chance and sinful amusements." The texts given to support this opposition are Romans 12:17; 1 Thessalonians 5:22; and 1 Peter 2:11. Romans 12:17, which is usually understood as paralleling the materials in Luke 6:27-30, states: "Do not repay anyone evil for evil, but take thought for what is noble in the sight of all." Thus the Brethren's Card based its case against gambling, in part, on the Golden Rule.

As the Brethren moved into the second half of the twentieth century, the increasing number of lotteries forced them to reaffirm their stance against lotteries and gambling in general. As early as 1958, Kenneth Morse, then editor of the *Gospel Messenger*, warned: "From our giveaway programs and our national contests it is only a short step to legalizing bingo games in churches and clubs throughout the country, and only a few more steps to providing for a national lottery (to support national welfare, of course). Then gambling will be not only a bigger-than-ever business but patriotic too."[7] By 1972 several states, including Pennsylvania, had initiated lotteries. An article in the *Messenger* that year listed six reasons why gambling is wrong. One of these reasons, poor stewardship, quoted Matthew's version of the Golden Rule (7:11-12) as a supporting text. After quoting the Matthew text, L. John Weaver, the author of the article, asked: "How different from this [the Golden Rule] is the lure of getting in gambling. The gambler assumes the right to take out of society more than he puts in."[8] Official reaffirmation of the Brethren opposition to gambling came in 1986. As already noted, this reaffirmation uses the Golden Rule texts as major support for the position.

Notes

1. *Minutes of the Annual Conference of the Church of the Brethren, 1985-1989*, comp. Annual Conference Office (Elgin, IL: Brethren Press, 1990), 310-311.

2. *Minutes of the Annual Meeting of the Church of the Brethren, 1778-1909* (Elgin, IL: Brethren Publishing House, 1909), 27.

3. Ibid., 71.

4. Ibid., 560.

5. J. H. Moore, *New Testament Doctrines* (Elgin, IL: Brethren Publishing House, 1915), 162.

6. Ibid., 166-67.

7. Kenneth Morse, "A Nation of Gamblers?" *Gospel Messenger*, 7 June 1958, 5.

8. L. John Weaver, "Gamble? You Bet Your Life," *Messenger*, August 1972, 31.

The Text in Today's World

We may think of the Golden Rule as simply a nice maxim for general social life or for instructing the children. That is not true. It is one of the most profound ethical guides ever uttered. That is especially true for us in the American culture. Americans have been known from the beginning as individualists. The well-known nineteenth-century French analyst, Alexis de Tocqueville, in his famous study of America (*Democracy in America*), generally praised the social structure of the new world except for its intense sense of individuality. Robert Bellah, in his recent study, *Habits of the Heart,* pointed to the same problem. Our individualism leads to social violence, excessive poverty, family dissolution, fractured communities, all the ills of a *laissez faire* social structure. But lest we feel isolated in our problems, we must note that no century has been as violent as this one. The horror of Stalin's Russia or Hitler's Germany will surely mark our time in history as the one in which we least cared for our universal family. The effect of the Golden Rule has not been self-evident.

Much as we deplore the destructive individualism of this century, we must also note that our own Christian heritage has contributed to the lack of community. At our best we have confused the two maxims of Luke 6:27-36. We have come to believe that the heart of our faith is expressed in agape—unrequited love. We see it in God's self-giving on the cross (John 3:16). We have learned to give without expectation of return, to serve without asking for response, to sacrifice self for others. These are powerful sentiments, often stated in the New Testament. But in the Golden Rule, Jesus spoke of a mutual caring between those who are in a reciprocal relationship. We act toward the other as we wish to be treated.

So, to the peripheral of society, we act so that they may become involved in the decision making. To the oppressed we act so that they may find freedom. To the poor we act in such a way that they may gain a just share of the wealth. To act toward others without mutual expectations makes those others subservient and dependent. We should so act toward others that a reciprocal benefit is achieved. Only in that way does Christian community become possible. And that is the deeper meaning of the Golden Rule.

In addition to the service orientation of the Church of the Brethren, there is a strong sense of mutual aid and reciprocal support. Historically, the Brethren did do unto others as they wanted others to do unto them. In our day we need to bring to our society a new sense of that mutuality. We love and care for each other with the assumption that a community of mutual love and care is being developed. Except for "love of the enemy" our service to others will develop also communities of faith. Sometimes we have not seen this so clearly and have tried to serve without living out the Golden Rule.

The early Brethren used the Golden Rule as a basis for their opposition to gambling. One can hardly suppose Jesus or the community of Luke thought of gambling as a problem addressed by these verses. Yet the Brethren did discern the mutuality of the Golden Rule. Community depends on mutually developed justice and distribution of resources. Any system which allows arbitrary distribution of resources will destroy the sense of peace and justice in the faith community. Gambling, especially lotteries, does just that. Furthermore, gambling encourages those who do not receive a fair distribution to "take a chance" for a better life. Instead, they and we should participate financially in the development of a society where mutual justice prevails.

CASE STUDY

The Union Hospital System runs several hospitals in a large metropolitan area. The Union Development Council, a part of the larger system, is charged with the task of raising funds for the several hospitals, especially the two struggling inner-city hospitals. Besides approaching local corporations and foundations, the Development Council also organized golf outings and fishing trips. One popular project was a new car raffle. It was held annually on behalf of the two inner-city hospitals. The raffle usually resulted in an $8,000 gift to each hospital. The grant was normally used for needed equipment in the much used emergency room. The grant was both needed and appreciated.

A rather wealthy, conservative Christian layman began to object to the raffle. He argued that people should give to the hospitals because they wanted to give, not because they might win a prize. Furthermore, he argued, the Christian faith opposed any form of gambling, even for a good cause. After some heated discussion the Development Council voted to cancel all such raffles.

1. Has your community ever held a turkey raffle or any other such fund raising event? Do you know a church that has? Did you think it was right?

2. If you fell on hard times, would you appreciate it if your friends held a raffle on your behalf?

3. Ought you to do good for others by means of a lottery?

On Counting the Cost

Luke 14:25-33 (NRSV)

Now large crowds were traveling with him; and he turned and said to them, [26]"Whoever comes to me and does not hate father and mother, wife and children, brothers and sisters, yes, and even life itself, cannot be my disciple. [27]Whoever does not carry the cross and follow me cannot be my disciple. [28]For which of you, intending to build a tower, does not first sit down and estimate the cost, to see whether he has enough to complete it? [29]Otherwise, when he has laid a foundation and is not able to finish, all who see it will begin to ridicule him, [30]saying, 'This fellow began to build and was not able to finish.' [31]Or what king, going out to wage war against another king, will not sit down first and consider whether he is able with ten thousand to oppose the one who comes against him with twenty thousand? [32]If he cannot, then, while the other is still far away, he sends a delegation and asks for the terms of peace. [33]So therefore, none of you can become my disciple if you do not give up all your possessions."

Luke 14:25-33 (BNT)

Several groups were walking along with him, when suddenly he turned and said to them, [26]"If there are any persons going along with me and they do not reject their father, and mother, and spouse, and children, and brothers, and sisters, yes, even their own personhood, they are not able to be my disciples. [27]And those who do not bear their cross and follow after me, are not able to be my disciples. [28]For which one of you, wishing to build a storage shed, does not sit down first and determine the cost of construction, to see if there are enough funds to complete the job? [29]Otherwise, after you have laid the foundation and then cannot finish, all those watching will tease you, [30]saying, 'This person here began to build and was not able to finish the job!' [31]Or what general, about to enter into combat with another general, would not first sit down and consider whether it is possible, with only ten thousand soldiers, to withstand the attack of twenty thousand? [32]And if it is not possible, while the enemy is still at a distance, the general will send an envoy to seek the terms for peace. [33]So then those of you who cannot set aside everything that is yours cannot be my disciples."

The Text in Its Biblical Setting

In the center of the Gospel of Luke we find a long section (9:51—18:14) which has no parallels in the Gospel of Mark and an order which is quite different from the Gospel of Matthew. It is difficult to assess the full import of this section, but it does deal heavily with the mission of the disciples and with the nature of discipleship. Our section deals directly with the decision to become a disciple (cf. one of the first narratives of the total section, 9:57-62). Verses 25-27 have parallels in Matthew, but verses 28-33 are peculiar to Luke.

The structure of the text is quite clear. There are four sets of sayings:

Verses 25-26:	Disciples may have to reject their families.
Verse 27:	Disciples are called to bear the cross.
Verses 28-32:	Disciples must count the cost of their decision.
Verse 33:	Disciples must set aside everything.

As we have already noted (see Session 3), a series or set of sayings often should be interpreted in the light of the last item of the series. Taken individually the sayings in a set might appear to mean one thing, but taken as a complete set they may mean something else. We will assume that verse 33 determines the meaning of the entire passage here.

The statement by Jesus in verses 25-26, that disciples will need to "hate" their families, must be the harshest saying in the New Testament. The Greek word *miseo* can mean hate in the sense of a *passion against* someone or something (as in Matt. 24:9). But *miseo* here can hardly refer to a passionate abhorrence. Love of, or honor of, father and mother was one of the Ten Commandments and one upheld by Jesus (Mark 10:19). He strongly admonished those who tried to avoid caring for their parents (Mark 7:9-13). And he himself showed care for his mother (John 19:26-27). In regard to husbands and wives, few teachers in antiquity held as firmly as did Jesus to the finality of the marriage bond (Mark 10:1-12). Even if he did ask his disciples to leave their spouses, they clearly ignored this saying. For not only were they married but they took their mates with them (1 Cor. 9:5). Finally, it would be hard to believe that the very teacher who called for us to cease hating our enemies would then advise us to hate those closest to us (see Session 3).

It is from our control saying, verse 33, that we begin to understand what *miseo* does mean here: Discipleship entails such fervent loyalty to Jesus and the kingdom that nothing else has equal value. We "love," "serve," and "are devoted to" God, but we "hate" and "despise" mammon (Matt. 6:24; see Session 3). We "hold fast" to what is good, but we "hate" what is evil (Rom. 12:9, where the Greek word for "hate" is a synonym of *miseo*.) The term *hate* then in Luke 14:25-26 means to "reject as an ultimate value" everything but the kingdom. Because of the high value of the family in the Judeo-Christian tradition, the family is the most difficult to "hate." Yet Jesus did speak of his natural family as less important than God's family (Mark 3:31-35), and the disciples apparently did leave their ancestral homes (Luke 18:28). Paul warned that a person overly concerned about marriage and family might put devotion to the Lord in second place (1 Cor. 7:32-35).

The second of the four sayings—on taking up the cross—also presents difficulties for the interpreter. Should it be taken literally or figuratively? And, if figuratively, in what sense? The Greek word translated "take up" means primarily to "bear a burden." Many readers assume the disciple is one who bears burdens rather than tries to escape them. But this ignores the meaning of *cross*. The cross was a Roman way of execution. Later it came to be the primary artistic symbol of the Christian faith, though not during the New Testament period. The only symbolic meaning available at the time the saying was formulated was, perhaps, as the letter *T* or *Tau*. The *T* was used by Ezekiel to designate those Jews who were pained by the sins of their fellow Jerusalemites (Ezek. 9:4-6). The early Christian writer Barnabas identified the mark of the *T* with the cross (Barnabas 9:8). If the symbolic interpretation is the correct one, then the phrase means "decide to take up the mark of a Christian." This fits very well with the next section, which deals with making a decision. If we are to take *cross* literally, then Jesus has invited us to martyrdom, for bearing the cross would be taking the path to execution by the Roman state. Some later Christians did just that, but there are few, if any, such invitations in the New Testament.

Perhaps we should assume a literal meaning for *cross*, with a figurative meaning for the saying as a whole. The last part of the preceding saying was the warning that discipleship might even mean the "hating" of one's own personhood. The saying about the cross may well build on that theme. Bearing a cross means ultimately the willingness to "execute" one's own person or self-will. In Mark 8:34 the disciple is invited to "deny self" and carry the cross. Apparently "denying one's person" and taking up the cross were parallel or equivalent sayings (and Matt. 10:38-39 could have the same meaning).

In contrast to the first two sayings, the third presents no complications. Jesus advises the disciple to be prudent in the decision to follow him, just as a homeowner is prudent about the cost of constructing a storage shed or a military leader is prudent about a potential battle. What is peculiar is the utter uniqueness of this teaching in the New Testament. The same Jesus who advised selling all for the pearl of great price, doing anything to purchase the field with a treasure in it, not to be concerned about food or drink and clothing for tomorrow, turning the other cheek, offering unilateral love to the enemy, not storing up more than is necessary in barns—the same Jesus now advises the disciple to sit down and carefully consider this matter of being a disciple. Despite the uniqueness of the saying (only here in Luke), the point is consistent. In seeking after the reign of God, we must set aside all else or put it in the background. That is the cost which must be considered. The cost is to risk one's own personhood for the sake of the reign of God.

The three sayings finally culminate in verse 33. The reference of the saying is not just to wealth. The disciple must be willing to make *everything* secondary to the following of Jesus. The teaching of the New Testament is not ascetic or dualistic. The family is good; the created world is good; a sense of identity is good. But the true disciple places nothing before "following Jesus."

The Text in Brethren Life

The theme *counting the cost*, based upon Luke 14:28, became very significant among the early Brethren. In fact, even before the initial baptism of the eight in 1708, the theme appeared in a letter written by Hochmann von Hochenau (1670-1721), a radical Pietist leader to whom the early Brethren looked for spiritual guidance. He wrote to Alexander Mack (1679-1735) and George Grebe, a gunsmith who was among the first eight Brethren, in reply to a letter in which Mack and Grebe asked Hochmann's reactions to their desire for adult baptism by trine immersion. Written by Hochmann during his imprisonment at Nürnberg, where he had been arrested for preaching, the letter says: "One must, therefore, first carefully count the cost, if one will follow after the Lord Jesus in all the trials which will certainly follow from this. Without this true following of Jesus Christ, the water baptism will help little or not at all, even if it were to be performed on adults after the example of the first Christians. God does not look on the outward but rather on the inward—the change of heart, and the sincerity of the heart."[1] According to Donald Durnbaugh, in his introductory remarks to the letter, "This is the first known expression of the theme which was to become so important for the early Brethren and their descendants."[2]

That the theme remained lodged in Alexander Mack's mind can be seen in the fact that he notes Luke 14:27 in the concluding remarks of his *Rights and Ordinances* (1715), which is arranged as a conversation between a father and a son. The father says: "If you have learned from Him [Jesus] the teaching as it is outwardly commanded in the [New] Testament, so that you will remain steadfast in it, and resolve yourself to sacrifice your life, your property, family, yes, all that you have in the whole world, rather than waver from His teaching—you must become used to taking His cross upon you daily with denial of your will. Otherwise, you cannot be a disciple of the Lord Jesus, much less an heir of His Kingdom (Luke 14:27)."[3] While Mack directly mentions only 14:27, his comments summarize well the entire theme of Luke 14:25–33: Following Jesus is foremost in the life of discipleship.

Mack also wrote a hymn which bears the title "Count Well the Cost." This hymn appeared in the first Brethren hymnal, printed in Germany in 1720. The first verse, as translated by Ora W. Garber (1903-1981), runs thus:

> Christ Jesus says, "Count well the cost
> When you lay the foundation."
> Are you resolved, though all seem lost,
> To risk your reputation,
> Your self, your wealth, for Christ the Lord
> As you now give your solemn word?[4]

In a sermon first presented in 1985, Durnbaugh points out that this hymn was used at early Brethren baptismal services. Furthermore, says Durnbaugh, "early Brethren had cause to count the cost most carefully because their baptism was illegal under the imperial laws of the time. Those joining the movement with their baptism as adults had all been previously baptized as infants. With this rebaptism they put themselves under the death penalty as part of the hated Anabaptist movement."[5] Because rebaptism was an act of civil disobedience, early Brethren indeed paid the cost. Some were forced from their homes, and their property was confiscated. Sometimes they were even beaten and tortured, and in a few instances their children were taken from them because they were considered unfit parents.[6]

Two specific examples of how early Brethren suffered for their beliefs and actions are the stories of Christian Liebe and the Solingen Brethren. Liebe (1679-1757), a Brethren leader, journeyed from the Palatinate, his home, to Bern, Switzerland in 1714. His purpose was to minister to the local brethren, but, unfortunately, the city government of Bern was in the midst of actively suppressing the Anabaptists in the city and anyone who gave them aid and comfort. Liebe, who admitted that he was there to minister and give comfort, was arrested and sentenced to life as a galley slave along with several Anabaptist ministers. After spending the winter in a crowded prison, they were transferred to a Sicilian galley ship where they remained chained for two years. There Liebe would have remained for life had it not been for the intervention of Dutch Mennonites and others on behalf of Liebe and the ministers. Unfortunately, the release in 1716 did not come in time for two of the Anabaptist ministers who had already died in their chains.[7]

The six Solingen Brethren were arrested in 1717 because they practiced adult baptism. They were imprisoned in Düsseldorf, where they remained several months for questioning about their beliefs by the theologians of the established churches—Roman Catholic, Lutheran, and Reformed. Eventually each of the three churches made recommendations for the punishment of the six. The Catholics recommended execution, the Lutherans recommended the galleys, and the Reformed recommended hard labor for life. The authorities took the recommendation of the Reformed Church, and the six were condemned to a life of hard labor at the fortress of Jülich. Fortunately, with the help of several Dutch gentlemen, the six Brethren were released after four years of labor. A complete account of the imprisonment was written by William Grahe, one of the six, and his account can be found in Durnbaugh's *European Origins of the Brethren*.[8]

Once the Brethren emigrated to Pennsylvania and enjoyed religious toleration, there seems to have been less emphasis in Brethren writings placed upon the theme of counting the cost and the words of Luke 14:25-33. This does not mean, however, that there has not been any cost to count for the Brethren. With each war in which the United States has become involved, Brethren have had their pacifist convictions tested; and some have had to pay a price for those convictions. (See chapter 6.)

Even in the twentieth-century American climate of religious freedom, Brethren young men have had to choose between prison and cooperation with the US military system. A few have chosen prison or, recalling Mack's *Rights and Ordinances*, they have chosen to lose their liberty rather than waver from the teaching of the New Testament. Art Gish refers to Luke 14:33 when giving testimony at the 1973 trial of Mike Stern, a Church of the Brethren member who refused to register with the selective service system. Preceding the reference to Luke, Gish says: "Some of the themes that I have been stressing, and I know Mike has heard me talk about this, is that the real essence of the Christian faith is discipleship. Whether we are going to follow and be obedient to Jesus Christ. It's not only a question of worshiping him and accepting certain theological tenets, but the great question is whether we're going to be obedient and follow, which really means surrendering your whole life to God's will."[9]

Given the Brethren emphasis on the themes of counting the cost and pacifism, Durnbaugh's reaction when Ronald Reagan used Luke 14:31-32 to support the buildup of the American military is not surprising. Concerning Reagan's misinterpretation of the text, Durnbaugh says: "The attempt of the President to exploit this misunderstanding of the biblical passage for his military expansion, unparalleled in peacetime, is not simply a display of biblical ignorance; it approaches blasphemy in claiming divine warrant for belligerent arms policy, made possible only by slashes in resources for human needs."[10]

Notes

1. "Hochmann von Hochenau to Grebe and Mack," in *European Origins of the Brethren*, comp. and trans. Donald F. Durnbaugh (Elgin, IL: Brethren Press, 1958), 113.

2. Ibid., 110.

3. Alexander Mack, *Rights and Ordinances*, in *Europeans Origins of the Brethren*, 404.

4. Alexander Mack, "Count Well the Cost," in *European Origins of the Brethren*, 408.

5. Donald F. Durnbaugh, "Counting the Cost of Peace" (Elgin, IL: Brethren Press, 1986).

6. Ibid.

7. *European Origins of the Brethren*, 217-240.

8. Ibid., 240-280.

9. Arthur G. Gish, Testimony given in "United States vs. Michael Edward Stern," C-9503, United States District Court, Eastern District of Washington, Spokane, 110-111 (1973).

10. Donald F. Durnbaugh, "Counting the Cost of Peace."

The Text in Today's World

The key to the Believers' Church lies in discipleship. For all the importance of the normal, family community, family does not produce discipleship. Religion in general may serve to create family cohesiveness, to promote local moral qualities and support those customs most helpful to the civil community, all of which are good and necessary functions. But neither does religion generate discipleship. Discipleship calls us to follow Jesus, to go beyond our local religious customs and join in an adult community which asks for a voluntary, freely offered commitment, a community which offers in return a commitment not unlike that of the family. It is in this context that adult faith and trust develop.

From the Believers' Church perspective, the most important years of one's life would be that time when one leaves home and enters into the adult community. At that time all the other things we have studied now become important: the willingness to be faithful, the willingness to risk unilateral actions, the willingness to love persons outside one's local, family community. What was seen as necessary then for the development of faith remains true today. The cost of discipleship would be the price of rising above the family community, one's own self-interests, and placing trust in the body of Christ. It is not the intention of the call to discipleship to destroy the familial community. Quite the contrary, it is a release from possessiveness which allows us to really enjoy life. Such a "giving up," however, can be very painful, hence the powerful image of the cross as the symbol for such discipleship.

What is surprising in the text is the emphasis on considering the cost in advance of the decision. Much of the New Testament urges us to take action regardless of the cost. Yet here a potential disciple is urged to consider the cost of building a storage shed, and a general is commended for considering whether there are sufficient forces available to win the victory. Both motives are necessary in the Christian life. The parables of Jesus stress both the surprise character of what is to come and also the need to prepare for its coming. Like the people working in the highways and byways, we never know when we will be called to the great banquet. At the same time, the ten maidens were urged to make provisions for having enough oil no matter what happened. The ten maidens were to be ready regardless of the time. Likewise, this text stresses preparedness by knowing the cost. In the New Testament it is possible to make plans, though it is not possible to control life by our planning.

Some have spoken of the cost of discipleship in personal heroic terms. The ones who have picked up their crosses are the individuals who have given away everything and suffered much: the St. Francises, the Joan of Arcs, and the martyrs of the church. The emphasis falls on how individuals have been faithful on their own. In Brethren history, discipleship and sainthood have a very different flavor. Brethren are not inclined to pick out individuals and honor them for the saintly quality of their lives. Rather, we celebrate congregations and communities which have truly counted the cost of discipleship. It is not coincidental that we have produced far more congregational histories than we have biographies of individual saints or heroes. When we do point to the discipleship of specific individuals, it is not usually their inward saintliness that we lift up, but rather the way in which their lives embody the concerns of the faith community. The call to discipleship then is a call to churches to consider what it means, what it costs, to function as communities of faith and love.

Case Study

During the cold winter weather and especially at night, Chicago's O'Hare airport served as a "hotel" for about 100 of Chicago's homeless. To get rid of this "nuisance" and "secure" the premises, the airport authority ruled that anyone in the airport after 10 p.m. must hold a valid airline ticket. Concerned about the plight of these doubly homeless, a church in the western suburbs of Chicago met to determine what might be done. After considerable weighing of the pros and cons, they offered, on a temporary basis, to open their doors to the O'Hare homeless. The decision created an outrage in the community. The neighbors of the church did not want so many homeless in their area. The church met to reconsider their offer.

1. The church council tried to count the cost of their action. Do you think they should have been more prudent? Should they have checked with the neighbors before making the offer?

2. Should the church quit worrying about the "cost"? Would you assume that if the action is right and is God's will, then the church should rightly suppose, in faith, that all will go well?

3. Should the church consider the detrimental effect on their church and then go ahead with their plan knowing they will "pay" for it?

On the Love Feast

Luke 22:14-23 (NRSV)

When the hour came, he took his place at the table, and the apostles with him. [15]He said to them, "I have eagerly desired to eat this Passover with you before I suffer; [16]for I tell you, I will not eat it until it is fulfilled in the reign of God." [17]Then he took a cup, and after giving thanks he said, "Take this and divide it among yourselves; [18]for I tell you that from now on I will not drink of the fruit of the vine until the reign of God comes." [19]Then he took a loaf of bread, and when he had given thanks, he broke it and gave it to them, saying, "This is my body, which is given for you. Do this in remembrance of me." [20]And he did the same with the cup after supper, saying, "This cup that is poured out for you is the new covenant in my blood. [21]But see, the one who betrays me is with me, and his hand is on the table. [22]For the Son of Man is going as it has been determined, but woe to that one by whom he is betrayed!" [23]Then they began to ask one another, which one of them it could be who would do this.

Luke 22:14-23 (BNT)

When the hour came, he came to the table, and his disciples were with him. [15]And he said to them, "I have wanted to share this Passover with you before I suffer. [16]For I say to you that I will not eat it until it is fulfilled during the reign of God." [17]And taking the cup and giving thanks he said, "Take this and share it among yourselves. [18]For I say to you that from now on I will not drink of the fruit of the vine until the reign of God comes." [19]And taking the bread and giving thanks he broke it and gave it to them saying, "This [breaking of the bread] is my body given for you. Do this [breaking of bread] as an act of remembering me." [20]And after dinner in a similar manner he took the cup, saying, "[The drinking of] this cup creates the new covenant through my blood poured out for you. [21]Behold, even now the hand of the one who will betray me sits with me at the table. [22]For the Son of Man is proceeding as was destined; nevertheless, woe be to the person through whom he is betrayed." [23]And among themselves they began to ponder which one of them was about to do this thing.

The Text in Its Biblical Setting

Our practice of the love feast is based primarily on accounts of the last supper or Passover found in this narrative and its parallels in Mark 14:22-26 and Matthew 26:26-30. Paul recounted the event in his first letter to the Corinthians (1 Cor. 11:23-25). The story of the last supper Jesus ate with his disciples and the washing of feet can be found also in John 13:1-30, though that account does not reflect the Passover celebration. Both the Agape meal (1 Cor. 11:17-22; 2 Pet. 2:13[?]) and the Eucharist, the primary celebrations of the Christian church, presumably derive from this meal ordained by Jesus himself. Yet that history has been the most controverted and debated issue in our Christian tradition.

The Passover celebrated liberation from Egyptian bondage (Exod. 12). The celebrative meal must have consisted of a cup of wine which had been blessed and a meal of lamb (cooked whole on a spit) with various prescribed herbs. Interspersed were standard prayers and questions. At some time in Jewish tradition, an agricultural festival, the Feast of Unleavened Bread, was joined with the more political, historical Passover (Exod. 12:14-40). As an agricultural festival it celebrated the barley harvest. At that time the rotten grain (leavened) could be discarded. For that reason leaven appears in the New Testament as an evil influence (Matt. 16:6; 1 Cor. 5:7).

The Passover was not a sacrificial meal. It celebrated the liberation of the Jews and the passing over of the Hebrew children when the Egyptian first-born were killed (Exod. 12:22-23). God's elect, the Hebrew people, then became a living, redeemed first-born (Exod. 13:11-16). When the Jews celebrated the Passover, they remembered God's act of deliverance, their moving toward the promised land, and the grace of God's continuing faithfulness.

The story of the last supper includes most of these elements. The Lukan account, somewhat different from the others, develops as follows:

vv. 14-16	Preparation for the Passover
vv. 17-18	Institution of End-time Cup
v. 19	Act of Breaking Bread of Remembrance

v. 20   Act of Drinking Cup of the New Covenant
vv. 21-23   Reflection of the Betrayal

It is a meal of remembrance (*anamnesis*, v. 19). It remembers the suffering and death of Jesus, our paschal lamb (1 Cor. 5:7). It reenacts the event which defines Christianity, the breaking of the body of Jesus and the pouring out of his blood.

It is clear that something like the Passover meal, or a Jewish meal of hope, lies behind the Lukan account. The meal anticipates the nearness of the reign of God. After the cup of the blessing, Jesus speaks of a next meal in the end-time. At this point a very interesting problem must be noted. The most highly regarded (and majority of) manuscripts of the New Testament contain verses 19b-20. This creates a last supper in which there is a cup of the blessing, the breaking of bread, and the cup of the new covenant. No other account of the last supper or the early Christian eucharist contains these two cups. Some ancient manuscripts omit 19b-20. In that case there is no bread of remembrance and no cup of the covenant. The meal is simply an end-time meal (Passover or Feast of Unleavened Bread). The first Christians must have celebrated such a meal. It is the breaking of bread mentioned in Acts 2:46; it is the communion mentioned by Paul in 1 Corinthians 10:16; it is the meal described in the early Christian document, the *Didache*.

What happened in Luke 22:14-23? Did Luke first describe a simple Jewish end-time meal and then early copyists added the meal of remembrance (vv. 19b-20; the translators of the RSV assumed it was added and so omitted it)? Or did Luke describe both meals as one and then some later copyists, seeing how unique it was, took out the meal of remembrance (the translators of the NRSV and the BNT assume it was taken out later so they include it)? We will never know. But thanks to Luke we know there were two celebrations in the early church: one a meal of end-time expectation and another which reenacted the suffering and death of Jesus.

It seems very likely that the meal of expectation merged into the agape or love feast. Probably the early Christians often ate together. They began with the cup of blessing and then ate a meal. The meal concluded with a prayer of hope, *maranatha* (Aramaic for "Our Lord, come"). Sometimes, or perhaps every time, there was an additional celebration: a reenactment of God's redemptive act in Christ. That celebration, known as the eucharist, began with the breaking of the bread or body and concluded with the establishment of a new covenant through the drinking of wine, the pouring out of the blood.

Because it is a reenactment (much like the Passover), the emphasis is on action: the breaking of the bread and the drinking of the wine.

The Text in Brethren Life

The Brethren love feast consists of three major elements: the feet-washing, the Lord's supper, and the communion. These three are preceded by a time of preparation which generally includes prayer, hymn singing, the reading of Scripture, and self-examination. One or more community meals were also part of the activities surrounding the love feast when slow travel meant that people had to spend several hours in transit. In fact, during the nineteenth century, it was not unusual for the love feast to be part of a two-day event. Under such circumstances the love feast was usually held only once a year. Today, however, love feast is typically held twice a year, often on the evening of the Thursday before Easter and the evening of World Communion Sunday in October. In addition, communion is sometimes held on Sunday morning during worship without the other elements of the love feast. Since feetwashing will be dealt with in the next chapter, this chapter will focus on the love feast as a whole and on the Lord's supper and communion.

Obviously the biblical texts used by the Brethren to verify the elements of the love feast included the accounts of the last supper in the four Gospels (John 13; Luke 22:14-23; Mark 14:12-25; Matthew 26:17-29) and Paul's directions about the supper in 1 Corinthians 11. Basically, what the early Brethren did was combine the activities described in these texts to arrive at the love feast. Alexander Mack, Jr., (1712-1803) speaks of this combining of texts as "a glorious harmony for a believing soul."[1] Of course, the harmonizing of texts sometimes causes difficulties. In another letter to his friend John Preisz (1751-1829), Mack, Jr., discusses the question of whether separate blessings are to be given over the bread and cup. Turning to the biblical texts, Mack notes that Matthew and Mark indicate separate blessings while Luke and Paul are not as definite. Luke 22:19-20 implies, says Mack, "that the giving of thanks over the cup was here included in the giving of thanks over the bread." However, Mack goes on to point out that a separate blessing was given over the cup mentioned in Luke 22:17. Thus Mack concludes: "It is . . . not very surprising for us that the two holy evangelists Matthew and Mark recorded [this] in such a manner that the witness of the holy evangelist Luke had to divide the word for greater clarity and indicate to us what kind of a cup it was over which the Lord pronounced a separate public thanksgiving."[2]

In his "Essay on the Lord's Supper," John Kline (1797-1864), Brethren martyr during the Civil War, cites Luke 22:19. The essay was written sometime before 1845 when it was published in a booklet on baptism by Peter Nead (1796-1877). In the essay Kline argues that the Lord's supper is not the same as the communion and that the supper is not to be identified with the Jewish Passover meal. In making these arguments, Kline quotes Luke 22:19 to show that "the ordinance of the breaking of the bread, and partaking of the cup, is . . . to remember the broken body of Christ, which as mangled, and lacerated by the lash, in Pilot's judgment hall, and by the nails and Spear on the Cross; and of his shed blood, which was shed for the remission of sins."[3]

Among the published accounts are two in-depth descriptions of nineteenth-century love feasts. One by H. R. Holsinger (1833-1905), the leader of the Progressive Brethren movement in the 1880s, is thought to be representative of the middle of the century.[4] The other by Phebe Earl Gibbons, a Quaker, is of a love feast held near Mount Joy, Pennsylvania, in 1871.[5] These two accounts complement each other well, since Holsinger emphasizes the content of the services while Gibbons provides many details about the food, the accommodations, and the activities which occurred outside the meetinghouse. From the two accounts a typical love feast can be projected.

The love feast itself was part of a two-day event, usually beginning on Saturday morning and ending on Sunday morning. In attendance were the brothers and sisters from neighboring congregations as well as from the congregation holding the love feast. Also in attendance were curious visitors, such as Gibbons herself, and people seeking free food and lodging. Sometimes these visitors created disturbances outside the meetinghouse while the services were taking place inside. On Saturday morning there was preaching followed by dinner which was served to both members and visitors. Holsinger states that the dinner might last until 3:00 in the afternoon and that from three to nine hundred people might be served. Gibbons lists the food served: "fine Lancaster County bread, good and abundant butter, apple-butter, pickles, and pies."[6] After the dinner another service was held which Holsinger describes as an *examination*. At this service, 1 Corinthians 11:28 was used as a basis for one or more sermons. In the Gibbons account, the dinner was followed by the election of a minister.

Following the afternoon service, benches and tables were set up for those who would partake of the evening love feast. First came the feetwashing which included the reading of John 13. After the feetwashing came the Lord's supper which consisted of bread, beef or mutton, and soup made from the broth of the meat, according to Holsinger. Visitors, however, did not participate in this meal but were fed earlier, as in Gibbon's case, in the kitchen. Following the supper came the communion of the bread and wine interspersed with readings from the scripture, hymns, and prayers, as well as preaching.

The communion ended the events of Saturday but, since there was to be more preaching on Sunday morning, those who could not return to their home for the night slept in the upstairs of the meetinghouse. This upstairs was divided in half so that men slept on one side of a partition and women on the other. Gibbons reports that most of the adult men and women rose about four o'clock on Sunday morning. Those who stayed overnight washed at the pump and were given a cold breakfast. Then several hours of preaching, praying, and singing began. Following these services, according to the Gibbons account, a midday meal was served to over five hundred people. Gibbons also indicates that the leftovers from the four meals were distributed to the poor regardless of their church membership.

Luke 22:19-20 was cited in a report at the 1900 Annual Meeting concerning the method by which sisters participated in the serving of the bread and cup. Evidently the usual practice was for the men to break the bread and pass the cup to each other, while the elder in charge broke the bread and passed the cup to each woman individually. As early as 1879 a query came to Annual Meeting as to whether the sisters might follow the same practice as the brethren. Since the request was not granted, similar queries came in 1885, 1891, and 1899. As a result of the 1899 query, a committee of three men was appointed to report back at the next meeting. In their report they cited several texts, including Luke 22:19-20, to support their recommendation that the men should follow the same method as the women. Since the texts cited described Jesus breaking the bread and giving it to his disciples and likewise passing the cup to each, the committee decided that the method being used by the women was more biblical. The Annual Meeting, however, did not accept their recommendation. Thus another query came in 1906, another committee was appointed, and several more years elapsed before women were granted the same privilege as the men in 1910.

Given the uniqueness of the love feast among the Brethren, it is not surprising that it has been a popular topic in Brethren publications over the years. Among the Brethren leaders who have written tracts or pamphlets on the topic are J. H. Moore (1864-1935), D. L. Miller (1841-1921), D. W. Kurtz (1879-1949), and William Beahm (1896-1964). Books on the topic include J. W. Beer's *Jewish Passover and the Lord's Supper* (Lancaster, PA: Inquirer Printing and Publishing Company, 1874); D. B. Gibson's *Lord's Supper* (Elgin, IL: Brethren Publishing House, 1902); and Vernard Eller's *In Place of Sacraments* (Grand Rapids, MI: Eerdmans, 1972). Often in such publications verses from Luke 22 are either cited or quoted. For example, Moore's tract, titled "The Lord's Supper," quotes Luke 22:20 to show that Jesus and his disciples had a supper in addition to the communion. Likewise, Gibson (1836-1921), evangelist and minister, quotes Luke 22:19-20 in his argument that the Lord's supper and the communion are not the same.

Perhaps the most used theological explanation of the love feast in the twentieth century is a pamphlet titled "The Brethren Love Feast" by William Beahm, Brethren missionary and seminary professor. Originally published in 1942, it has been reprinted several times. Today it is still used to explain the love feast to new members and non-Brethren. After explaining each of the three elements of the love feast, Beahm ends the pamphlet by discussing the meaning of the love feast as a whole. According to Beahm the love feast is the "interrelationship between our religious experience and our social relations, between the power of God and our human needs . . . . Any attempt to curtail the evening's ceremony so as to speed it up, or any attempt to streamline it so as to reduce wind resistance among the sophisticated, is to jeopardize its richer significance."[7]

Notes

1. "Mack-Preisz Correspondence, " in *Brethren in Colonial America*, ed. Donald F. Durnbaugh (Elgin, IL: Brethren Press, 1967), 235.

2. Ibid., 234.

3. John Kline, "An Essay on the Lord's Supper," in *Brethren in the New Nation*, comp. and ed. Roger E. Sappington (Elgin, IL: Brethren Press, 1976), 178.

4. H. R. Holsinger, *Holsinger's History of the Tunkers and the Brethren Church* (Lathrop, CA: the author, 1901), 249-255.

5. Phebe E. Gibbons, *The Plain People* (Lebanon, PA: Applied Arts Publishers, 1963), 8-15.

6. Ibid., 9.

7. William Beahm, "The Brethren Love Feast" (Elgin, IL: Brethren Press, [1971]), 14.

The Text in Today's World

In terms of history there are few texts, or narratives, more important than the account of the last supper. The story was passed on very early as one coming from the Lord (1 Cor. 11:23). Today it still actively conveys the heart of the Christian faith.

Because the last supper appropriates the Passover, the central message is that of divine liberation. As God freed the Hebrew people from the Pharaohs, so Jesus on the cross frees us from sin, alienation, oppression, and any form of enslavement. The heart of the Christian good news is that we are "free at last." Probably later theology has inappropriately shifted the emphasis more toward sacrifice and the appeasement of God's wrath. While sacrifice does play a role in the New Testament (Heb. 10:12) and the cross does lead us to self-giving (Luke 14:25-33; see Session 10), more central yet is liberation from those bondages which keep us from full life and joyful communion with God and God's children. That is the message of both the Jewish Passover and the last supper.

The Lord's supper consists of more than the idea of liberation. It is, in itself, an act of liberation. Some Christians understand the bread and wine as sacraments wherein the faithful receive for themselves and in themselves the crucified Lord. Others take the bread and cup to be a symbol of the death and resurrection of Jesus. But we understand that the bread and cup are *not* the body and blood of Jesus. It is the act of breaking the bread which is the body and the act of drinking of the cup which is the formation of covenant. By breaking (*do this!*) the bread with each other, we free each other from bondages. By drinking the cup together we form a new covenant (*testamentum*) community. Of course, Jesus Christ is really present with us as we do these things. One might even argue Jesus Christ *is* us (the body).

The eucharist involves one kind of action: in it we remember the death and resurrection of Jesus and by acting out that event we recreate the liberating power of the gospel. At the same time, the text also has a meal. In the meal (love feast), the new community celebrates the bonding which has brought it together. Perhaps the meal need not be directly attached to the eucharist. Most churches show some sign of it in their communion services. But a local faith community must eat together in the recognition of their unity. Furthermore they should bring food (*oblatum* or offering) and share it with the others (1 Cor. 11:17-22; Acts 6:1-2; 2:43-47). By eating together with equality and joy, the God-given freedom and trust can actually be realized among us. Every person present knows that what she or he eats and offers will have been accepted by the faith community. We have become "someone" in a community that cares for us.

Through the centuries many churches have modified the love feast and eucharist to suit their particular needs and faith. Historically, the Church of the Brethren may have stressed the requirement of membership more than intended in the New Testament. To be sure, participation in love feast and the eucharist does signify active participation in a faith community. But, at the same time, the last supper as described in the New Testament also creates the occasion for redemption and liberation. As the Church of the Brethren extends itself here and abroad it will come to understand that *doing* the meal, the bread, and the cup is a major means of sharing the good news.

Perhaps some revision will be necessary. The old custom of the Dunkers may have been useful. Anyone in the community was invited to the love feast (the meal). In that way hungry persons could be fed, and the unchurched could experience the care of the faith community.

Case Study

Shortly after First Church in Chicago was rebuilt (1989), the faith community celebrated a love feast and communion. The deacons had prepared just enough places for those present. However, one member left after the feetwashing. About the same time there was a knock on the front door. One of the men went upstairs to see who was there. Eventually he returned with a Stephen Miller who had just been released from a halfway house and Bethany Hospital. He was hungry and lonely. There was one empty place so he was invited to sit there. He ate the love feast with the faith community (with apologies for the meager fare). He sang the songs and he prayed the prayers. When it came time for the bread and cup he stayed and took part. When it was all completed the community gave him some food and said farewell. Stephen Miller was never seen again.

1. First Church had just agreed on a policy for participation in the love feast and communion. Christian discipleship was a minimal requirement. The deacons did not ask any questions of Stephen Miller. Did they violate the meaning of the love feast when they invited Miller to stay and eat with them?

2. Does the love feast and communion signify the community of believers or does it create faith and community? If you think it creates faith, then who should decide who can come to the table?

3. Many Christians speak of the real presence of Christ at communion. Was the presence of Stephen Miller (a poor, hungry person) the real presence of Christ? Was the action of accepting Stephen Miller the real presence? How do you understand that Jesus is really with the faith community when it breaks bread?

On Washing Feet

John 13:1-17 (NRSV)

Now before the festival of the Passover, Jesus knew that his hour had come to depart from this world and go to the Father. Having loved his own who were in the world, he loved them to the end. [2]The devil had already put it into the heart of Judas son of Simon Iscariot to betray him. And during supper [3]Jesus, knowing that the Father had given all things into his hands, and that he had come from God and was going to God, [4]got up from the table, took off his outer robe, and tied a towel around himself. [5]Then he poured water into a basin and began to wash the disciples' feet and to wipe them with the towel that was tied around him. [6]He came to Simon Peter, who said to him, "Lord, are you going to wash my feet?" [7]Jesus answered, "You do not know now what I am doing, but later you will understand." [8]Peter said to him, "You will never wash my feet." Jesus answered, "Unless I wash you, you have no share with me." [9]Simon Peter said to him, "Lord, not my feet only but also my hands and my head!" [10]Jesus said to him, "One who has bathed does not need to wash, except for the feet, but is entirely clean. And you are clean, though not all of you." [11]For he knew who was to betray him; for this reason he said, "Not all of you are clean." [12]After he had washed their feet, had put on his robe, and had returned to the table, he said to them, "Do you know what I have done to you? [13]You call me Teacher and Lord—and you are right, for that is what I am. [14]So if I, your Lord and Teacher, have washed your feet, you also ought to wash one another's feet. [15]For I have set you an example, that you also should do as I have done to you. [16]Very truly, I tell you, servants are not greater than their master, nor are messengers greater than the one who sent them. [17]If you know these things, you are blessed if you do them."

John 13:1-17 (BNT)

Before the feast of the Passover, knowing that the hour had come for him to depart from this world and go to the Father, Jesus, who had loved his own in the world, did for them a consummate act of love. [2]Even though the devil had already put it into the heart of Judas, son of Simon Iscariot, to betray him,[3] knowing that the Father had put everything in his hands, and that he had come from God and was going back to God, [4]he rose from the table, while they were still eating, took off his outer garments, and tied a towel around his waist. [5]Then he poured water into a basin and began to wash the feet of the disciples. And he dried them off with the towel tied about his waist.

[6]Then he came to Simon Peter who said to him, "Lord, you are not about to wash my feet, are you?" [7]And in reply Jesus said to him, "Right now you do not realize what I am doing, but when everything is finished you will know."

[8]"Peter said to him, "You absolutely will never wash my feet!" Jesus replied, "If I do not wash you, you will not be able to receive life from me."

[9]Simon Peter said to him, "In that case, Lord, not only my feet, but my hands and head also."

[10]Jesus said to him, "People who have already taken a bath hardly need to wash up (except for their feet), for they are clean all over. And you all are clean, though not each one of you." [11]For he knew the one who was going to betray him. That is why he said, "Not every one of you is clean."

[12]Then after he had washed their feet, put on his clothes, and again reclined at the table, he said to them, "Do you understand what I have done to you? [13]You call me 'teacher' and 'lord,' and that is appropriate for you to do, since I am. [14]If then I, the one who is lord and teacher, washed your feet, you also ought to wash one another's feet. [15]For I have given to you a paradigm, that as I have done to you, you also ought to do. [16]For I tell you the truth, a slave is not greater than his lord, nor an apostle greater than the one who sent him. [17]If you know these things, you are fortunate if you do them."

The Text in Its Biblical Setting

Most of the favorite passages of the Church of the Brethren deal with the nature of discipleship. This passage is no exception. In chapters 1 to 12 of the Gospel of John, Jesus deals primarily with his relationship to Palestinian Judaism. The narrative, called by many the Gospel of Signs, shows how the wine of Christianity exceeds the water of Judaism (2:1-11); how the community of Jesus Christ will replace the community of the temple (2:13-22); how Jesus is wiser than the leaders of Israel (3:1-15); how the source of Christianity is more satisfying than the source of Judaism (4:1-54); how Jesus is the true manna from heaven (6:1-71).

From chapter 13 on, Jesus deals more with his relationship to the world. The theme of chapters 13 to 20 is the "lifting up of Jesus" so that he might be "glorified" (3:14; 13:31). In this first narrative of chapter 13, the washing of feet, Jesus tells how the disciples might have a part or share in that glory (v. 8).

It is not to encourage imitation of Jesus that the story is included, but rather to point to a basic truth about faith. Jesus says that he has washed the feet of the disciples as a *hypodeigma* (13:15, "example" in the RSV). In the Greek language *hypodeigma* is a synonym of *paradeigma*, the root word for our English word "paradigm." Both words were used in Greek philosophy in the sense of a "pattern" or "example" from which copies are made (for example, the pattern of the tent in Exod. 25:9; likewise in Heb. 8:5). Persons from the past who ought to be emulated are also "paradigms," somewhat in this sense (see Jas. 5:10). Since the Bible does not share the presuppositions of Greek thinking, however, it is not very often that we find the two words used to mean "pattern." More often they refer to events used by God to point to divine truth. In the Greek Old Testament (not the Hebrew, from which our English versions are translated), the bones of the kings of Judah are a paradigm (Jer. 8:2). In the book of the prophet Nahum, the destruction of Nineveh is to serve as a paradigm (Nah. 3:6; in the NRSV: "spectacle"). So, in the biblical material, a paradigm is a key event or experience which teaches a lesson or points to a truth. So Jesus did this final act of love, prior to the cross, as an indication, or paradigm, of how persons might share in his glory.

Jesus washed the feet of all the disciples, but the text focuses on Peter. There can be no doubt that Peter generally represents all the disciples. Not only is he the rock (John 1:42; Matt. 16:18), but he normally speaks for all the others. He made the confession at Caesarea

Philippi (Mark 8:30); he spoke for the group at the transfiguration (Mark 9:5); he was the first disciple chosen (Mark 1:16); and he was the first to witness the resurrection (1 Cor. 15:5; John 20:6).

In the Gospel of John, Peter keeps that representative role, as in this passage, but he and the rest of the twelve have been supplanted by another figure, the beloved disciple. The beloved disciple was probably called first (1:37); at the last supper he lies closer to Jesus than Peter (13:23–24); he goes with Jesus into the hall of the high priest while Peter denies knowing Jesus (18:15-17); he beats Peter to the empty tomb (20:4); and he is the first to recognize the risen Lord by the Sea of Galilee (21:5). In fact, John makes it clear that the beloved disciple replaced the "historical" Jesus as the son of Mary (19:25-27). John allows the beloved disciple to supplant Peter in these ways in order to make a point about discipleship. True discipleship does not hinge on having the official apostolic credentials of the twelve. It does not depend merely on having seen the saving facts of the Christian faith (as stressed in 1 Cor. 15:1-5; Acts 1:21-22; 2 Pet. 1:16). Instead, it depends on having a close relationship with the incarnate Lord, on knowing the Father through the Son (John 8:19; 14:9), on loving and being loved by Jesus (13:1) and on being willing to share what one has received from the Son, that is, being willing to lay down one's own person (15:13; 13:37-38) for others.

The author of the Gospel of John wishes to stress this kind of discipleship in the text before us. There are two foci of the feetwashing as an act of discipleship. First, Jesus divested himself of his outer garments, knelt down, and gave of himself as a servant to his disciples. That act of Jesus is to be emulated (13:14). True disciples will give of themselves to others. That is the new commandment, and only commandment (!), which Jesus gives at the end of the meal (13:34). In that way disciples can be known (13:35). The other focus has often been overlooked. When approached by Jesus, Peter refused to have his feet washed. That is not to be emulated. Peter was the chief of the disciples, the one who later (by the time of the writing of John) was known as the primary apostolic source of the Christian faith; yet Peter was reluctant to be on the receiving end. But the Jesus of the Gospel of John says there is no way to participate in his glory except by having one's feet washed, that is, receiving true life from the incarnate Lord (13:8). True discipleship entails both giving in love to others (that is, washing *their* feet) and receiving life from the Son through the church (that is, having *our* feet washed).

From this perspective the saying in verse 16 now makes sense as an interpretation of the feetwashing paradigm. We hardly needed to be told that a slave is not greater than the master, and that the one who is sent is not greater than the one who sends (NRSV). In Matthew (10:24) and Luke (6:40), the saying implies that the fate of the disciples cannot be expected to improve over that of the master (Jesus). They, too, will be persecuted. But in John the saying means that the "apostle" (translated in the NRSV as "messenger") cannot be greater than the Lord who sends. The apostle, too, must receive life from the Son, as did the beloved disciple, and must share that life in love with others. Peter was at first unable to lay down his person in that way (13:37-38), but finally he is willing "to feed the sheep" (21:15-19).

The Text in Brethren Life

John 13:1-17 is the biblical source for the Brethren practice of feetwashing, which has been an element of the Brethren love feast since the beginning of the sect in Germany. The fact that feetwashing was a practice of the first eight brothers and sisters can be seen in a November 1708 letter from Hochmann von Hochenau (1670-1721) to Count Frederick Ernest von Solms, a ruler with Pietist leanings. In this letter, which is Hochmann's reply to the Count's request for his opinion on the Brethren baptism, Hochmann says: "If the members of Christ wish to wash one another's feet in Christian freedom, out of love for Jesus and sincere humbleness, who will deny it to them, for Jesus has indeed specifically commanded it (John 13 in entirety)."[1] Alexander Mack (1679-1735), in his explanation of the Lord's supper, also speaks of feetwashing and John 13. Says Mack: "When, however, the believers gathered in united love and fellowship and had a supper, observing thereby the commandments of the Lord Jesus that they wash one another's feet after the example and order of the Master (John 13:14, 15), yes, when they broke the bread of communion, drank the chalice (the cup) of communion . . . that alone could be called the Lord's Supper."[2]

Traditionally the Brethren have understood feetwashing as having a twofold meaning. These two meanings are well presented by William Beahm (1896-1964) in his pamphlet "The Brethren Love Feast." Cleansing or purification, says Beahm, is the more obvious meaning of the feetwashing practice. Of course, it is not the feet which are being cleansed, but the heart which is cleansed of sin. Whereas baptism is the initial act of purification and regeneration, feetwashing enables the believer to continue to be cleansed from sin and thereby remain in the love of God. Placed as it is at the beginning of the love feast, the feetwashing ceremony prepares the believer for the meal and the bread and the cup. Through purification the believer is brought into proper relationship with God. The cleansing aspect of feetwashing applies, of course, to the person whose feet are being washed. The second meaning of feetwashing applies primarily to the one who is doing the washing. By stooping to wash another's feet, the believer is showing his willingness to love and serve others. The believer is, to return to the language of the first meaning, being purified of his pride and desire for superiority through an act of humble service. It was the pride and self-seeking among the disciples which prompted Jesus to initiate feetwashing at the last supper. By washing their feet he showed them the true attitude of a disciple and thereby quelled their pride, the primary obstacle to Christian fellowship.[3]

Given the emphasis on service among the Brethren in the twentieth century, the act of feetwashing can easily lead to self-righteousness and self-sufficiency. Pastors are advised to warn against the sin of self-righteousness at the beginning of the feetwashing service with these words: "We do violence to the heart of this act if we suppose that by stooping to wash one another's feet we rise in status in the Kingdom. We do not kneel to demonstrate humility, but to remember the service of the life of Christ, and to let that memory fill us with inspiration and determination."[4] Concerning the sin of self-sufficiency, Dale W. Brown observes: "Each one should be open to be served as well as to serve in order to combat the sin of self-sufficiency, pride, and the striving for power. For this reason each person should have his or her feet washed."[5]

Unfortunately, feetwashing has sometimes caused problems among the Brethren. Two particular problems which feetwashing posed were those of time and mode. The time problem centered on the question of when the service of feetwashing should occur during the love feast. An open letter written by Alexander Mack, Jr., (1712-1803) describes the problem well.[6] According to the letter, the early Brethren first practiced feetwashing after the meal and the bread and cup. Later they washed feet after the meal but before the bread and cup. Finally, after someone knowing Greek explained to them that Jesus washed the disciples' feet before the supper, they turned to washing feet before the meal. It was Mack's opinion that feetwashing was properly placed before the meal, but the fact that he defends his opinion so vehemently, and yet so humbly, reveals that there was much dissension among the early Brethren over the issue. Eventually it became the accepted practice among the Brethren to have feetwashing at the beginning of the love feast.

The problem of the mode of feetwashing plagued the Brethren in the 1800s. The debate was between the double mode and the single mode. Double mode, the generally accepted mode among the Brethren of the nineteenth century, involved one person washing and another person drying the feet of several brothers or sisters. The single mode, practiced by some of the western Brethren, involved a person washing and drying the feet of a neighbor and the neighbor in turn washing and drying the feet of the next person. While the generally accepted mode was the double mode, fifteen of the sixteen queries which appeared before Annual Meetings between 1812 and 1881 concerning feetwashing centered on the desire to change from the double mode to the single mode.[7] The reason for these queries was not only the desire to change the mode, but the fact that some congregations already practiced the single mode.

Such diversity of practice and thought greatly disturbed the conservative element of the denomination, who felt that there must be uniformity of practice and thought among the true followers of Christ. Eventually these conservatives, who favored the double mode, broke away from the Brethren and formed the Old German Baptist Brethren. Although the reasons for the split were much deeper than the mode of feetwashing, there is no denying that feetwashing was one of the issues. H. R. Holsinger (1833-1905), himself the leader of the progressives who also split from the Brethren, makes the following comments about the controversy over the mode of feetwashing in the context of his discussion about the Old German Baptist Brethren: "It is remarkable that an intelligent body of such devoted people should suffer themselves to become alienated from each other in regard to the manner of observing an ordinance which was instituted for the special purpose of uniting them more closely . . . . In all the controversies that ever disturbed the Tunker fraternity [the Brethren] none was so prolific in the propagation of bad feeling, harsh sayings, and unholy conduct as was that upon the mode of feetwashing."[8]

Today the mode generally practiced by the Brethren is the single mode, and the meaning most emphasized is that of service. A variation on the service theme can be found in Vernard Eller's discussion of feetwashing in his book *In Place of Sacraments* (1972). Eller begins by pointing out that those gospel versions of the last supper which do not include the feetwashing emphasize *what Christ did for us* through the bread and the cup. In John's version, however, there is also an emphasis on the *believer's commitment* to and role in Christ's body. Whereas the bread and cup represent Christ's body broken for the believer, the feetwashing represents the believer's giving his or her body to be broken for others by means of service. Says Eller: "With the bread and cup alone, the service concludes with the participation as mere *recipients* of the body *of Jesus*. The feetwashing makes them pledged and active members of the body *of Christ*."[9]

In the latter half of the twentieth century, concern has arisen about the decline of the practice of feetwashing in conjunction with communion. In 1969 Warren M. Eshbach observed: "Because many within the denomination no longer find any meaning in the service, it is being alternated with the regular Sunday morning Eucharist service." In light of this trend, Eshbach calls for a reinterpretation of feetwashing. Rejecting "the closed and separate attitude of the Brethren in the nineteenth century" and "the liberal attitude of dismissal in the twentieth," Eshbach turns to the eighteenth-century Brethren understanding of feetwashing where he finds "a sense of discipleship in man's daily relationship with other persons . . . . a sense of sharing that love with other persons that was made manifest by God in Christ."[10] Writing in 1986 Dale W. Brown observes: "Some Brethren have been embarrassed to participate in such a service in our contemporary culture; others feel that the attitude and manner of the participants often lead to pride rather than humility. For most Brethren, however, the rite of feetwashing remains an integral, meaningful part of the total love feast."[11]

Notes

1. Hochmann von Hochenau, "Hochmann von Hochenau to Count von Solms," in *European Origins of the Brethren*, comp. and trans. Donald F. Durnbaugh (Elgin, IL: Brethren Press, 1958), 126.

2. Alexander Mack, *Rights and Ordinances*, in *European Origins of the Brethren*, 364.

3. William M. Beahm, "The Brethren Love Feast" (Elgin, IL: Brethren Press [1971]).

4. *Pastor's Manual: Church of the Brethren* (Elgin, IL: Brethren Press, 1978), 43.

5. Dale W. Brown, "Worship," in *Church of the Brethren: Yesterday and Today*, ed. Donald F. Durnbaugh (Elgin, IL: Brethren Press, 1986), 69-70.

6. Alexander Mack, Jr., "A Letter Concerning Feetwashing," in *Brethren In Colonial America*, ed. Donald F. Durnbaugh (Elgin, IL: Brethren Press, 1967), 463-469.

7. Kerby Lauderdale, "Division Among the German Baptist Brethren" (Independent Study, Bethany Theological Seminary, 1968), 4.

8. H. R. Holsinger, *Holsinger's History of the Tunkers and the Brethren Church* (Lathrop, CA: the author, 1901), 417.

9. Vernard Eller, *In Place of Sacraments* (Grand Rapids, MI: Eerdmans, 1972), 112.

10. Warren M. Eshbach, "Another Look at John 13:1-20," *Brethren Life and Thought* 14 (Spring 1969):123-124.

11. Brown, 70.

The Text in Today's World

With the problem of mode now past history, Brethren probably will continue to wash feet as a mark of their discipleship. Biblical precedent and the servant motif are strong motivating factors, so the influence of John 13 on our worship life is not likely to lessen. However, we should be careful not to let the "service" motif swallow up the total meaning of the passage. Early Brethren saw in feetwashing a continuing process of purification as well as an act of service. Perhaps the author of the Gospel of John was not thinking in exactly these terms, but was surely making a similar point. In the Christian life there is an initial point of change, a rebirth in John's terms. But the Christian life depends on a continual process of receiving new life from Jesus and passing that life on to others. Washing feet represents that in the Fourth Gospel. The disciples received Jesus' ministry to them and then passed on that service to one another and other persons.

The Gospel of John sees the Christian life as flowing like sap through the trunk to the branches (John 15). We stop that process if we refuse to minister or be ministered to. Apparently Peter was willing to serve, but unwilling to be served. We too can foul up the process of redemption by supposing that we have arrived, that we no longer need the ministry of the church or each other. The meaning of John 13 for us today is that we give up our pride in ourselves and accept the ministry of Jesus and the church. Then we may effectively serve others.

There is yet another level at which John 13 speaks to us today, that of the form which our worship should take. Brethren historically have had both a practical religion and a participative kind of worship. Brethren have looked askance at intellectualizing the faith or creedalism. And like the Eastern Orthodox, Brethren would rather reenact life in their worship than merely watch clergy carry out a prescribed liturgy. As the Orthodox reenact the drama of the feetwashing on the Thursday prior to their Easter, so the whole love feast, including the washing of feet, has been a very dramatic element in Brethren life. There is perhaps no better form of Christian education and no better "service" than actually acting out our worship. Whatever changes occur in Brethren liturgy ought to be in the direction of more participation rather than less.

In the particular drama of the washing of feet, life as a whole is linked to worship in a very powerful way. This particular "service" affirms that life itself is an arena for serving God and being served by God, calling us to see common, even mundane, everyday events and everyday things as occasions for service. What we act out in the washing of feet at communion can take place then at many other points of the life of the church as well, at church suppers, picnics, meetings, coffee hours, study groups, etc. It is a lifestyle that often marks the Christian in the world, a kind of quiet, almost unnoticed helpfulness in even simple things. In this sense, too, feetwashing is a continuing paradigm for the worshiping faith community.

Case Study

There is no movement afoot in the Church of the Brethren to alter the function or mode of the feetwashing service. No doubt, however, many congregations have practical difficulty with the practice. Still other congregations find powerful ways to use the tradition. But, for the sake of understanding, let us suppose Dunkerdale wishes to revitalize the tradition of washing one another's feet. Some of the members have travelled to the Near East and Africa. They have experienced the washing of hands where a host passes a basin and towel around the table before a meal. Some congregations have already substituted handwashing for feetwashing. Dunkerdale decides, at its Nurture meeting, to make the shift.

1. Would you accept the substitution?

2. Does discipleship mean doing what was original or doing its current, everyday equivalent?

3. Of what faith value is doing the ordinance as it was done in the New Testament?

Session 13

On Hospitality and Mutual Aid

John 13:31-35 (NRSV)

When he had gone out, Jesus said, "Now the Son of Man has been glorified, and God has been glorified in him. [32]If God has been glorified in him, God will also glorify him in himself and will glorify him at once. [33]Little children, I am with you only a little longer. You will look for me; and as I said to the Jews so now I say to you, 'Where I am going, you cannot come.' [34]I give you a new commandment, that you love one another. Just as I have loved you, you also should love one another. [35]By this everyone will know that you are my disciples, if you have love for one another."

John 13:31-35 (BNT)

When, then, he came out, Jesus said, "Now the Son of Man is glorified, and God is glorified in him. [32]If God is glorified in him, God will also glorify himself by means of him, and so will glorify him immediately. [33]Little children, I am with you just a little while. You will look for me, but just as I have said to the Jews that they were unable to go where I am going, so I say the same thing to you now. [34]A new commandment I give to you—that you love one another. As I have loved you, so you love one another. [35]So everyone will know that you are my disciples, if you express love for one another.

The Text in Its Biblical Setting

John 13:31-35 occurs in the first chapter of what we call the Gospel of Glory. The first twelve chapters of John depend heavily on another writing called the Gospel of Signs. The author of John has used this source to develop for the reader a narrative about Jesus which uses the signs as faith symbols (water into wine, healing of the official's son, making the blind man to see, and others). This section about signs ends when Jesus arrives in Jerusalem and the Passion narrative begins. John 13 begins with the final meal and the episode of feet-washing. Gradually the discourses and narrative lead to the cross where the glory of God is made manifest for all to see.

We think of glory as overwhelming presence. The word glory translates a Greek word *doxa*, which in turn translates a Hebrew word *kabod*. Its most common usage meant weight or heaviness but soon was extended to wealth or power (Exod. 14:18; Isa. 61:6). For a person it can also refer to her or his reputation, fame, and influence (Job 29:20). When ascribed to God the term means powerful presence, as in the early Psalm 29. It could well be that the glory of God sits on the Ark in this Psalm (see 1 Sam. 4:21-22). God's glory was also present through the fire and the cloud (Exod. 40:34-38). It was the glory of God which led the Israelites out of Egypt, through the wilderness, into the promised land and went before them into victorious combat with their enemies.

In the Gospel of John the Word has become flesh and dwells among us (John 1:14). As the incarnate Word, Jesus walked among the people, and he brought to them the opportunity for ultimate life (John 4:13-14). But in chapter 13 the direction changes. Jesus is headed for the cross. There on the cross the glory of God will be known to all the world. Jesus will be lifted up for all to see (3:14-15; 12:30-33; 17:1-5). In contrast to the Hebrew Scriptures and even the apostle Paul, that presence or glory on the cross does not signify liberation, redemption or reconciliation, but love. Jesus on the cross is a sign of God's love for us, a love we as disciples have for each other and the world (17:26).

The "new commandment" to love one another raises a number of questions. Love is hardly new as a Judeo-Christian expectation (Hos. 3:1; Lev. 19:18). What is new is to make it the only ethical norm. John did just that. There are no other ethical admonitions in the Gospel of John. The disciples will be known by their love for each other. What is love? Obviously it describes the condition of a relationship. In the New Testament there are three different words for love, each of which reflects a slightly different understanding of the love relationship. There is a term for love as might be expressed between sisters and brothers or just good friends (*philos*). It is marked by concerned friendship and loyalty (John 11:3, 11). Another word, used less often, describes the relationship between two people joined by agreement (covenant) or attraction. These persons form an intimate relationship in which there is a mutual benefit for all parties concerned. One thinks, of course, of this love as that which may exist between men and women (*eros*). John, however, speaks most often of love as *agape*, a love which gives without asking anything in return. It is sometimes called unrequited love.

Agape love as seen on the cross best describes God's love for us. It signifies a gift given to us regardless of our response. Indeed, for Paul, we can only be freed if the gift requires nothing from us. It is an act of love which changes our lives. Because of that love, nothing can separate us from God (Rom. 8:39). One does note that our human communities, known for their covenantal relationships, are a result of the gift of God in Christ, not a condition for it (1 Cor. 8:9-13).

Love was expressed yet another way in the Fourth Gospel. The author of the Gospel of John understood God's love as a new kind of life (John 3:16; 10:10). God gave that new life in Jesus who in turn gave it to us. Jesus in John does not ask for anything in return. There are no demands or commandments. Rather we are only asked to "pass it on" (John 21:15-17). Of course, if we fail to pass it on, we may lose it (John 12:24-25). That is the new commandment, then. It is not a responsive obedience to God but a passing on of God's love to others.

The Text in Brethren Life

According to Donald F. Durnbaugh, "the Brethren are best described as a Radical Pietist movement which accepted an Anabaptist view of the church."[1] For both the Anabaptists and the Pietists, hospitality and mutual aid were important characteristics of Christians. In fact, Menno Simons (1496-1561), the founder of the Mennonites, included "sincere and unfeigned love of one's neighbor" as one of the signs by which the true church is known. He quoted John 13:35 as biblical support for this sign.[2]

Though he didn't quote the Gospel of John, Michael Frantz (1687-1748), a leader among the colonial Brethren, highlights the importance of hospitality and mutual aid based on Christian love. In a section on "the outward communion with God" (love of others) Frantz writes: "From this [Luke 3] it is to be understood that he who has two portions, be it food or clothing, house, property, livestock, money or whatever his neighbor needs for his life's necessity, then love should compel him to give to his brother and to his neighbor and to do as he can for their need. Love has no aim or measure as to how much one should give. Rather, it helps and gives gladly of its own volition as long as it has something and is able to help."[3]

In his book *Primitive Christianity* (1834), Peter Nead (1796-1877) includes a section titled "Hospitality and Alms-giving" in which he specifically quotes John 13:35. At the beginning of the paragraph in which he quotes this verse, Nead says: "It is very evident, that if the members of the church are in love and fellowship towards one another, they will not suffer their poor brethren and sisters, if it lies in their power, to want for any of the necessaries of life."[4] Nead also emphasizes that "the children of God will not only be kind and charitable to their own brethren in the Lord, but also to the children of men in general."[5]

Examples of Brethren hospitality and giving abound. Alexander Mack (1679-1735) is said to have been a wealthy miller who became poor because he shared his goods with the early Brethren in Schwarzenau when they suffered economic persecution because of their beliefs. Christopher Sauer (1695-1758), who related to the Brethren but was not a member, was sometimes called the "Good Samaritan of Germantown" because of his practice of providing aid to immigrants arriving in the New World. During colonial times a poor box was often kept in the meetinghouse. Individuals contributed to this box, and the deacons emptied it and distributed the funds to the needy.

In the nineteenth century it was common for Brethren to invite tramps into their homes and seat them at the table with the family. According to a record kept by Susan Landis of Montgomery County, Pennsylvania, each year from five to seven hundred tramps received hospitality at the Landis home. At the Michael Zigler home in Broadway, Virginia, a separate room was kept for tramps. It was furnished as well as the other rooms in the house and called the Plaugher room after one of the tramps who used it regularly twice a year.

It was not uncommon for the *Gospel Visitor* to have articles with such titles as "True Love," "Brotherly Love," and "Love." Often in these articles John 13:34-35 was quoted. One particular article titled "Brotherly Love in the Early Christian Churches," by a Dr. Neander, opens with a reference to John 13:31-35. The writer then cites examples from the writings of the church founders of how the early Christians provided "for the support and maintenance of the stranger, the poor, and the sick, of the old men, widows, and orphans, and of those who were imprisoned for the faith's sake."[6]

Because of the Brethren emphasis on mutual aid, which often took the form of providing for widows and orphans, helping a sick neighbor, and barn raisings, Brethren were opposed to insurance companies throughout much of their history. In 1879, however, Annual Meeting allowed members to establish mutual aid societies to insure against disaster, so long as Brethren principles were not compromised. As a result, several mutual aid societies were formed. Chief among these was the Brethren Mutual Aid Society of Northeast Kansas, which began in 1885 as a district organization that insured against fire and storm damage. Over a hundred years later, it is still operating. Under the name Mutual Aid Association, it now offers coverage to all members of the Church of the Brethren.

As the Brethren moved into the twentieth century, the terms *hospitality* and *mutual aid* tended to be replaced by the terms *service* and *stewardship*. The concept of service has already been dealt with in chapter 7. Stewardship came to refer primarily to the giving of money to support Brethren programs and institutions. While financial contributions are certainly appropriate and necessary, the practice of hospitality on a face-to-face basis was less emphasized. At the midpoint of the century, an article appeared in the *Gospel Messenger* titled "Hospitality—A Dying Practice?" In the article, the author, D. Eugene Lichty, contrasts current Brethren practices with those fifty years earlier. These contrasts include the fact that Brethren now build houses with so few bedrooms that there is no space for overnight guests; the fact that Annual Conferences are held in convention centers and not hosted by local churches on Brethren farms; and the fact that Brethren no longer invite visitors home for dinner after Sunday worship. At one point, Lichty asks: "Does this semicentennial contrast mean anything more than a change in styles? For the average American whose Christianity is only a Sunday affair perhaps it does not. But for Brethren who mean to be brothers, it indicates the decline of one mark of brotherhood, namely, hospitality."[7]

In recent years, however, the concept of hospitality has received new emphasis. In a critique of church growth principles, Donald E. Miller, then a professor at Bethany Theological Seminary, suggested that the Brethren reclaim their role as a hospitable people and use that hospitality as a method of evangelism. As a conclusion Miller writes: "My hope is that we will come to know growth in the full biblical sense by exercising hospitality, which is almost lost in many of our congregations. Hospitality seems to move against the grain of modern transient society, yet the admonition to be hospitable was born in the transiency of earlier ages. To become a hospitable people who are proud to proclaim the faith in which we believe is the basis for church growth in our time."[8]

In a follow-up article, Kenneth L. Gibble elaborates on hospitality evangelism. Gibble goes to Henri Nouwen for further understanding of the hospitality concept. According to Nouwen, hospitality is providing space for the stranger to "enter and become a friend instead of an enemy."[9] Such an approach does not promise numerical growth, but it gives people the freedom to discover God at work in their lives. Says Gibble: "I believe hospitality evangelism is a model that ought to be explored and tested by the Brethren. It is not for every congregation. But I believe it is in keeping with the best of Brethren heritage and theological rootage."[10]

Notes

1. Donald F. Durnbaugh, "Mutual Aid in Ministry to God's World," *Brethren Life and Thought* 23 (Spring 1988):91.

2. Menno Simons. "A Clear Reply to Gellius Faber," in Donald F. Durnbaugh, *Every Need Supplied* (Philadelphia: Temple University Press, 1974), 87.

3. "The Doctrinal Treatise of Michael Frantz," in *Brethren in Colonial America*, ed. Donald F. Durnbaugh (Elgin, IL: Brethren Press, 1967), 453.

4. Peter Nead, *Primitive Christianity, or a Vindication of the Word of God* (Staunton, VA: Kenton Harper, Printer, 1834), 145.

5. Ibid., 147.

6. Dr. Neander, "Brotherly Love in the Early Christian Churches," *Gospel Visitor*, August 1857, 224.

7. D. Eugene Lichty, "Hospitality—A Dying Practice?" *Gospel Messenger*, 9 September 1950, 10.

8. Donald E. Miller, "Brethren and Church Growth," *Brethren Life and Thought* 25 (Winter 1980):23.

9. Kenneth L. Gibble, "Hospitality to Strangers," *Brethren Life and Thought* 26 (Summer 1981):187.

10. Ibid., 188.

The Text in Today's World

Hospitality has been a hallmark of the Christian community from its inception. In the Pastoral Epistles it is said only those who show hospitality should be elected as leaders in the faith community (1 Tim. 3:2). For the first 250 years, the church met in homes, so hospitality became an important element in the very existence of the church. This was especially true when traveling evangelists came through (3 John 5). The author of the Didache (ca. 120 A.D.) urged the local congregation to be hospitable to such traveling leaders, though for no more than three days (Didache 11:3-6).

After Christianity became the dominant religion, the meaning of hospitality shifted. The church itself, or the bishop's church, became a place of hospitality. Persons who were under attack could find refuge in the church. The safety of the church building would not be violated even by the state. So the hospitality of the church shifted to that of a sanctuary—a safe place. At the same time the church, especially, monastic institutions, became charitable establishments. In the church those in need could find food, clothing, and medical attention.

As indicated in the section of Brethren history, during the Reformation the meaning of hospitality shifted again. For the Left Wing (Anabaptist) it meant not only an open home for others, including homeless, but also a sense of mutual aid for members of the community.

Today we are once again in shifting times. Christian hospitality still remains one of the marks of the church and still carries many of the earlier stances. For many the open home, though limited, remains the best sign of hospitality. Guests are shown hospitality by a meal, visit, or room in a private home. Among Believers' Church types, hospitality has become something of a fun way to travel. Members open their homes to travelers and in turn are received by others anywhere in the world. This "mennoniting your way" serves the same function we saw in the Didache. In a similar way the return to hospitality evangelism picks up the function of the early house church. The good news spreads by invitations to visit in private homes. In this way prospective Christians realize that the faith community is more than an idea or a personal decision, but starts with a new community context where care and support can be found.

At the same time, the medieval sense of sanctuary continues in a somewhat different way. Just as Brethren participated in the underground railway during the Civil War, so also a number of congregations have offered themselves as sanctuaries for persons from central America who have not legally entered the United States, but who would be harmed if they returned to their own country.

Most churches also continue the medieval sense of charity. Depending on the circumstances, one can find in local congregations a food pantry, a soup kitchen, a clothing supply, baby blankets, and many other helpful materials. These are an important element of hospitality. Brethren would do well, however, to stress once more a wider sense of mutual aid. "Charity" can create undesirable forms of co-dependency. In our stewardship we need to stress that everyone participates mutually in the program of the local congregation. No one should be placed in a position of subservient dependency. The author of the Didache was right: if hospitality cannot be mutual, it had better be sharply limited.

Case Study

Having become convinced that General Noriega was not only aiding drug dealers, but also had disallowed a legitimate election in Panama, the United States sent in troops to "arrest" him. The American military looked for him several days before it finally became clear that he had sought sanctuary in the Vatican embassy and it had been granted. Although the Vatican had no sympathy for General Noriega, and although it risked fostering displeasure from the American government, still the Catholic Church argued it had a tradition of offering sanctuary to *anyone* who needed it. Theologically and historically the church and the embassy had no choice—the hospitality of the church was available even to Noriega.

1. Should your local church offer sanctuary to *anyone* who seeks it? Have you ever offered sanctuary? Describe it.

2. Does your church presently offer sanctuary to illegal aliens from Central America? If so, how did you make the decision? If you don't, why don't you? If no one has asked for sanctuary (and so no policy is necessary), would you grant it if they did?

3. Do you think the Roman Catholic church did the right thing with General Noriega?

Session 14

On Secret Societies

John 18:19-24 (NRSV)

Then the high priest questioned Jesus about his disciples and about his teaching. [20]Jesus answered, "I have spoken openly to the world; I have always taught in synagogues and in the temple, where all the Jews come together. I have said nothing in secret. [21]Why do you ask me? Ask those who heard what I said to them; they know what I said." [22]When he had said this, one of the police standing nearby struck Jesus on the face, saying, "Is that how you answer the high priest?" [23]Jesus answered, "If I have spoken wrongly, testify to the wrong. But if I have spoken rightly, why do you strike me?" [24]Then Annas sent him bound to Caiaphas the high priest.

John 18:19-24 (BNT)

Then the high priest asked Jesus about his disciples and about his teaching. [20]Jesus answered him, "I have spoken openly to the world. I have always taught in the synagogue and in the temple, where the Jews all gather. I have said nothing in secret. [21]Why do you question me? Ask the ones who heard what I said to them. Look here, they know what I said." [22]As he said these things, one of the servants standing nearby struck Jesus and said, "Is this any way to answer the high priest?" [23]Jesus answered him, "If I have spoken falsely, then testify about what is false. But if I have spoken correctly, why do you strike me?" [24]Then Annas, leaving him bound up, sent him to Caiaphas the high priest.

The Text in the Biblical Setting

While the Gospel of John stresses living the truth (being reborn), as revealed to us in Jesus, the Revelator, there are also social components to the good news. These components are not always easy to see. One occurs frequently enough for us to be fairly certain about it:

believing in Jesus the Christ means a literal, public break with one's past. We can see this most clearly in the story of the man born blind (chapter 9). Though the man born blind has no preconceived ideas about Jesus, he does know that he was blind and now can see (9:25). Though the Jewish leaders question his experience and new sight (9:18), his parents and neighbors confirm something new has happened (9:20-21). Eventually the reality of his new life brings him into conflict with the Pharisees (9:30-33). At that point they expel him from the synagogue (9:34).

Once we have determined that the Jesus of the Fourth Gospel called people to public acknowledgment of their faith, we do see other examples. In chapter 5 a sick man who acknowledges Jesus causes a major conflict between Jesus and the religious leaders. In chapter 3 the Jewish leader Nicodemus comes *at night* to speak to Jesus. Jesus urges him to be reborn and come out into the light (3:19).

By the time John was written (about the year 95), it was not only Jews who confessed Jesus as Christ. Surely these other folk saw in the story of the man born blind a reflection of their own decision to follow Jesus. They must have seen in chapter 9 a discussion of their own anguish in forsaking the past and publicly believing in Jesus.

A major concern may have been for persons like the God-fearers mentioned in Acts (Cornelius in 10:1-3 or Lydia in 16:14). They believed in God but, for various reasons, could not make a public commitment to Judaism. Perhaps the Gospel of John calls for Jewish sympathizers to make a public confession of faith in Jesus and to abandon their closet faith. Even more serious, perhaps, were the growing number of gnostics, people who intellectualized or spiritualized their faith. Their faith was conveyed in obscure stories and strange language, e.g., the Gospel of Thomas and *The Gospel of Truth*. Theirs was not a fear of the public eye but a desire to have secret knowledge (*gnosis* in Greek) of God as shared by a few close comrades. We know that the hymn which introduces the Gospel of John (1:1-14) was used to contradict those who denied the historical and public nature of the incarnation.

The section John 18:19-24 needs to be understood in this light. It stands in the arrest and trial story. Jesus has finished praying and now enters a garden across the Kidron. There he is approached by Judas, some temple guards, and some Roman soldiers. Judas attempts to betray Jesus and hand him over to the guards. That cannot be done. Jesus acknowledges quite openly who he is (18:5). In fact, he invites the guards to arrest him (18:8). Jesus was taken before Annas, the father-in-law of Caiaphas, the High Priest. In the Synoptics Jesus goes before the High Priest alone, but in the Gospel of John we have a witness to the trial—the beloved disciple himself (18:15). It is this disciple who makes public an event which might otherwise have occurred in the secret chambers of the High Priest (see v. 22 on the confusion about the identity of the High Priest).

In this pre-trial interview with Annas, Jesus is asked about his disciples and about his teaching. Jesus responds as he has done throughout the Gospel. There is no secret teaching. There is no conspiracy. There is no small in-group of disciples. Everything has been said and done in public. His response not only denies the charges of a secret movement, but it also supports what we have already seen: Jesus calls for public confession of the faith, just as he himself taught and appeared openly before the people and the leaders.

The Text in Brethren Life

John 18:20 was often cited by Brethren writers of the nineteenth and twentieth centuries as part of their arguments against membership in secret societies. Such citations are found in both short tracts about secret societies and longer writings about Brethren beliefs and practices. The writer of the tract titled "Secret Societies and the Word of God" says: "In John 18:20, Jesus is replying to a question at His trial. The question is regarding His disciples and His doctrine. If Jesus had belonged to a secret society, and had communicated His instructions in secret, the fact would have at once appeared."[1] J. H. Moore (1846-1935), writing about oath-bound societies in his book *New Testament Doctrines* (1915), states: "Jesus, at one time, defined his policy in dealing with the public by saying: 'In secret I have said nothing.' He also declared that he had spoken 'openly before the world' (John 18:20)."[2]

The first mention of Brethren opposition to secret societies in the minutes of Annual Meeting occurred in 1804. In response to a query as to "what is to be done with brethren who join the Freemasons," the meeting stated that because of "many trifling things, frivolities, and unfruitful works . . . it is considered highly improper for brethren to be members in their association." The meeting went on to say that brethren should not have fellowship with anyone who wanted to remain with the Freemasons.[3] Throughout the nineteenth century, the issue of membership in secret societies continued to come before Annual Meeting. Twice in the minutes John 18:20 is cited—in 1859 as part of a query and again in 1878 as part of a response to a query. The secret group most often mentioned in the minutes are the Freemasons. But other groups are also named, including the Sons of Temperance (1847), the Odd Fellows (1852), the Know-Nothings (1855), and the Grange (1872). Early opposition of the Brethren to labor unions was due in part to the fact that Brethren equated unions with secret societies (1908).

According to Martin G. Brumbaugh (1862-1930), both Christopher Sauer (1695-1758) and Christopher Sauer, Jr., (1721-1784) were opponents of secret societies. Brumbaugh theorizes that Sauer, Jr., intentionally missed a dedication at the Germantown Academy, even though he was a trustee of the academy, because Masonic rites were part of the ceremonies.[4] Elder George Wolfe (1780-1865) and his brother Jacob (1778-1823), both Brethren leaders on the frontier in Illinois, are said to have joined the Masonic fraternity. However, "on duly considering the nature of their mistake they withdrew from the lodge and ever afterward remained true to the principles of the church regarding oathbound and secret societies."[5]

Not only was the issue of secret societies found in the writings and minutes of the 1800s. The issue was also the subject of a major debate on at least one occasion. According to Mary N. Quinter (1863-1914), her father James Quinter (1816-1888), publisher and editor of several Brethren periodicals, affirmed the proposition "The Principles of Freemasonry are Inconsistent with the Principles of Christian Truth" in a debate with Elder McKinney (Christian Church) in Miami County, Ohio, in September 1869.[6]

Probably the most unusual piece written by a Brethren about secret societies is Henry Holsinger's article "Is the Standing Committee a Secret Organization." Holsinger (1833-1905), the Progressive Brethren leader, listed the similarities between a standing committee meeting and a lodge meeting. These included: (1) meets in a separate room, (2) has a door keeper, (3) meets behind closed doors, (4) excludes the press, (5) admits only those in the third degree of ministry, (6) has secrets which cannot be revealed.[7] Without doubt such a comparison was offensive to many Brethren leaders of Holsinger's day.

Frederick Dove (1895-1952), a professor at Bridgewater College for over twenty years, discussed the position of the Brethren on secret societies in his book *Cultural Changes in the Church of the Brethren* (1932). After reviewing the minutes of Annual Meetings on the topic, Dove concludes: "Altho these declarations of the church regarding secret orders have not been repealed, they are not strictly observed and members of the church become members of secret fraternities without any risk of excommunication. The church has turned her attention away from these personal matters toward more constructive moral issues and religious problems."[8]

In spite of Dove's conclusion, concern about secret societies came before the Annual Conference again in 1952. A query asked for a restatement of the Brethren understanding of the New Testament teaching related to oath-bound and secret societies. A study committee was appointed and reported back in 1954. The report, as adopted, began by stating that only a small percent of the Brethren were members of secret societies and that such membership was only a problem for a few churches. Then, for the benefit of the congregations having problems, the report restated the Brethren opposition to secret societies and concluded by calling the church to become so vital and to provide such genuine fellowship that fraternal orders would not be needed.[9]

Most recently a 1988 issue of the BRF Witness was devoted to secret societies. Included is a lengthy article titled "The Masonic Lodge—A False Religion" by Larry Graybill and an editorial on the Freemasons by Harold Martin. The editorial quotes John 18:20 as evidence that "organized secrecy . . . is contrary to the very spirit of the Gospel."[10]

Notes

1. "Secret Societies and the Word of God," Tract No. 285 (Elgin, IL: Brethren's General Mission Board, n.d.), 5.

2. J. H. Moore, New Testament Doctrines (Elgin, IL: Brethren Publishing House, 1915), 147.

3. Minutes of the Annual Meetings of the Church of the Brethren, 1778-1909 (Elgin, IL: Brethren Publishing House, 1909), 26.

4. Martin Grove Brumbaugh, History of the German Baptist Brethren in Europe and America (Elgin, IL: Brethren Publishing House, 1899), 412. See footnote.

5. J. H. Moore, Some Brethren Pathfinders (Elgin, IL: Brethren Publishing House, 1929), 82.

6. Mary N. Quinter, Life and Sermons of Elder James Quinter (Mt. Morris, IL: Brethren's Publishing Co., 1891), 46.

7. [Henry R. Holsinger], "Is the Standing Committee a Secret Organization?" Progressive Christian, 27 June 1879.

8. Frederick Denton Dove, Cultural Changes in the Church of the Brethren (Elgin, IL: Brethren Publishing House, 1932), 167-68.

9. Minutes of the Annual Conferences of the Church of the Brethren, 1945-1954, comp. and ed. by Ora W. Garber (Elgin, IL: Brethren Publishing House, 1956), 216-17.

10. Harold S. Martin, "Editorial," BRF Witness 23:1 (1988), 2.

The Text in Today's World

Brethren of the nineteenth century saw in John 18:19-24 an admonition to avoid secret societies. It should be said immediately that their perception was correct. Jesus of the Gospel of John did call for expressions of faith and a discipleship which were open and public. He must have spoken sharply to Annas on the matter—the identity of my disciples and the content of my teaching is known to everyone. At least a guard slapped Jesus for being so sharp in his answer. Secret societies build their power on secret rites and secret knowledge (*gnosis*). Those who possess such private information develop with others a powerful comradery. Christians cannot give themselves to such societies without destroying their relationship to the faith community and to the Lord of all, Jesus Christ. A person cannot serve two masters.

But Jesus actually spoke more of himself and his disciples. He said his movement was not a secret organization. A number of scholars have thought of the early church as a sectarian organization. They mean to say that the early church expected the end of the world; it exercised strong authority over its members; it maintained strong boundaries over against the world; it exercised an ethic of love among members only; it held its resources in common. The words of Jesus in John speak of a much more open church which called for public affirmation and visible membership. By warning against secret societies our foreparents also warned against making the church a closed society. The church of the Gospel of John had no hierarchy; there were no saving sacraments offered by priests only to believers; membership rights and responsibilities were held equally by women and men; no dogmas separated believers from non-believers.

Some among us may be tempted to make of the Church of the Brethren a closed sect, an isolated family of faith. That will not likely happen, and it may never have been our heritage. But, in contrast, others might like to see us more mainline Protestant, so that our decisions could also become public policy (like the Jewish leaders in the story). The Gospel of John offers another way: we live out our faith in a parabolic fashion. We are a community of love, but we do it openly. We appear before the public eye, we meet with national leaders. Jesus taught as he did in the parables in order to question the *status quo*. The author of the Gospel of John calls for a community of love which constantly makes public its faith.

Case Study

In an eastern district of the Church of the Brethren, a task force on ministry to the deaf determined that there was sufficient need to seek special resource materials and a part-time minister. Representative deaf persons and members of the task force approached the district for financial support. The district was sympathetic but uncertain about its priorities. They asked for help from the Parish Ministries Commission. When the district board met to determine its response to the task force, they first met in executive session with a consultant. Later, in public session, they gave their decision to the group representing the deaf.

1. Do you think any board or committee of a church should meet in executive (private) session. If so, under what circumstances?

2. In the case described, did the task force for deaf ministry have a right to participate in a decision which so vitally affected their future and ministry?

3. Someone has defined a minority as a group asked to leave when a committee goes into executive session? Does that seem reasonable to you?

4. Do you think a church board could make a decision about personnel or about program priorities if the persons involved were present at the meeting?

Session 15

On Not Conforming

Romans 12:1-2 (NRSV)

I appeal to you therefore, brothers and sisters, by the mercies of God, to present your bodies as a living sacrifice, holy and acceptable to God, which is your spiritual worship. ^{2}Do not be conformed to this world, but be transformed by the renewing of your minds, so that you may discern what is the will of God—what is good and acceptable and perfect.

Romans 12:1-2 (BNT)

So, by the mercies of God, I beseech you who are members of the Christian family, be willing in your relationship to each other to place yourself on the altar as a living sacrifice, which is a life set apart for God and well-pleasing to him. That would be worship in the truest sense of the word. ^{2}And do not be conformed to this age, but be transformed by a mindset which anticipates renewal, so that you can try out those things which are God's will—that which is good, that which is pleasing to God, and that which is ultimate in nature.

The Text in Its Biblical Setting

Romans 12 is a passage favored not only by Brethren but also by the entire church down through history. The theology of Paul is not always easy to understand, so for some persons the ethical sections such as this one become a window for understanding the great apostle. In Romans 1—8 Paul pounds out that powerful statement of Christian faith which has so influenced Christianity through the centuries. In chapters 9—11 he reflects, in something of an interlude, on what relationship exists between the new faith and Israel. In chapter 12 Paul returns to the train of thought he left in chapter 8. As is usual for Paul, he moves from theological to ethical considerations by means of the Greek word *parakalo* ("I beseech"). Both in the New Testament epistles and in other letters of the time, the word *parakalo* introduces a series of directions which follow information just given to the readers (see 1 Th. 4:1; 2 Th. 3:12; Eph. 4:1). So the admonitions of Romans 12 follow the "gospel" of chapters 1—8. Some of the material clearly has a Pauline flavor, but there are more Jesus-like sayings here than in any other chapter outside the Synoptic Gospels.

For Paul, ethics invariably accompanies faith. We cannot be justified before God by what we do (Rom. 1:16-17; Gal. 3:11), but the new covenant with God in Christ will result in appropriate action. What Romans 12 sets forth then is an ethical stance which derives from and is made possible because of the previous "mercies of God." These previous mercies consist not only of personal experiences of the grace of God but also the historical events of salvation, especially the death and resurrection of Jesus Christ. Paul has recounted these historical mercies in the preceding chapters of Romans, especially chapters 9—11 (see 9:14-23; 11:28-36).

On the basis of these mercies Paul can ask the reader to display the same mercy toward others. The analogy he chooses to describe this human mercy is that of a "living sacrifice" of the Christian's "body." What is this "body" of which Paul speaks? It must be argued that Paul is speaking of the Christian community as a whole, not just individuals. We have already noticed that "body" has corporate meanings (see Session 4, p. 35). Further, the word for body, *soma*, is hardly ever used to mean the total organism of an animal, and in the Old Testament never used of that animal as a sacrifice. So, though it seems natural for us to speak of a body being sacrificed, it would not have been so in the Jewish sacrificial system. There the term used was *basar*, which was translated *sarx* in Greek and means "flesh." So the term "body" surely means something more than an individual body, namely, the corporate relationship of the person within the Christian community.

Paul says then that we should be willing to place our bodily relationships on the altar as "living sacrifices." In the ancient world it was common to appease the gods by means of sacrifices, especially through sacrificing the firstborn (Exod. 11:5; 13:12). The purpose of the Exodus, however, was that Israel might be a *living* firstborn people (Exod. 13:15). As a living sacrifice, the Israelites became a kingdom of priests and a holy nation (Exod. 19:6). Paul speaks the same way of the first Christians who, instead of sacrificing other things, are to become themselves living sacrifices in the process of relating to one another in the Christian community. Such is the nature of true worship.

Paul uses here the term *latreia*, a term related to our word *liturgy*. We do, indeed, speak of worship as a service, but we have lost the radical sense of that. In the Greek world, *latreia* meant work or service, but in the Greek translation of the Hebrew Scriptures (the Septuagint) the term, and its cognates, refers to divine service, such as service of sacrifice. For example, Moses consistently asked Pharaoh to let the Hebrew people go "serve God on the mountain" (Exod. 3:12). By that he surely included the offering of sacrifices (Exod. 5:3). In the New Testament, the same sense of sacrifice continues but always with service in mind. For example, Jesus says to the disciples that the day is coming when those who kill the disciples will think they are doing a service for God (John 16:2; make a sacrifice?). Paul pulled the term out of the Exodus narrative. The Christian community is to become the living sacrifice, the firstborn, just as God chose the Hebrew people at the time of the first Passover. To serve God in that way is true service and worship.

In verse 2 Paul goes on to describe our calling with yet another concept from his Jewish heritage, that of the old age and the new age. The idea of two ages derives from apocalyptic Judaism, which was a movement within Judaism during the time between the testaments. These Jews believed that the present evil age was passing away and that a new age, in which God was king, was close at hand. Jesus spoke of this coming kingdom, and Paul too believed that the present age was soon to be ended (1 Cor. 7:26; 1 Th. 5:1-2). The whole thrust of early Christianity was to challenge people to forswear the values of this age and live according to the values of the coming age—even while living within this age.

Paul uses this apocalyptic structure as a basis for his ethics: We are not to conform to the values of this passing age, but to live now according to the values of the endtime. It is not the world as God's creation or the world of other people that we are to reject, but rather the warped value system of the world in the present era. Anticipating the renewal of all things which is on its way, we are to let renewal begin in our own approach to life ("mindset"). In that way we will be free to try out those things which are God's will rather than live for our own self-protection. This venture is what Paul attempts to spell out, then, in the remainder of Romans 12—15.

The Text in Brethren Life

Historically, Romans 12:1-2 was used among the Brethren to support the doctrine of nonconformity to the world. In many ways

142   Texts in Transit II

nonconformity was replaced by the doctrine of simple living during
the second decade of the twentieth century, as already discussed in
chapter 4. Nonconformity, however, is really a more inclusive term
than simple living. J. H. Moore (1846-1935), writing during the decade
of the development of the simple living doctrine, describes well the
historic Brethren understanding of nonconformity. According to
Moore, nonconformity "relates itself to every phase of the new and
consecrated life. It applies to character, methods of doing business,
attending places of amusement and other places wholly unbecoming
the Christian profession, as well as places of residence, houses of
worship, occupations, and even the clothing that is worn."[1] Two
terms closely associated with nonconformity are *a separate people* and
a peculiar people. By *separate people* the Brethren have meant that they
understand themselves as separated from the unchristian ways of the
world which, in turn, has made them appear to be a *peculiar people*.

One of the early extensive discussions of nonconformity in Brethren literature is found in Peter Nead's (1797-1877) *Theological Writings*
(1850). Nead has a chapter entitled "Non-conformity to the World,"
in which he quotes Romans 12:1-2 as well as John 17:16, 1 Timothy
2:9, and several other New Testament passages. Concerning nonconformity Nead says: "The church of Christ should be distinguished
from the world in the inward and also the outward man. Christ tells
us, that the tree is known by its fruits; Mat. 7:16. When we can discover
no difference in conduct between the world and those who profess
not to be of the world, we conclude that the difference is in name only,
which in this respect is worse than nothing. The most of the world's
recreations are sinful—an abuse of time, and should be abandoned."[2]

A second lengthy discussion of nonconformity is found in an
editorial by Henry Kurtz (1796-1874) in the *Gospel Visitor*. This editorial, which presents the third general principle of the Fraternity of the
German Baptists, as the Brethren were called in the mid-1800s, extends from the third through the sixth issues of Volume I of the *Visitor*.
Kurtz begins the editorial by stating: "The *third* principle, which the
Brethren hold to be of primary importance, and requisite for every
member to study and observe, is—*Humility* and *Nonconformity to the
world*."[3] After an extensive discussion of humility, Kurtz turns to
nonconformity. Using Romans 12:2 as one of his texts, he says that the
word *world* in Romans 12 is not the world which God created with its
seasons and natural laws that provide fruits at harvest time. It is,
rather, the "present evil world of mankind, which has been deceived
by Satan into disobedience and proud rebellion against God and his
laws, and which has so readily and foolishly imbibed that wicked

principle of their deceiver—pride;—this world it is, to which we are NOT to be conformed."[4] Over against this world, says Kurtz, stands the church or the kingdom of Christ. The members of this church are often tempted to conform to the manners, fashions, and customs of the world; but they must remain "a body distinct and separate from the world, a peculiar people."[5] Now, continues Kurtz, in order to maintain nonconformity, our Brethren ancestors might have made rules and laws to govern the practice of the principle, but they did not. The practice has been left to the guidance of the Scripture and the Holy Spirit in the individual member. Each person follows the principle as he or she will and is admonished only for gross violations.

The most obvious aspect of Brethren nonconformity in the nineteenth century was dress; and it is primarily to the question of dress that numerous Annual Meeting articles on nonconformity spoke during that century. The 1804 minutes of Annual Meeting state that people desiring to join with the Brethren should be told that the new fashions in vogue in the world are contrary to salvation and that when they are willing to lay aside such fashions, they will be cheerfully baptized. In 1817 minutes is this statement: "Concerning conforming to the world in wearing fashionable clothing and everything that is high . . . . It was considered, that when a member should herein be found guilty, he should be admonished; and if the admonition would not be heeded, we could not hold such in full fellowship."[6] By 1849 the Annual Meeting had mellowed on the issue of nonconformity. The question was stated thus: "Whether it would not be agreeable to the gospel, to advise those members, who have been in the church two or three years, and are still conformed to this world, not to come to communion until they deny themselves, and become transformed from the world?" The reply of Annual Meeting was that such members should be admonished but that the Meeting could "not erect a standard . . . to authorize the church to prohibit such members from partaking of the communion."[7]

This change in attitude about dress eventually led to the abandonment of the prescribed dress and other outward signs of nonconformity, coupled with the development of the doctrine of the simple life. Interestingly, by 1923 neither nonconformity nor Romans 12:1-2 are listed on the Brethren's Card. However, the card does include the Brethren opposition to such things as immodest dress, games of chance, membership in secret societies, and taking oaths. Opposition to such items is based, in part, on the doctrine of nonconformity. Also noteworthy is the fact that nonconformity is not featured in either the 1966 Annual Conference report on the "Theological Basis of Personal

Ethics" or the 1980 Annual Conference paper on "Christian Life-styles." Of course, as with the Brethren's Card, these two papers do include some practices once related to the nonconformity doctrine.

In spite of the lack of specific references to nonconformity in official Brethren statements of the twentieth century, the doctrine is covered by some Brethren authors. A Brethren guide to church membership for senior highs and adults, *Becoming and Belonging*, Volume 2, contains a section on nonconformity. Listed among the biblical teachings on the subject is Romans 12:2, and in speaking about a member's responsibility for nonconformity, the guide urges members to live in dynamic tension with the world by being active in the world without being conformed to the ways of the world.[8] Art Gish, in *Beyond the Rat Race*, quotes Romans 12:2 and notes that just as Paul realized that the new realities ushered in by Jesus Christ were in conflict with the old structures of the world, so must Christians realize that their faith stands in judgment of present-day culture.[9] A 1985 pamphlet titled "Nonconformity" by Ron Martin-Adkins indicates that nonconformity for the late 1900s calls people "from commercialism and overconsumption to living on only as much as you need, from national security and the saving of one's own life to serving all of life, and from making-it-on-your-own individuality to responsible covenant with others before God."[10] Martin-Adkins then quotes Romans 12:2.

Notes

1. J. H. Moore, *New Testament Doctrines* (Elgin, IL: Brethren Publishing House, 1914), 134.

2. Peter Nead, *Theological Writings on Various Subjects* (Dayton, OH: the author, 1850), 124-125.

3. Henry Kurtz, "The Fraternity of German Baptists," *Gospel Visitor*, June 1851, 37.

4. Ibid., (August 1851), 71.

5. Ibid., (September 1851), 87.

6. *Minutes of the Annual Meetings of the Church of the Brethren, 1778-1909* (Elgin, IL: Brethren Publishing House, 1909), 40.

7. Ibid., 108.

8. Ercell V. Lynn, ed., *Becoming a New Person in Christ* and *Belonging in the Christian Fellowship* (Elgin, IL: Brethren Press, 1964), 2:84-87.

9. Arthur G. Gish, *Beyond the Rat Race* (Scottdale, PA: Herald Press, 1973), 168.

10. Ron Martin-Adkins, "Nonconformity" (Elgin, IL: Church of the Brethren General Board, [1985]). Pamphlet.

The Text in Today's World

As Kenneth Shaffer has shown in the section on Brethren history, Romans 12:1-2 was used largely to support a way of life that differed from the surrounding culture. However, over a long period of time allegiance to any one style of dress and culture becomes a matter of conforming rather than nonconforming. In recent years Brethren came to realize that this passage did not support a continuing concern for a specific approach to culture, such as the plain garb typical of the early twentieth century. Brethren, however, became keenly aware of the meaning of dress during controversies over school dress codes and gang colors. Obviously one can be tagged as belonging or not belonging by the way one dresses. But as indicated, this passage blesses neither culture nor counterculture.

Paul was not concerned about avoiding Roman culture as such. He was much more concerned that we not become enslaved to any cultural expression, be it that of the established society or that of the counterculture. In 1 Corinthians 6:12, he insisted that all those who had to express their freedom by doing something other than what the majority did surely were enslaved to their marks of freedom. The Christian should be able to become involved in any one of a number of different ways of life without being enslaved by it (1 Cor. 9:19-23). For the Christian who lives in hope of the coming kingdom, there should be nothing in this world which has ultimate significance. A person is free in Christ at that point only. Anything less becomes slavery once more. Such a person does not "leave" this world, however. Such a person is now free to move here and there to support those things which seem appropriate for the service of God. Such persons can say "Yes" to life because they are not consumed by the "No" of compulsive conformity. This was the freedom Paul had in mind (2 Cor. 1:15-22).

If Christians are not bound by either social expectations or the denial of social expectations, then the church is more fully able to act as a living sacrifice. The church ought not protect cultural values except as they help persons. Nor should the church oppose cultural values except as they hinder persons from seeking the kingdom. Because a church choir does not need to meet the standards of culture, it should be able to include persons who cannot sing well but who need the *koinonia* of singers. By the same token, a church softball team can include persons who cannot play well but who need the ministry of an athletic fellowship. We are saying at the same time, however, that a Brethren congregation may indeed have a choir and a softball team, even though they are cultural phenomena. The church is free to do its ministry as a living redemptive group, because it has no hang-up about the ultimate value of anything in this life. Perhaps few passages are more important to the Believers' Church today than this one. We need to recapture a vision of Christian existence in a non-Christian world.

Paul describes the existence of the Christian community between the times as that of a living sacrifice. He calls it the true worship of God, which involves living in the new age while the world still abides by old values and standards. Such lives, though they are costly, serve as a sacrifice to God and point to the coming reign of God. Mainline liturgical worship services often leave Brethren feeling somewhat inept. It isn't just a matter of standing, sitting, kneeling, and responding. Many simply lack the sense of occasion. The sense of occasion for Brethren comes more often when the moment calls for a word of kindness, a touch of support and healing, an act of reconciliation, a witness for peace and justice. True worship is serving God while the world is being transformed.

Case Study

Summer Valley Church of the Brethren faced a crisis. The roof on the church leaked badly. It appeared that a new roof was required. Furthermore, as winter approached it became clear that a new furnace was required if the congregation were to meet in its usual place. Two contractors had indicated a total cost of no less than $15,000. The church simply did not have that kind of money in its budget. The pastor suggested they consult with a Methodist layman, well-known in the area for his skill in raising money for such groups as the Boy Scouts. At the Stewards meeting he suggested they borrow the money, make the repairs, and at the same time, start a special capital gifts campaign. He suggested he could organize the campaign for a small percentage of the amount. He would need some members and the pastor to make initial large pledges of, say, $5,000. Then he could tell the rest of the congregation of the sacrificial giving of these dedicated board members. They would almost surely give about the same amount. The Methodist consultant said it always worked with the Boy Scouts.

1. Does the success of such methods make them commendable for the church of Jesus Christ?

2. How would you expect the faith community to differ from society as a whole?

3. How should Summer Valley raise the $15,000?

Session 16

On the Holy Kiss

Romans 16:3-16 (NRSV)

Greet Prisca and Aquila, who work with me in Christ Jesus, [4]and who risked their necks for my life, to whom not only I give thanks, but also all the churches of the Gentiles. [5]Greet also the church in their house. Greet my beloved Epaenetus, who was the first convert in Asia for Christ. [6]Greet Mary, who has worked very hard among you. [7]Greet Andronicus and Junia, my relatives who were in prison with me; they are prominent among the apostles, and they were in Christ before I was. [8]Greet Ampliatus, my beloved in the Lord. [9]Greet Urbanus, our co-worker in Christ, and my beloved Stachys. [10]Greet Apelles, who is approved in Christ. Greet those who belong to the family of Aristobulus. [11]Greet my relative Herodion. Greet those in the Lord who belong to the family of Narcissus. [12]Greet those workers in the Lord, Tryphaena and Tryphosa. Greet the beloved Persis, who has worked hard in the Lord. [13]Greet Rufus, chosen in the Lord; and greet his mother—a mother to me also. [14]Greet Asyncritus, Phlegon, Hermes, Patrobas, Hermas, and the brothers and sisters who are with them. [15]Greet Philologus, Julia, Nereus and his sister, and Olympas, and all the saints who are with them. [16]Greet one another with a holy kiss. All the churches of Christ greet you.

Romans 16:3-16 (BNT)

Greet Prisca and Aquila, my co-workers in Christ Jesus, [4]who have risked a great deal on my account. Not only I, but all the churches of the Gentiles thank them. [5]Greet also the congregation which meets at their house. Greet my beloved Epaenetus who in Asia was the first of those in Christ. [6]Greet Mary who labored much among you. [7]Greet Andronicus and Junia, members of my family who shared imprisonment with me. They are noteworthy among the apostles, and were in Christ before I was. [8]Greet Ampliatus, my beloved in the Lord. [9]Greet Urbanus, our co-worker in Christ, and my beloved Stachys.

[10]Greet Apelles, well thought of in Christ. Greet the household of Aristobulus. [11]Greet my relative Herodion. Greet those in the household of Narcissus who are in the Lord. [12]Greet Tryphaena and Tryphosa, women who labor much in the Lord. Greet my beloved Persis, another woman who labors much in the Lord. [13]Greet Rufus, eminent in the Lord, and his mother (and mine). [14]Greet Asyncritus, Phlegon, Hermes, Patrobas, Hermas, and the brothers and sisters with them. [15]Greet Philologus, Julia, Nereus and his sister, and Olympas and all the saints with them. [16]Greet everyone with a holy kiss. All the churches of Christ greet you.

The Text in Its Biblical Setting

Some parts of the Bible are seldom read. One thinks of the genealogy in Genesis 5 or the families in Numbers 26. The list of greetings in Romans 16 would also rank high among the texts not often read and not often used in sermons or educational curricula. But for those who read the New Testament often and who are specifically interested in the life of the early church, these personal greetings can be very informative. Let's note some of the things apparent in this series of greetings.

The Names. In this list there are few classical Roman names, though a name like Andronicus certainly has a long Roman heritage (2 Macc. 4:31-38). The names Junia and Julia are classical, and these two women could be of noble origin. Normally a Roman man had two classical names such as Titus Justus in Acts 18:7. As a matter of fact, since Romans was written from Corinth, the Gaius of 16:23 probably is Paul's well-to-do friend Titus Justus (see 1 Cor. 1:14); so his full name would be Gaius Titus Justus, a complete Roman noble name. Most of the names in this list are virtue names like Ampliatus (ample), Urbanus (urbane), or Philologus (lover of words or talkative). Such names invariably point to slaves or freed. The "freed" have been slaves but have found ways to buy or gain freedom. In such a case they have kept their slave name. Often they then retained, in addition to the slave name, the name of the owner. It may be quite significant that no such example of this occurs in the New Testament. We know the later church did not indicate who was noble and who was slave. Had that equality already begun in the New Testament period (Gal. 3:27-28)?

Gender. In Gal. 3:27-28 Paul proclaimed an equality of master and slave, male and female. These lists usually indicate that he took the equality seriously. Later church leaders and translators have not always stressed this equality. Feminine names like Prisca, Tryphaena, Tryphosa, and Julia are easy to spot. More difficult has been Junia (NRSV) in verse 7. It might be masculine but probably is not. In the New Testament there is no other woman named as an apostle except Junia in 16:7, though the Phoebe of Romans 16:1 must have been a well-known and influential minister (see NRSV footnote). In fact, some translators and churches have been reluctant to have the unknown man Andronicus and the woman Junia be listed as apostles and persons who became Christians before Paul did! It is little wonder that earlier translations changed Paul's "sister" and apostle Junia to the man Junias.

Family. The Mediterranean world was much more family-oriented than our more individualistic society. The threat of losing family, or being shunned by family, was a powerful negative force in that society. The possibility of being shamed by one's family was nearly intolerable. The first Christians had to deal with the probable loss of family when a person became a disciple of Jesus. In the Gospels, Jesus said that people who left brothers and sisters, mothers and fathers to follow Jesus would receive many more in return (Mark 10:28-31). Little wonder then that the new faith community frequently used family designations to describe their new relationship in Christ. Paul speaks of the community as brothers and sisters (v. 14). Indeed, he speaks of Andronicus, Junia, and Herodion as relatives (vv. 7, 11). We would suppose Paul meant some special relationship within the family of God. In the same vein, he can refer to the mother of Rufus as his own (v. 13).

The Faith Community. The incredible couple, Priscilla and Aquila, have done it again! They have formed a house church in Rome, as they had done also in Ephesus (1 Cor. 16:19) and likely in Corinth (Acts 18:2). Through the second century, we know of no other form of church than house churches. We assume there were in every major city of the Mediterranean world homes where about fifty to seventy-five Christians met. It seems strange then to hear of only one such house church in Rome, that of Priscilla and Aquila. Presumably the others also met in house churches, but perhaps not in homes as we know them. Rome was a densely populated city. There were far more apartments, or *insulae*, than houses. Do we have here lists of people belonging to an apartment church (vv. 14-15)? If so, what was their faith life like? Since they would have lived next door to each other, did they meet daily for meals and worship as in Jerusalem (Acts 2:46)? Did they share some property in common (Acts 2:44)?

In a world that stressed family relationships so intensely, we would expect to see in the faith community the marks of family. Besides the names, the sharing in common, and eating together, the earliest Christians greeted each other as if they were family. In the Jewish world the kiss was indeed a family kiss. A son and father, Jacob and Isaac, would kiss (Gen. 27:26-27). Brothers, Esau and Jacob, would kiss (Gen. 33:4). A mother kisses her daughters-in-law, Naomi with Ruth and Orpah (Ruth 1:9). We seldom hear of an erotic kiss such as occurs between the two lovers in Song of Songs (1:2; 8:1). So, as a mark of the new family in Christ, the Apostle Paul asks the Christians of Rome to greet each other with a kiss, a practice he calls for at the end of several letters (1 Cor. 16:20; 2 Cor. 13:12; 1 Th. 5:26; cf. 1 Pet. 5:14).

The Text in Brethren Life

On the basis of Romans 16:16 and four other New Testament verses (1 Cor. 16:20; 2 Cor. 13:12; 1 Th. 5:26; and 1 Pet. 5:14), Brethren have used the kiss as a form of greeting. Variously referred to as the holy kiss, the kiss of charity, and the Christian salutation, it is exchanged between people of the same sex. Typically it is combined with a handshake (the right hand of fellowship). During the twentieth century, the exchange of the holy kiss among members of the Church of the Brethren has come to be limited, for the most part, to the time immediately after one person has washed and wiped the feet of another during the love feast.

In earlier days, however, the holy kiss was used more frequently. A reference to its use in the eighteenth century is made in the following excerpt from a letter by Alexander Mack, Jr., (1712-1803) to John Preisz (1751-1829):

> As regards Brother Cornelius Nice, he has had his name put on the list for the drill. He seeks to remove himself from the congregation as much as possible and no longer likes to be called a brother. He refused the kiss to Brother Christopher Sauer when he spoke to him. When I learned of it and also spoke to him, I did not offer it to him. Thus he would be as good as expelled but we should gladly have more patience to see whether he might repent.[1]

Peter Nead (1796-1877), writing in 1834, recommended the use of the holy kiss when Brethren met for worship, at the time of baptism, and twice during the love feast. Even M. G. Brumbaugh (1862-1930), writing in 1899, described its use "at the close of the Lord's Supper or love feast, and just before the Communion" and "at any other appropriate occasion upon the meeting or parting of those of like precious faith."[2]

Nead includes an entire section in his *Primitive Christianity* (1834) on the holy kiss. He begins by quoting Romans 16:16, as well as two other verses concerning the kiss, and then states: "I will venture to say, that we have not, in the Bible or Testament, a plainer command of any thing, than of the observance of the Holy Kiss."[3] Nead also discusses the meaning of the kiss. The use of the kiss between the Lord's supper and the communion, says Nead, reminds members "to be true to one another—not to forsake one another in times of tribulation—but, as John says, to lay down their lives for the brethren." In the next paragraph Nead continues: "The spiritual import of this performance is spiritual affection, and is intended to promote mutual love among the fraternity."[4]

Annual Meeting minutes reveal that the practice of the holy kiss was not without problems. Between 1797 and 1885, questions concerning the kiss came up at more than twenty different meetings. As early as 1797 concern was raised about the neglect of the kiss in some congregations. While the meeting affirmed the use of the kiss, the response implies that the kiss was being neglected because some members were ashamed of it. Evidently shame also lay behind the question which came to the 1856 meeting: "Does Christian fellowship, according to the gospel, forbid, or require, or leave it optional for brethren when meeting in cities, towns, or at public gatherings, when extending the salutation of the hand, to accompany the same with the salutation of the holy kiss?"[5] Whereas the 1797 meeting affirmed the kiss, the 1856 meeting made it optional in public.

Another problem which developed concerning the kiss had to do with white members who refused the kiss to black members. Concerning this issue, the Annual Meeting of 1835 stated: "But inasmuch we receive our fellow members with the holy kiss, and there is repugnance in some of our white members to salute colored persons in this manner, the colored members should bear with that weakness, and not offer the kiss to such weak members until they become stronger, and make the first offer."[6] This decision, which had been reaffirmed in 1845, was called into question at the 1875 meeting. That year a query came asking Annual Meeting to make no distinction on the basis of color or race as to the use of the holy kiss. While the meeting granted the request, it also asked members to continue to bear with each other.

No doubt due to the problems and questions related to its use, the holy kiss was a popular topic in Brethren publications of the second half of the nineteenth century. Several articles about the kiss appeared in the *Gospel Visitor*. In November 1858, the *Visitor* answered a question about the use of the kiss with this statement: "It should be practiced by Christians when they meet at their meetings for worship, and when their performances call for a special manifestation of love and union. But when they meet frequently, or daily, and for the transaction of their ordinary or temporal business, we do not think it necessary to practice it at every such meeting."[7]

Two tracts were also published on the kiss in the late nineteenth century by the General Missionary and Tract Committee—one by Salome A. Stoner Myers (1863-1894) and one by J. H. Moore (1846-1935). The one by Myers, who taught "Sacred History" and "Sunday School Normal Work" at Mt. Morris Academy and College, is the longer and more scholarly of the two tracts. She begins by noting the use of the kiss in early societies such as Greece and Persia. Next, she discusses its use in biblical times. Finally she reviews the use of the kiss among the early Christians by citing second-century writers, such as Tertullian and Justin, and church historians, such as Lange, Godet, and Bloomfield. In closing Myers says: "Compared with the commands of the Old Testament, this is beautiful, simple, easy to fulfill. And inasmuch as it increases peace, union, love and higher Christian fellowship among the members of Christ's body, its observance is of prime importance."[8]

The kiss, under the designation of *the Christian salutation*, is included on the Brethren's Card as revised in 1923. On the card it is listed among the New Testament rites observed by the Brethren, and Romans 16:16 is cited as the basis for the rite. No specifics, however, are included on the card as to when the kiss is to be observed.

In 1932, Frederick Dove (1895-1952) claimed that the Brethren no longer greeted each other with the holy kiss when they met, with the exception of some older and more conservative members. He further noted that after the passing of the kiss was made optional between the supper and communion in 1913, that practice also ceased to exist. According to Dove the kiss was still being used in 1932 only "between brethren and brethren and sisters and sisters just after the rite of feet washing has been observed, between the one serving and the one served."[9] And so the practice continues to be observed to this day.

Notes

1. Sander Mack to John Preisz, in *Brethren in Colonial America*, ed. Donald F. Durnbaugh (Elgin, IL: Brethren Press, 1967), 360.

2. Martin G. Brumbaugh, *A History of the German Baptist Brethren in Europe and America* (Elgin, IL: Brethren Publishing House, 1899), 556.

3. Peter Nead, *Primitive Christianity, or a Vindication of the Word of God* (Staunton, VA: Kenton Harper, Printer, 1834), 120.

4. Ibid., 120-121.

5. *Minutes of the Annual Meetings of the Church of the Brethren, 1778-1909* (Elgin, IL: Brethren Publishing House, 1909), 159.

6. Ibid., 60.

7. "Concerning the Kiss of Charity," *Gospel Visitor*, November 1858, 344.

8. Salome A. Stoner Myers, "The Christian Salutation," in *The Brethren's Tracts and Pamphlets* (Elgin, IL: Brethren Publishing House, 1900), lacks ongoing paging.

9. Frederick Denton Dove, *Cultural Changes in the Church of the Brethren* (Elgin, IL: Brethren Publishing House, 1932), 151.

The Text in Today's World

Normally characterizations of American denominations lack precision and might even create more confusion than clarity. H. Richard Niebuhr did try to describe the nature of different churches in his useful *The Social Sources of American Denominationalism*. Following some of his distinctions, we might say that the mainline churches (state churches in earlier discussions) seek to train children in such a way that they move into adulthood as responsible members of the church and citizens of the state. More individualistic denominations, like Baptists, are more concerned that children come to accept the Lord as their personal Savior. That is, personal salvation becomes the key to adulthood. Anabaptists have yet another basic concern. While they wish to emphasize the power and sanctity of the family, adulthood comes with the shift from the family of origin (parents and children) to the family of faith. The second community is not a state, a parish, or any geographically inclusive social unit. It is a voluntary association of Christians who have formed a new family.

We have made much of the communitarian nature of the local congregation. In order for the local congregation to remain a family, it will exhibit the characteristics of a family. Consequently loyalty, mutuality, caring, eating, playing, singing, praying, all become essential aspects of this new family. As can be seen in the discussion, the early Brethren also found in the familial kiss of the early church a sign of family for our time. While that adaptation was quite appropriate, few would argue that the kiss as such must be kept by the Church of the Brethren. Relegating the kiss to a spot in the love feast does little to keep the sense of family. Some visible marks of family are absolutely necessary, however. If the "kiss" disappears, the sense of family will also have disappeared, and if the sense of family disappears there will no longer be any need for the Church of the Brethren. Doing the Holy Kiss did not create a sense of family in the early church. Nor can it create one today. To the contrary, kissing results from a sense of family. To demand a kiss actually destroys the spontaneity and genuine affection the kiss signifies. Even though many cultures still kiss as a sign of friendship and bonding, it would appear the kiss no longer serves that function for Brethren. Is there an equivalent sign of family among the Brethren?

Perhaps Brethren have shifted from the Holy Kiss to the Holy Hug. The hug has many advantages. It allows an easier crossover between gender and age lines while still signifying the family. Some Brethren have suggested that our freedom to touch one another during times of celebration, suffering, and worship has become an equivalent for the kiss. Surely most people cannot develop into adulthood and maintain a mature life without fairly frequent touch from another person. Whatever the future, Brethren will not shy from greeting each other as sisters and brothers in the same family.

Case Study

A couple recently immigrated from the Pacific Rim, joined a Church of the Brethren in California's Bay area. They were delighted with the church's warmth, teaching on service and peace, concern for the world, and free style of worship. At their first love feast, however, they withdrew from the feetwashing. The pastor also noted that at other church functions they tended to step back when someone moved to touch their shoulder or hug them. The pastor spoke to them about the feetwashing. They were not negative about the practice, but they told the pastor about their own culture where touch was not common even in the family. They wanted to be part of their new American community but felt they could not bring themselves to even touch everyone, much less hug them, kiss them, or wash their feet. The pastor brought their problem to the Nurture Commission.

1. Should the members of the faith community continue to welcome this family with touches and hugs? How important is it that they learn the "Brethren family way"?

2. Should members of this Church of the Brethren learn how to signify family to this new couple and greet them in terms of their family system (respect, honor)? Which is more important: that they know the "Brethren way" or that they know this faith community is family?

3. Does it really matter? Why not let people greet each other in whatever way they wish?

On Chemical Dependency

1 Corinthians 6:12-20 (NRSV)

"All things are lawful for me," but not all things are beneficial. "All things are lawful for me," but I will not be dominated by anything. [13]"Food is meant for the stomach and the stomach for food," and God will destroy both one and the other. The body is meant not for fornication but for the Lord, and the Lord for the body. [14]And God raised the Lord and will also raise us by his power. [15]Do you not know that your bodies are members of Christ? Should I therefore take the members of Christ and make them members of a prostitute? Never! [16]Do you not know that whoever is united to a prostitute becomes one body with her? For it is said, "The two shall be one flesh." [17]But anyone united to the Lord becomes one spirit with him. [18]Shun fornication! Every sin that a person commits is outside the body; but the fornicator sins against the body itself. [19]Or do you not know that your body is a temple of the Holy Spirit within you, which you have from God, and that you are not your own? [20]For you were bought with a price; therefore glorify God in your body.

1 Corinthians 6:12-20 (BNT)

"All things are lawful for me," but not everything is beneficial. "All things are lawful for me," but I will not be enslaved by anything. [13]"Food is for the stomach, and the stomach is for food." But God will destroy both of them. And the body is not for fornication, but for the Lord, and the Lord is for the body. [14]And God has raised the Lord and by his power will raise us. [15]Do you all not know that your bodies are members of Christ? Shall I then take the members of Christ and make them members of a prostitute? Absolutely not! [16]Do you not know that the one who has intercourse with a prostitute becomes one flesh with her? For, it says, "The two shall become one flesh." [17]And the one who has intercourse with the Lord is one Spirit. [18]Flee fornication. Every sin that a person does is outside the body. But the one who is unfaithful sins against his/her own body. [19]Do you not know that this body you all have is the temple of the Holy Spirit among you, a temple you all have from God, not from yourselves. [20]For you were bought with a price. All of you, then, glorify God in your bodies.

The Text in Its Biblical Setting

Most of 1 Corinthians was written as a letter in response to questions posed by one or more of the house churches in Corinth. Those questions begin in 7:1. Chapters 1-6, written in response to news from Chloe's people (1:11), ends with the passage 6:12-20. Chloe had shared with Paul the news of conflict among some of the house churches (1:12). It would appear the major difficulty was caused by the Christ house church. That congregation was composed of members who had taken seriously Paul's news of freedom. Their spiritualism (some call it gnosticism) led them to pride in their faith (1:26-31; 4:7), disregard for law (5:1-5), disdain for the historical Jesus (12:1-3), and sexual abstinence (7:1-6). One of their several slogans, perhaps even picked up from Paul, was "All things are lawful for me," a summary of their new sense of freedom.

In chapters 1—6, Paul consistently shows how they have misunderstood the nature of the Christian life. They suppose they have arrived in the reign of God, when actually they, like him, are living between the times of the present age and the coming new age (4:8-13).

In his closing statement (6:12-20) he uses two arguments: 1) our marks of freedom can enslave us; 2) the body of Christ requires commitment. Both arguments are basic to Paul's perception of Christianity. The first occurs in 6:12-13. He agrees that all things are lawful. He does not mean we can do anything we wish. He only means there are no laws which, when obeyed, will commend us to each other and to God. His short argument against the Christ house church is powerful. If you must do something in order to show to yourself and others you are free, then you are enslaved. Paul is yet to mention food offered to idols, but he could be thinking of it. If you must eat food offered to idols in order to show that you are free in the Lord(and there is no reason why you cannot), then you are enslaved to that mark of freedom. If you are *really* free, you may or may not do those things which appear to be mere customs, antiquated religious laws, useless moralities, or whatever. But why would you want to? That is the second issue.

The second reason has to do with the meaning of membership in the body. In chapter 8 Paul will say that if eating meat offends another member of the body, then he will never eat meat again (8:13). Yes, we are free, but not free to destroy the faith community, the body of Christ. For Paul, food and the stomach will be destroyed at death, but the sense of body belongs to the Lord. And at the end-time, God will raise both the Lord and the body. The body is of ultimate value. Food and physical organs are not.

In the rest of the section, Paul argues that in our freedom we may attach ourselves to another body, a body of the old age. In order to convey his intent, he used the analogy of fornication or prostitution. Normally a writer such as Paul tells us when he is using an analogy by using "like" (3:10), but sometimes there is no particular hint. We must then decide according to the context. In this case there has been no hint of problems with prostitution (in fact, the difficulty with the Christ group was quite the opposite!). The issue is that there has been a misuse of freedom.

An analogy has two parts to it: the vehicle (the apparent story or metaphor) and the tenor (the intended meaning). For example, Jesus compared seeking the reign of God with buying a pearl of great price. The buying and selling of pearls is the vehicle. Seeking the reign of God is the tenor. Only the tenor is intended. But the vehicle must be convincing or the analogy collapses. The vehicle about prostitution is true. One can become one flesh with a prostitute. Consequently some readers have, with good reason, taken the vehicle as the meaning. They suppose Paul is struggling with sexual excesses at Corinth. But actually Paul is more likely concerned about the body of Christ and members who use their freedom to risk joining themselves to other "bodies," or communities. After all, the body of Christ is the temple of the Holy Spirit (3:16-17; 6:19;).

Regardless of the interpretation, 6:18 presents problems. In terms of the vehicle (sexual sins), why is every sin but a sexual sin outside the body? Are not theft, falsification, murder, and rejection of one's family also sins against the body? In terms of the tenor or meaning, would not anyone who returns to the old age endanger the body? Or put another way: if an action does not affect the corporate body, can it possibly be called a sin? Perhaps this is Paul's point: what some people at Corinth call sin may actually be only private concerns (e.g., food laws).

Freedom does not come with any particular action. One cannot wear something, eat something, do something, or use something which then makes the person free. Freedom is a gift of God. Paul uses the image of slavery as yet another analogy of freedom (v. 20). In the ancient world a slave could be freed by paying the price of purchase. Actually some persons sold themselves into slavery (bankruptcy) and later paid back the price of their purchase. More likely, though, a slave was freed by someone else. Liberated slaves were called freedmen (and women). Paul says that God has paid the price (Christ on the cross) to free us, and that as the body of Christ we all should honor (glorify) God in our freedom.

The Text in Brethren Life

While the term *chemical dependency* is relatively new, the problem existed among the Brethren while they were still in Germany. As early as 1715, Alexander Mack (1679-1735) noted in his *Rights and Ordinances* that drinking to excess "is a great sin."[1] Over the years Brethren have expressed much concern about the use of alcohol and tobacco. In recent years they have also begun to become concerned about the use of drugs (marijuana, heroin, cocaine), but the attention given to drug abuse by Brethren appears to be much less than the attention it receives in the larger society.

Without doubt the manufacture, sale, and use of alcohol is the form of chemical dependency about which Brethren have spoken and written the most. In addition to Mack's condemnation of excessive drinking, the Annual Meetings of the eighteenth century opposed the operation of distilleries by Brethren. The 1781 meeting reaffirmed an earlier decision that all Brethren should "put away" their distilleries. This counsel was evidently not followed because the minutes of 1789 indicate that the refusal of some members to do away with their distilleries was causing division in the church and that some Brethren even refused to participate in the love feast with members who still operated distilleries. It must be noted that the decision to put away distilleries had economic consequences. Farmers living on the frontier, especially during the Revolution, found it easier and cheaper to convert their grain into liquor before taking it to market.

Interestingly, Annual Meeting did not specifically condemn the *use* of strong drink until the 1830s. The minutes of 1833 indicate that a testimony was given at that meeting against using strong drink, and the minutes of 1835 state that Brethren should "by no means use distilled liquors for a common beverage nor offer it to those that work for them."[2] Even so, questions concerning drunkenness, not moderate use, most often came before the Annual Meetings for the next twenty years. According to one historian, "a serious ambivalence existed in the Brethren ranks about drinking. Many continued to use alcohol regardless of what the church taught."[3]

At first the Brethren refused to participate in the temperance movement as it swept across the country. As early as 1842, Annual Meeting advised members not to sign the pledge of total abstinence saying: "Inasmuch as our churches have always been testifying against intemperance, and even against the free use, the making and selling of ardent spirits, it is not advisable for members to put their hands to the pledge, or to meddle with the proceeding and excitement of the world on this subject."[4] Likewise, in 1867 Brethren were advised against joining temperance societies. In short, the Brethren were not to participate in the temperance movement because it was too worldly and too political.

While the Annual Meetings throughout the remainder of the 1800s continued to maintain the official position of noninvolvement with the temperance movement and refused to call for the passage of prohibition laws, the Brethren slowly moved toward both. In 1900 Annual Meeting stated: "It is the duty of the Christian church to mould temperance sentiment, without which no law can become operative. We urge the greatest possible efforts of the church to create such sentiment."[5] At the 1908 meeting the General Temperance Committee was created. Among its eight duties was the responsibility to circulate temperance literature and to assist districts and local congregations in organizing temperance meetings. Such meetings, however, were understood to be under Brethren auspices and not in cooperation with other temperance groups. And Brethren still shied away from active involvement in the political movement for prohibition. However, with the election of Martin G. Brumbaugh (1862-1930) as governor of Pennsylvania in 1915, the Brethren jumped into the political arena. By 1917 the temperance committee was calling for the passage of the eighteenth amendment, and the 1918 Annual Conference petitioned "the President and Congress for and urge[d] the enactment of laws to prohibit the waste of foodstuffs in the manufacture of alcoholic liquors."[6]

Once prohibition was law the Brethren concentrated on educating their youth about the evils of alcohol. Unfortunately, such education did not receive the same enthusiasm and financial support as the issue of temperance did during the first twenty years of the twentieth century. After the repeal of prohibition, the 1934 Annual Conference reaffirmed the position of total abstinence and condemned "the action of our government which for the sake of revenue has legalized and popularized the use of beverage alcohol."[7]

Since 1950 two major statements about alcohol have been adopted by the Brethren. A 1952 statement urged Brethren to abstain from the use, sale, and manufacture of alcoholic beverages and recommended educational programs as the best way to solve the alcohol problem. The 1976 report included a study of the use of alcoholic beverages among Brethren. The study revealed that drinking was particularly prevalent among the youth at Brethren educational institutions. While the report affirmed the traditional Brethren opposition to the use of alcohol, it also emphasized that alcoholism is an illness, stated that the church should not judge the alcoholic as uniquely sinful, and provided cautions to moderate drinkers.

Throughout much of their history Brethren have cited the biblical texts which condemn drunkenness, such as 1 Corinthians 5:11 and Ephesians 5:18, when they sought scriptural support for their views on alcohol use. In the twentieth century, however, they have turned from the texts which condemn drunkenness to the texts which emphasize responsible lifestyles. According to the 1976 report, 1 Corinthians 3:16-17 is one of the texts which guide the church in its convictions on alcohol. These two verses are interpreted to mean that "we are God's temple and have the obligation to keep ourselves in top shape."[8] A similar interpretation is given to 1 Corinthians 6:19-20 in a temperance curriculum published by the church for juniors in the 1950s.[9] In a 1985 pamphlet titled "Temperance," Curtis Dubble cites 1 Corinthians 6:12-20. According to Dubble the Brethren cherish this passage which admonishes Christians not to allow anything to enslave them. "When Paul says, 'Do you not know that your bodies are members of Christ?' he is saying much more than the popular religious jargon, 'Give your heart to Jesus.' Paul is saying, giving yourself to Jesus means giving your body also."[10]

As with alcohol use, the nineteenth century began with some Brethren using tobacco, including leaders such as the frontier preacher George Wolfe (1780-1865), and no official church position on such use. But the century ended with specific statements from Annual Meeting in opposition to both the use and production or sale of tobacco. Interestingly, Annual Meeting first spoke out against the use of tobacco (1817) before taking a position against the production of tobacco (1827), whereas in the case of alcohol the reverse was true. By 1889 Annual Meeting had decided that all delegates to the meeting had to abstain from tobacco, and in 1896 this decision was extended to include those who raised and/or sold tobacco. Obviously tobacco was included with alcohol in Brethren temperance publications during both the nineteenth and twentieth centuries. The Annual Conference of 1952 adopted a statement on tobacco which paralleled its statement on alcohol of the same year. The most recent action taken by the Brethren on tobacco was at the 1981 Annual Conference where a query was adopted calling for education and action programs to witness against the use and production of tobacco. Included in this query was a quote from 1 Corinthians 3:16-17. Thus the Brethren look to the same biblical texts for support of their position on tobacco as they do for their support of their position on alcohol.

Compared to their extensive statements and publications concerning alcohol and tobacco abuse, the Brethren have said little to date about the abuse of drugs such as marijuana, heroin, and cocaine. Of course, such drug abuse is a relatively new problem in the United States compared to alcohol and tobacco. Even so, as early as 1975 an article appeared in the *Messenger* calling for the Brethren to develop a drug policy.[11] Thus far the Brethren have not done so. Occasionally references to drug abuse are made in Annual Conference statements and resolutions on other issues. For example, drugs are mentioned in the 1976 report on alcohol, the 1981 World Mission Philosophy and Program paper, the 1987 statement on AIDS, and the 1987 resolution titled "A Quest for Order." In 1988 a whole paragraph was devoted to the problem of drug use in the resolution on "Responsible Citizenship in an Election Year." There exists a task force on substance abuse under the auspices of the Brethren Health and Welfare Association. This group includes drug addiction among its concerns. Finally, Graydon F. Snyder includes in his book on the faith community and health care a section on marijuana, stimulants, depressants, and a section on hallucinatory drugs. The biblical basis of his concern is covenant theology as expressed in the faith community of the New Testament. Drug abuse is wrong because it creates a false relationship with the faith community which forms (1 Cor. 4:7) and sustains the Christian.[12]

Notes

1. Alexander Mack, *Rights and Ordinances*, in *European Origins of the Brethren*, comp. and trans. Donald F. Durnbaugh (Elgin, IL: Brethren Press, 1958), 389.

2. *Minutes of the Annual Meetings of the Church of the Brethren, 1778-1909* (Elgin, IL: Brethren Publishing House, 1909), 61.

3. Richard V. Pierard, "The Church of the Brethren and the Temperance Movement," *Brethren Life and Thought* 26 (Winter 1981):38.

4. *Minutes of the Annual Meetings of the Church of the Brethren, 1778-1909*, 75.

5. Ibid., 719.

6. "Minutes of the Annual Conference of the Church of the Brethren," held at Hershey, PA, June 11-12, 1918, 5.

7. "Minutes of the 136th Annual Conference of the Church of the Brethren," 46.

8. *Minutes of the Annual Conference of the Church of the Brethren, 1975-1979*, comp. Phyllis Kingery Ruff (Elgin, IL: Brethren Press, 1980), 194.

9. Hazel M. Kennedy, "Temperance in My Life, Pupil's Book" (Elgin, IL: General Brotherhood Board, n.d.), 14.

10. Curtis W. Dubble, "Temperance," Brethren Faith Pamphlets (Elgin, IL: Church of the Brethren General Board, [1985]).

11. Russell Yohn, "Drug Use and the Church," *Messenger*, December 1975, 31-33.

12. Graydon F. Snyder, *Tough Choices* (Elgin, IL: Brethren Press, 1988), 88-93.

The Text in Today's World

It may be too simple, but it surely is true that the freedom of one generation is the slavery of the next. One generation frees itself by wearing long hair, while the next frees itself by wearing hair short. One generation finds freedom in slacks, another in dresses. Except for the immediate context, there is no real meaning to this. Unless we are conscious of our own relativity, we can easily become enslaved to something of no ultimate value. That is exactly Paul's meaning in this passage. There is no freedom we can gain on our own. There is only the *gift* of freedom which does not require of us any act or sign. It is Christ who did the act; our sign of freedom is the cross. We are free, indeed!

Brethren especially have seen in this powerful passage a call to the real freedom in Christ, and not one which depends on some habit that can enslave us. There are two aspects of the problem. If God has paid the price to liberate us, then we dishonor God and our own faith by submitting to any enslavement. Put in other terms, it is most futile to accept freedom and then, to preserve it, take on more enslavement. In our time some of the most enslaving habits are those connected with chemical dependency. People find a kind of freedom in using alcohol, tobacco, or drugs. Besides the sense of liberation from societal norms, the drugs themselves often give one an emotional sense of freedom. Our tradition has not stressed so much the ill effects of the substances themselves, as the anguish of the enslavement to or dependency on this false sense of freedom.

The second concern arises from Paul's discussion of prostitution. The shift to some other loyalty destroys loyalty to Christ and the faith community. Paul noted several such shifts in loyalty: use of the legal system, or eating of meat offered to idols. But any enslavement would have the same effect. Chemical dependency is especially dangerous because it can create the sense of peace where peace does not exist. The alcoholic can suppose all is well in the community when, in fact, just the opposite is true. This makes us suspect any chemical which can create a false sense of community well being. Surely alcohol and drugs, perhaps tobacco and coffee, can create such an effect. More problematic are personality-altering drugs used to counteract manic-depressive states or to make children with learning disorders more placid, or whatever personality state is desired. Is it appropriate to construct through chemical means a form of community which depends on chemicals rather than human interrelationship? One can hardly deny the use of drugs for the benefit of those who are handicapped in some way. But a social unit guided by the Spirit would more likely find ways to adjust to the handicap than to force the person to conform.

Case Study

At Mack Church of the Brethren it was well-known that one of the church school teachers was an alcoholic. No one for sure knew whether he was recovering, active, or perhaps dry. His wife said he was doing okay, and his children said they didn't need any help. Nevertheless, the teacher, John Sauer, had changed jobs three times in the last twelve years and his giving to the church had noticeably dropped. One Sunday he came to church with the smell of alcohol on his breath. During the opening worship he sang louder than usual. On Monday the pastor talked to Mr. Sauer who said everything was under control. The pastor feared there was serious codependency with Sauer, both in his family and in the church. So he called a special session of the executive committee. He asked them what should be done with Brother Sauer.

1. Would you suggest Mr. Sauer leave the church?

2. Would you ask Mr. Sauer to give up his teaching responsibility?

3. Would you make his continuation as a teacher dependent on entering a rehabilitation program?

4. Would you propose the formation of an Alcoholics Anonymous at the church?

5. Would you accept the family's word that there is no problem?

Session 18

On the Prayer Veil

1 Corinthians 11:2-16 (NRSV)

I commend you because you remember me in everything and maintain the traditions just as I handed them on to you. [3]But I want you to understand that Christ is the head of every man, and the husband is the head of his wife, and God is the head of Christ. [4]Any man who prays or prophesies with something on his head disgraces his head, [5]but any woman who prays or prophesies with her head unveiled disgraces her head—it is one and the same thing as having her head shaved. [6]For if a woman will not veil herself, then she should cut off her hair; but if it is disgraceful for a woman to have her hair cut off or to be shaved, she should wear a veil. [7]For a man ought not to have his head veiled, since he is the image and reflection of God; but woman is the reflection of man. [8]Indeed, man was not made from woman, but woman from man. [9]Neither was man created for the sake of woman, but woman for the sake of man. [10]For this reason a woman ought to have a symbol of authority on her head, because of the angels. [11]Nevertheless, in the Lord woman is not independent of man or man independent of woman. [12]For just as woman came from man, so man comes through woman; but all things come from God. [13]Judge for yourselves: is it proper for a woman to pray to God with her head unveiled? [14]Does not nature itself teach you that if a man wears long hair, it is degrading to him, [15]but if a woman has long hair, it is her glory? For her hair is given to her for a covering. [16]But if anyone is disposed to be contentious—we have no such custom, nor do the churches of God.

1 Corinthians 11:2-16 (BNT)

I appreciate very much that you always remember me, and that you hold fast to the traditions just as I passed them over to you. [3]I wish you to know that Christ is the head of every husband, the husband is the head of the wife, and God is the head of Christ. [4]Every man who prays or prophesies with his head covered puts his head to shame. [5]Every woman who prays or prophesies with her head uncovered puts her head to shame. She might as well have her head shaved. [6]Indeed if a woman does not cover her head, then let her cut off her hair. If a woman is ashamed to have her hair cut or to have her head shaved, then let her cover her head. [7]For while a man ought not to cover his head, since he is the image and presence of God, the woman (wife) represents her husband. [8]For the husband does not derive from the wife, but the wife from the husband. [9]For the husband was not even created for the sake of the wife, but the wife for the sake of the husband. [10]For this reason the wife ought to place a sign of authority on her head—for the sake of the angels. [11]Nevertheless in the Lord a wife is not considered apart from her husband, nor is the husband considered apart from his wife. [12]For just as a wife is a wife because she has a husband, so also a husband is a husband because he has a wife. And everything derives from God. [13]Now what do you think? Is it appropriate for a woman to pray to God with her head uncovered? [14]Does not nature itself teach us that long hair on the man is a disgrace, [15]but long hair for a woman is glorious? For her hair was given to her as a covering. [16]If anyone seems to be upset by this, we have no other practice than this, nor do the churches of God.

The Text in Its Biblical Setting

This passage has always been a difficult one (as verse 16 indicates), but in these days, when the relationship between man and woman is so problematic, it is especially difficult. It is not the task of exegesis to make the text more clear or more acceptable than it really is. If persons in Paul's own day had difficulty with his advice, the present interpreter should not attempt to erase whatever it is which is objectionable. Nevertheless, few passages have been more misunderstood in modern times than this one, so some explanations are in order.

Perhaps only one thing is obvious: There are women in the church at Corinth who are not wearing coverings on their heads. This fact has created a problem at Corinth. It also stands at variance with the practice in all the other churches at the time. Paul would like for these women to wear a covering.

Paul was aware of the sexual function of a woman's hair (11:15a), but he does not mention modesty as a reason for wearing a covering. Rather he contends that a woman who uncovers her hair might as well have no hair at all (vv. 5b-6). In the ancient world a shaved head for a woman could imply lewdness, punishment, or mannishness. Possibly Paul scorns the "uncovered" group at Corinth as women who look like prostitutes (v. 6). But it is more likely that mannishness is actually the issue, because the problem of sexual differentiation was a greater issue at Corinth than sexual immorality.

As we saw in Session 15, Paul would have Christians live according to the values of the new age rather than be conformed to this passing age. Paul said very clearly that in this new age there was no Jew or Greek, no male or female, no slave or master (Gal. 3:28; cf. 1 Cor. 12:13). Apparently there were in Corinth those sincere, perhaps overzealous, Christians who took Paul's teaching very much to heart. Some had so obliterated sexual distinctions that they had denied the sexual relationship (1 Cor. 7:1, 5). Some think the overly zealous Christians at Corinth all belonged to a specific house church called the Christ group (1:12). It was probably a nascent gnostic movement. Paul answered this movement toward unisexism at Corinth by stressing the importance of the sexual dynamic (7:4) and by insisting that Christians were to stay in whatever calling they had for this age (7:17-28). It would seem probable that 1 Corinthians 11:2-16 deals with the same issue, that is whether sexual distinctions should exist in a community that lives according to the values of the coming age. For some reason, probably because of Greco-Roman society, a head covering for women became the point at which sexual distinction became a church problem. That is, were women free to worship with their heads uncovered, as did the men? The passage makes the most sense if taken this way.

What arguments did Paul marshal to convince the women that their heads should be covered? He begins by arguing from a commonly accepted "household ethic" which had become a part of Christian teaching (11:3-5a). In the Roman world it was popular to list an order of responsibilities: people to king, wife to husband, children to parents, slave to master, and the like. The early Christians and, in fact, even some Jewish groups adapted this structure for their own teaching. In this passage Paul adapts the "household list" to say that the church (represented by Christ) is responsible to the will of God; the households, represented by the fathers or husbands, are responsible to the church (Christ); and individuals in the families, represented by the mother or wife, are responsible to the father or husband.

Obviously there is nothing final about the lists, even this list. Paul does not mean that women are inferior to men any more than he meant that it was God's will for slaves to obey their masters forever (see 1 Cor. 7:21). In the Pauline churches women participated fully in church life by preaching and leading in worship (1 Cor. 11:5), by holding major offices of ministry (Rom. 16:1), and by leading itinerant evangelistic teams (Rom. 16:3), among other things (see Session 16). It is an error to suppose that submission destroys equality. Everyone submits. But one of our basic problems in life is to suppose mutual submission will destroy us rather than free us (Gen. 3). Likewise, it is an error to suppose that submission to God has no implications for submission in this life. Submission to God will be marked by an analogous submission in the human world because our covenant to God cannot be separated as a type from our covenants with each other (best stated in 1 John 3:16-17). But we must not use this insight to create a third error, the error of believing that any particular order of submission is final. Paul made it clear that this is not true (Gal. 3:28) as did Jesus also (Luke 20:34-38 and parallels). The *order* of submission is a sociological factor which varies from time to time. The *fact* of submission is of ultimate faith significance. Both the men (5:1-5; 6:5; 11:7, 14) and the women at the Christ house church apparently were testing the issue of submission to the faith community. In this passage Paul addresses primarily the women.

At first glance, the order Paul upholds here seems to have little to do with the question of women alone covering their heads. If the covering as such is a sign of submission, then Paul should advise the men to wear hats in church and the women to wear veils whenever they are in the presence of their husbands. That Paul urges only women to cover their heads reflects the particular problem in the Corinthian church to which we alluded earlier, the problem of persons wanting to wipe out all sexual distinctions (gender neutrality). Women are urged to cover *their* heads when they lead worship because the covering affirms womanliness in their cultural setting. This is the thrust of Paul's second argument, in 11:5-6: if the women dress like the men who lead worship (no covering), then they might as well do away with their physical sexual characteristics (hair), too. If the women do not want to take this step, then they should stop trying to "be like men" in church, which means they should cover the head.

In verses 7-9 Paul argues from Genesis 2 that women were created as mates for men; therefore, women are indeed secondary in the order of creation. This has nothing to do with covering the head but does support the order mentioned by Paul in 11:3. Of course, male and female do not exist in Genesis 2 until the creation of woman from the androgynous Adam (Gen. 2:23). Paul recalls this in verses 11-12. In verse 11 he reminds us that ultimately there is no such order ("in the Lord," that is, in the end-time community). In verse 12 he actually corrects his earlier assertion by noting that men and women were created for each other!

This leaves the perplexing statement in verse 10. Presumably for the Church of the Brethren this would be the key sentence, because here women are admonished to "have a symbol of authority for her head" (NRSV). The term veil in Greek does not occur at all. Only much later was that word substituted for the Greek word *exousia*, which means *authority or power*. Since it appears that a wife is to have something on her head, some modern translators still put the word "veil" in the text, with a footnote indicating the underlying word is *exousia*. Note, however, that "head" has been used two different ways in the passage, sometimes as a head which can be covered or uncovered and sometimes as that person or entity which is the source or head. Here I think both meanings are intended in a kind of play on words. So I would translate the verse: "For this reason, that is, because of the angels, a wife ought to have her sign of authority on (regarding?) her head."

Angels refer here to godlike institutional powers which maintain order in life. Since God is the ultimate power to whom we are responsible (11:3), sons of God or angels refer to penultimate institutions such as the state or city or even the church (Rev. 2—3). So verse 10 is a decisive argument for order. If some order is not maintained, the structures of society will be destroyed. It is to this same concern that Paul returns in verse 16. Only you in Corinth are having trouble with this issue, Paul says. Why don't you do like the rest of the churches and take the need for order seriously? In any case the point is clearer than the argument itself: women and men have equality in Christ, and men should dress as men even as women should dress as women.

The Text in Brethren Life

Paul's comments in 1 Corinthians 11:2-16 have provided the Brethren, as well as other Christian groups, with biblical support for the practice of having female members wear prayer veils. Actually the term *prayer veil* is predated by the term *cap*, which was the term used among the Brethren in the nineteenth century. According to Esther Rupel, in her dissertation concerning prescribed dress among the Brethren, the change from the term *cap* to the term *prayer veil* was due to change in custom. In the nineteenth century it was the custom for the cap to be worn each day at home as well as at public religious functions. With the coming of the twentieth century, however, Brethren women turned from wearing the cap at home to wearing it only at public worship services. Logically, the cap then became known as a prayer veil or prayer covering.[1]

The first mention of the prayer veil in the minutes of Annual Meeting, as noted by Henry Kurtz (1796-1874) in *The Brethren's Encyclopedia* (1867), occurred in 1848 with the question of whether single women members had to wear a prayer veil as the married women did. The response was a unanimous *yes*, with a reference to 1 Corinthians 11. Kurtz appends an interesting note on the matter, in which he suggests that in cases which concern the women of the church, a committee of elderly sisters should be appointed to consider the question. Such action, says Kurtz, "would seem to be consistent with the principles of equality (see Gal. 3:28) and their verdict would perhaps have more weight with their younger sisters."[2]

Peter Nead (1796-1877), in his *Primitive Christianity* (1834), firmly supports the use of the prayer veil. After quoting 1 Corinthians 11:4-6, Nead says: "Now, it is plain from the above, that women in divine service, and especially when engaged in praying or prophesying, should have their heads covered."[3] Next, Nead rejects the theory that long hair on a woman is sufficient covering when she prays or prophesies. Lastly, Nead explains why a woman must wear a veil. He says: "According to ancient custom, a cover on the head was a sign of subjection and respect to superiors; and it was owing to the woman being under subjection to the man, according to the word of our Lord, (see Gen. iii, 16), that she should, in divine service, especially when praying or prophesying, have a cover on her head."[4] For support, Nead quotes 1 Corinthians 11:3.

A very different interpretation of the prayer veil is presented by S. Z. Sharp (1835-1931) in his article titled "The Token of Authority," which appeared in the *Gospel Messenger* in 1896. Sharp begins by explaining that the article is a synopsis of a study of 1 Corinthians 11:1-16 done at a "Bible Term." The Greek text was used for the study, and the best Greek scholars among the Brethren were present. Four days were spent studying and discussing the sixteen verses, and over a hundred people participated. After this introduction, Sharp presents a verse-by-verse explanation of the sixteen verses. It is in the discussion of verses 10-12 that the changing interpretation of the prayer veil is most noticeable. Concerning these verses Sharp reports the following: "Although woman's relation to man, as arranged by creation, is not to be disturbed, yet woman may have power delegated to her to pray and prophesy in public on condition she wears on her head this token of delegated power, since in Christ there is no distinction of sex, while in nature this distinction must remain."[5]

As the Brethren moved into the twentieth century, the use of the prayer veil lessened. Because of the neglect of the prayer veil, the Quinter Church, in 1925, requested that an interpretation of the prayer veil practice as presented in 1 Corinthians 11 be made by the Annual Conference. A committee of three was appointed to make the study and to report back to the conference of 1926. The report summarized 1 Corinthians 11, specifically stated that a woman should wear a prayer veil because she is the glory of man and because it brings a woman "into right relationship for angel ministry," and affirmed that Paul's arguments in 1 Corinthians apply to all Christian churches, not just to the church at Corinth.[6]

Interestingly, Frederick Dove (1895-1952), after noting that dress among the Brethren of the 1930s is primarily the same as in the society at large, goes on to report that in 1931 he attended a meeting of nearly a thousand Brethren in a conservative district where "all the women, with the exception of one visitor, wore bonnets, and most of them the *prayer covering.*"[7] While today it would not be possible to find a district where most of the women wear the prayer veil, some conservative sisters still do wear it. This is particularly true among those related to the Brethren Revival Fellowship. In fact, a 1971 issue of the *BRF Witness* contains an article by James F. Myer affirming the use of the "head veiling" on the basis of 1 Corinthians 11:1-16. Myer's understanding of these verses follows Peter Nead's interpretation, not the interpretation given by Sharp.[8]

Notes

1. Esther Fern Rupel, "An Investigation of the Origin, Significance, and Demise of the Prescribed Dress Worn by Members of the Church of the Brethren" (Ph.D. diss., University of Minnesota, 1971), 137-38.

2. Henry Kurtz, *The Brethren's Encyclopedia* (Columbiana, OH: the author, 1867), 60.

3. Peter Nead, *Primitive Christianity, or a Vindication of the Word of God* (Staunton, VA: Kenton Harper, Printer, 1834), 165.

4. Ibid., 166.

5. S. Z. Sharp, "The Token of Authority," *The Gospel Messenger,* 28 March 1896, 195.

6. *Minutes of the Annual Conferences of the Church of the Brethren, 1923-1944* (Elgin, IL: Brethren Publishing House, 1946), 34-36.

7. Frederick Denton Dove, *Cultural Changes in the Church of the Brethren* (Elgin, IL: Brethren Publishing House, 1932), 158.

8. James F. Myer, "The Head Veiling," *BRF Witness* 6:2 (1971), 3-6.

The Text in Today's World

Like Paul we, too, live between the times. We live between the revelation of truth (the New Testament) and the final consummation or victory of that truth in this world. How shall we live between the times? How shall we live in a world which does not recognize the very truth we have come to profess? Should we forget what we know to be true and simply live according to the standards of the present age? Surely not! Should we ignore the condition of the present age and live according to the truth regardless of the consequences? No, not that either! That was the situation at Corinth. Paul had told them plainly that what they ate, what they drank, and what they wore could in no way commend them to the Lord (1 Cor. 6:12-13). For that matter, neither could their status in society or their prior religion commend them to God (1 Cor. 7:17-24). In Christ there is no advantage for any particular sex, religious background, social status, race, or any other human distinction. Yet we live between the times. The reign of God has not yet come. If we live entirely according to God's reign, we may well destroy ourselves and others.

So Paul agreed, indeed insisted, that foods and drink had no religious value and were, therefore, harmless, yet he doubted the wisdom of flaunting meat offered to idols before those who still believed it was a sin. Doing the truth was not always the loving thing to do. We would surely agree with Paul that food and drink do not commend us to God, yet in light of the alcoholism in our society and the hunger in our world it is hardly appropriate or loving to ignore what we eat and drink. Paul insisted there was no difference between male and female in the end-time. Yet at a time of family fragility and growing hostility toward the church, he had to ask if it were appropriate and loving to ignore sexual differences and sex roles as defined by the then current culture, i.e., "the angels." We, too, could well ask whether, granted the total equality of male and female before God, we should attempt to live in these in-between times as if there were no differences between the sexes. Is that appropriate in our time? If not, what does equality mean for men and women today? If going beyond existing sex roles is appropriate, then what is the Christian responsibility for the order in which we find ourselves?

This is the problem with which 1 Corinthians 11 confronts us. There may be no point in bringing the particular Corinthian problem of a head covering into our day. But few passages in the New Testament are more pertinent to us than this one. The continuing problem is how to live with knowledge of the end-time before the end-time comes. Knowledge of the coming reign of God obviously affects the present order. Christianity did abolish slavery in the Roman Empire. Christianity did transform the role of women and strengthen the family. Christianity did transform attitudes and actions toward the poor and the outcast. Yet somehow Christianity never committed suicide by putting the truth in such a way that it totally demolished its life in the present age. The truth was tempered with love, but the truth was maintained nevertheless. The problem of the head covering was a problem in Corinth caused by different customs regarding sexual differences. We, too, know and believe that in Christ there is no distinction between male and female, husband and wife. Yet we exist in a world where, by custom, gender distinctions are made. As members of the faith community, we will object to many of these distinctions that affect job opportunities, wages, legal limitations, advertising, abuse, to name just a few. But as members of a faith community in a particular time, do we want to obliterate gender differences in dress or appearance, or even in some functions such as nurturing? The problem of living out the truth in love, especially in the realm of the critical issues like gender differentiation, is one the Christian community has always faced.

Case Study

A district recently had several vacancies for full-time pastors. The district executive was working overtime to fill these several vacancies. For one fairly large church, he suggested a woman from California who had pastoral experience. While the experience of this district with women pastors had been excellent, this specific local congregation had never called a woman as pastor. When the district executive presented her name, there was some approval but also some reticence. Fully aware of the delicacy of placing a woman pastor for the first time, the district executive cautiously attempted to ferret out the causes for reticence. One man said it might do for California, and even their congregation, but this town would not accept a woman pastor. Another man noted that Saint Paul had said women should be silent in the church. A third man, rather embarrassed, said he would not be able to worship with a young woman in the pulpit. If you were a member of the search committee would you say:

1. That gender should make no difference to a Christian, and note that the same Apostle Paul said there was in Christ no male or female?

2. That a woman would likely disturb (seduce?) some men, but that male pastors had done that to women for centuries?

3. That it was against federal law to discriminate against a job applicant because of gender. The church could be sued.

4. That you support the objections already made.

5. That every person should be evaluated on their own merit. So the church should grant an initial interview.

On Sunday Observance

1 Corinthians 16:1-4 (NRSV)

Now concerning the collection for the saints: you should follow the directions I gave to the churches of Galatia. [2]On the first day of every week, each of you is to put aside and save whatever extra you earn, so that collections need not be taken when I come. [3]And when I arrive, I will send any whom you approve with letters to take your gift to Jerusalem. [4]If it seems advisable that I should go also, they will accompany me.

1 Corinthians 16:1-4 (BNT)

Now concerning the contribution for the saints, do as I directed the churches of Galatia. [2]On the first day of the week each of you put aside something from your surplus and save it, so that a collection need not be taken when I come. [3]When I do arrive I will send, with letters, whomever you select to take your gift to Jerusalem. [4]If it seems appropriate for me to go also, then they can accompany me.

The Text in Its Biblical Setting

Chapter 16 of 1 Corinthians begins in Greek with the words *peri de*, "now concerning." Most of the letter called 1 Corinthians was written in answer to questions asked by a house church (or the congregations in Corinth). With the words *peri de*, Paul indicates that he is responding to a question. Those answers first begin in 7:1 where Paul responds to a question about marriage and remarriage. Other questions occur in 7:25; 8:1; 12:1; and 16:12.

Paul had suggested taking a collection to the church in Jerusalem. This is our first knowledge about the collection, mentioned later in 2 Corinthians 8—9; Galatians 2:10; and Romans 15:26-29. According to Paul in Galatians, the Jerusalem church had suggested during its so-called Apostolic Council that there be such a mutual sharing of resources. A number of reasons have been suggested for the collections: the famine mentioned in Acts 11:27-30; an earlier collection of goods for widows which exhausted resources in Jerusalem (Acts 6:1); or even a Christian temple tax (Matt. 17:24-27). In Romans, Paul actually referred to the collection as a *koinonia*, a mutual relationship made concrete by a gift from the new congregations to the mother church (15:26; cf. 2 Cor. 9:13). The collection differed from the ordinary congregational offering because it was taken from the surplus, not earnings.

The offering was taken on the first day of the week. The Jews, of course, worshipped on the last day of the week, the Sabbath. Written about 53 AD, this passage in 1 Corinthians 16:2 may be the first reference to the Christian practice of worshiping on the first day of the week.

Almost all cultures recognize the need for a day of rest. The term *shabat* means cessation or ending. So the Sabbath was the ending of a time period. The frequency of the rest, and its dating, depended then on the calendar. Since the Hebrew people reckoned time according to a lunar calendar, the end of a phase came every seven days. Other celebrations came in multiples of seven (like Pentecost, at the end of seven weeks, or the year of Jubilee, at the end of forty-nine years).

Eventually the keeping of the Sabbath became one of the basic commandments (apodictic law—a truth valid in any context). The fourth of the Ten Commandments, "Remember the sabbath day, and keep it holy," makes us aware that a primary relationship in life must be celebrated. A relationship that exists only as an idea or a principle eventually dies. Unless we stop ordinary work and take time to express our trust and hope in God, we finally have only a belief in the existence of God. This is a basic understanding of how covenant life operates.

Early Christians kept the same perception of the seventh day, except that their day shifted to the first day of the week. The reason for the shift cannot be ascertained. We do know from this passage that it must have occurred before the middle of the first century. If Christians were to be distinguished from Jews, they would have celebrated a different "day of rest." Many historians assume that differentiation first became apparent to the Romans because of events such as the destruction of Jerusalem and the persecution of Christians by Nero (65-70 AD).

From our later perspective, it appears that the first Christians dropped the Sabbath at the end of the week, a rest after six days, in order to celebrate the beginning of a new age on the first day of the week (Col. 2:16-17; Gal. 4:10). The first day of the week set the direction for the remainder of the week ahead. This must have been connected with the resurrection of Jesus on the first day of the week. We can see that in John 20:19 where the first Christian celebration occurred on the evening of the day Jesus was raised from the dead (note that the Gospel of John was written about 95 AD). One of the Apostolic Fathers, Barnabas, argued that God created light on the first day, and since Jesus was the light of the world (John 8:1), then we should celebrate the first day of creation (Barnabas 13:9-10). There is more to this argument than meets the eye. The early Christians were involved in an intense struggle with the worship of the sun god, Apollo or Helios. The birth of Jesus was placed on the winter solstice in order to counter, or absorb, the popular day of the sun. This explanation by Barnabas would be another attempt by Christians to subvert Roman worship of the sun god.

But this later argument hardly accounts for the "first day" noted in 1 Corinthians 16:2. We would be better advised to assume the "first day" signals the beginning of the new age.

The Text in Brethren Life

Throughout their history Brethren have observed the first day of the week (Sunday) as the Sabbath set aside for worship and rest. In this practice, they agree with the majority of other Christian groups. Twice, however, the Brethren have actively had to defend their observance of Sunday as the Lord's Day. First, in the 1720s Conrad Beissel came among the Brethren preaching sabbatarianism, the practice of observing Saturday, the seventh day of the week, as the true Sabbath. In the second half of the nineteenth century, the Brethren were again confronted by sabbatarianism. This time it was part of the teachings and practices of the Seventh-Day Adventist movement.

Johann Conrad Beissel (1691-1768) came to Pennsylvania from Germany in 1720, probably to escape persecution for his Radical Pietist beliefs. On his arrival he was apprenticed to Peter Becker (1687-1758), the first Brethren minister in colonial America, to learn the weaver's trade. The next year he left Becker in order to live the life of a hermit in the Conestoga wilderness. In 1724 Beissel again came in contact with the Brethren when leaders from Germantown arrived in the Conestoga area as part of the revival which began on Christmas Day, 1723. This time Beissel, along with several others, was baptized by Becker. Thus a new congregation was born at Conestoga, and Beissel was elected its leader. But tension soon began to develop between the Germantown congregation and Conestoga because Beissel practiced sabbatarianism, although at first he did not preach it. In 1728, however, a booklet by Beissel espousing sabbatarianism was published. By the end of the year, the Conestoga congregation had divided, with some members becoming followers of Beissel while others remained with the Brethren. In 1732 Beissel moved to the location on which the buildings of the Ephrata Cloister were later constructed, and around him the Ephrata Community developed.

The Brethren and the Ephrata Community shared many of the same beliefs and practices, including noncredalism, feetwashing, and trine immersion. Of course, there were also major differences between the two, such as Ephrata's emphasis on celibacy and personal revelation. The initial issue of contention, however, was over the Sabbath. The primary purpose of Beissel's 1728 booklet was to claim that the seventh day of the week is the true Sabbath, even for Christians. According to bibliographers, Beissel's book was the first German language book printed in Pennsylvania. While there is no known copy of this booklet still in existence, there is a copy of the English translation made in 1729 by Michael Wohlfahrt (1687-1741), a follower of Beissel. On the title page of the English translation, Exodus 20:10 is quoted, in part, as support for sabbatarianism. On the reverse of the title page, six other biblical texts are also given. The only New Testament text among them is Romans 2:12.[1]

Alexander Mack (1679-1735), after his arrival in Pennsylvania with the second group of Brethren in 1729, was quickly drawn into the dispute with Beissel. Mack attempted a reconciliation, but once that failed he evidently published a tract against sabbatarianism. No copy of this tract is known to exist, but references to it are found in other writings of the day.[2] While it is unfortunate that no copy of Mack's tract exists, there do exist Brethren arguments against sabbatarianism in Michael Frantz's (1687-1748) doctrinal treatise, mentioned in chapter 13. This treatise, published some twenty years after Frantz died, consists of 507 stanzas of poetry plus a prose section. Approximately fifty of the stanzas deal with an explanation of why Christians should observe Sunday as the Sabbath. According to Frantz, the Old Testament presents the law of Moses while the New Testament presents the grace of Jesus Christ. Since the Sabbath is part of the Mosaic law, Christians are not called to observe it. In fact, Jesus, as the Lord of the Sabbath, broke the Sabbath, thereby indicating that it is no longer to be observed. Furthermore, the New Testament does not contain a command to observe the Sabbath. Finally, since Revelation calls Sunday the Lord's Day, it should be observed as the Sabbath.[3]

During the second half of the nineteenth century, the Brethren again dealt with the question of which is the true Sabbath. Without doubt, the question came alive because of the growth of the Seventh-Day Adventist movement in the United States. In 1855 a lengthy article appeared in the *Gospel Visitor* titled "On the Christian Sabbath or the Lord's Day." The author argues for Sunday as the Christian Sabbath. His primary argument is similar to Michael Frantz's in that he understands the gospel dispensation as taking precedence over the Mosaic law. He also cites several New Testament texts to show the importance of the first day of the week to the early Christians. Included in these citations is 1 Corinthians 16:2.[4] In October of the same year, another even longer article appeared in the *Visitor* to refute the earlier article. At the beginning of this article, the *Visitor* gives an explanation as to why they are granting the author's request to publish an article which is not in agreement with the general practice among the Brethren. The explanation concludes with these words: "This is a rather singular request presuming greatly upon our liberality. Yet we have come to the conclusion, to gratify him this once. We have no fear that his arguments will disturb the minds of our readers."[5]

For the next several years, articles about the Sabbath continued to appear in the pages of the *Visitor*. Most supported Sunday as the Sabbath, but a few claimed Saturday as the Sabbath. Some of the pro-Sunday articles cited 1 Corinthians 16:2. In the 15 September 1864 issue, however, Henry Kurtz (1796-1874), then the senior editor, wrote an editorial stating that the Sabbath question was no longer to be discussed in the *Visitor*, except to answer those who objected to the observance of Sunday as the Sabbath. In short, the *Visitor* was to publish only articles which were pro-Sunday. No doubt this policy reflected the fact that earlier in the year Annual Meeting answered a question about how to handle a brother who keeps Saturday as the Sabbath thus: "Inasmuch as the old brethren have always observed the first day of the week as a day of rest and public worship, we think such a brother should be heartily admonished to conform to the order of the brethren and the gospel."[6]

Now that Annual Meeting had taken an official stand on the question, Brethren published even more material supporting Sunday as the Sabbath. R. H. Miller (1825-1892), the well-known Brethren debater, published an article on the subject in the 1869 *Visitor*. He devotes a long paragraph to 1 Corinthians 16:2 in order to show how the verse proves that the early Christians observed the first day of the week as the Sabbath. As part of his conclusion he says: "There is no fact more clear than that Paul points out the first day of the week in the same sense and in the same way that we would to-day if we were writing to a church that kept the first day of the week consecrated to the worship of God."[7] Revised editions of this article were later published in the *Primitive Christian* (25 April 1876) and the *Vindicator* (May and June 1876).

Several pro-Sunday tracts and pamphlets were published by Brethren in the last quarter of the nineteenth century. These include M. M. Eshelman's (1844-1921) "Sabbatism: The Law and Gospel Contrasted," G. J. Fercken's (1855-1930) "Saturday or Sunday,—Which?" and I. J. Rosenberger's (1842-1923) "The Sabbath and the Lord's Day." Even as late as 1938 the Tract Examining Committee of the Church of the Brethren published a pamphlet by James M. Moore (1876-1955), who taught Bible at Bethany Bible School from 1908 to 1917, titled "The Bible and the Sabbath." All four of these either quote or cite 1 Corinthians 16:2.

Notes

1. Julius Friedrich Sachse, *German Sectarians of Pennsylvania, 1708-1742* (Philadelphia: the author, 1899), 142-146.

2. Donald F. Durnbaugh, ed., *Brethren in Colonial America* (Elgin, IL: Brethren Press, 1967), 425.

3. Dale R. Stoffer, *Background and Development of Brethren Doctrines, 1650-1987* (Philadelphia: Brethren Encyclopedia, Inc., 1989), 97.

4. Aristobulus, "On the Christian Sabbath or the Lord's Day," *Gospel Visitor*, April 1855, 75.

5. "Which Is the True Sabbath?" *Gospel Visitor*, October 1855, 235.

6. *Minutes of the Annual Meetings of the Church of the Brethren, 1778-1909* (Elgin, IL: Brethren Publishing House, 1909), 228.

7. R. H. Miller, "The Seventh Day," *Gospel Visitor*, June 1869, 180.

The Text in Today's World

Although one comes into an occasional conversation with Seventh-Day Adventists or other sabbatarians, the issue which so plagued earlier Brethren no longer attracts our attention. In order to make a cogent argument for the Sabbath as the day of rest, one must hold the Hebrew Scriptures as highly authoritative. Brethren, with their slogan "the New Testament is our rule of faith and practice," find the Saturday argument singularly unconvincing. Our parents in the faith used 1 Corinthians 16:2 as proof that the early Christians had set aside Sunday as the day of rest and worship. They were undoubtedly correct.

The passage in 1 Corinthians 16:1-4 does not occur in one of Paul's well-known dialogical passages. To the contrary, he simply mentions the first day of the week as a matter of fact. In this little bit of instruction, we discover that Paul was taking a collection, that it was beyond what they ordinarily gave, and that it was to be banked on the first day of the week. All of this greatly interests those of us who have a historical concern for early Christianity, but it was the matter of Sunday worship which caught the eye of earlier Brethren. For our day there are several implications of considerable import.

The practice of a day of rest is in itself very important. For some people religion lies more in the realm of ideas, or in cosmic order, than in everyday practice. For such people, religious practices may seem irrelevant or even obnoxious. But the Judeo-Christian faith, though highly intelligent, does indeed engage in specific religious practices. The relationship to God is not simply a feeling or a vision. Like any other relationship there are concrete, incarnational elements to it. Those elements are best summarized by the day of rest in which the community celebrates its relationship to God, to the world in which it lives, and to each other as co-believers. To be sure, a covenant relationship must be constant, but such relationships also demand times of celebration and renewal. That time comes on Sunday, a day to glorify God and enjoy the world given to us.

In recent years anthropologists have convinced many of us that religious practices cannot necessarily be defended on pragmatic grounds. We may say that humans must rest every seven days, but can that be a basis for the Sunday observance? Whatever the answer, it must be said that religious observances mark the coherent unity of a group of people. Jews are marked by the Sabbath, Passover and kosher foods. Christians are marked by Sunday, the eucharist or mass, and Christmas. To rest on Sunday, to worship on Sunday and to renew covenant relationships—these mark one as a Christian. To disregard the Sunday rest does more than say that you are free to do as you please. It separates you from those who call upon the name of Jesus Christ. A person who wishes to be a disciple of Jesus would be very cautious about breaking away from any essential marks of the faith. Eventually such people would find themselves more in the community of "Sunday Times readers" than in the faith community.

While we may not be deeply disturbed by Sabbatarians (those who argue that Christians should rest on Saturday), we are distressed by "blue laws." If we say Sunday is essential for Christians, should we require Sunday to be a day of rest? Should we make it difficult for business to require employees to work on Sunday? The question seriously affects our daily lives and our faith community. But upon due consideration there is no choice. Brethren should not support "blue laws." There are two essential reasons: Brethren oppose the use of the state to enforce Christian customs and morality. That is the very essence of the "free church." On the issue of abortion, for example, Brethren advised members not to practice abortion but, at the same time, would not ask the state to enforce an anti-abortion law. So it is with "blue laws." We speak for the use of Sunday as a day of rest but cannot ask governments to close all but essential services. At the same time, we know there are many in our society for whom Sunday is not a special day. We Brethren not only recognize pluralism, but we rejoice in it. In a society that did not allow different religions, opposing political views, and various customs, Brethren would have little chance. Since we depend on the openness of a plural society, we can hardly suppress pluralism. Brethren will need to bite the bullet: individuals, with the support of the faith community, will need to find ways to celebrate Sunday without forcing everyone to the same conclusion.

Case Study

A Church of the Brethren building in the Northwest needed winterizing before the first snows fell. The Stewards called for a work day on the first Saturday of November. Only a few members of the church showed up, so the winterizing was not completed. On Sunday morning the chair of the Stewards stood up during announcement time and said, "We did not complete preparing the building for winter. According to the weather report the first snow will come this evening or tomorrow morning. So I am going to stay after church and finish the job. I would like everyone that can to stay with me." Immediately the pastor stood up and said, "As long as I am pastor of this church there will be no work day on Sunday. Sunday is the Lord's day." The chair of the Stewards walked out of the service.

The executive committee called an emergency session to talk with the pastor. How would you deal with the following questions raised at the meeting?

1. Was the pastor too strict in his interpretation of the Sunday observance?

2. Is work on the church building actually work?

3. There are obviously exceptions to the Sunday rest—the ox in the ditch problem. Would winterizing the church building prior to the first snow be one of those?

Session 20

On Reconciliation

2 Corinthians 5:16-21 (NRSV)

From now on, therefore, we regard no one from a human point of view; even though we once knew Christ from a human point of view, we know him no longer in that way. [17]So if anyone is in Christ, there is a new creation: everything old has passed away; see, everything has become new! [18]All this is from God, who reconciled us to himself through Christ, and has given us the ministry of reconciliation; [19]that is, in Christ God was reconciling the world to himself, not counting their trespasses against them, and entrusting the message of reconciliation to us. [20]So we are ambassadors for Christ, since God is making his appeal through us; we entreat you on behalf of Christ, be reconciled to God. [21]For our sake he made him to be sin who knew no sin, so that in him we might become the righteousness of God.

2 Corinthians 5:16-21 (BNT)

So from now on we do not consider anyone from a human point of view. Perhaps we had even considered Christ from a human point of view, but not any longer. [17]So if any are in Christ, they are a new creation. The old things have passed away—behold, the new have already come into being. [18]But actually all things come from God who reconciled us to himself through Christ and gave to us the ministry of reconciliation. [19]So God was in Christ reconciling the world to himself, not counting their trespasses against them, and placing in us the message of reconciliation. [20]So then let us be ambassadors for Christ, with God making his appeal through us: "We plead with you for Christ's sake, be reconciled to God. [21]He made the one who had not known sin to be 'sin' on our behalf, in order that we might come into a right relationship with God in him."

The Text in Its Biblical Setting

The letter found in 2 Corinthians 1—9 is at least the fourth letter of Paul to the Corinthian church. The first letter is not contained in our scriptures but is mentioned in 1 Corinthians 5:9. Apparently that letter from Paul evoked a response from the church. Then our book titled 1 Corinthians is actually Paul's reply to their correspondence (1 Cor. 7:1; see Session 17). But 1 Corinthians apparently did not solve all the conflicts at Corinth, so Paul himself returned to Corinth from Ephesus (2 Cor. 13:1). When this trip failed to produce reconciliation of the factions (1 Cor. 1:10-12), Paul wrote a rather angry letter which now can be found in 2 Corinthians 10—13 (see reference to the letter in 2 Cor. 7:8). Paul's cohort Titus then tried to bring about a reconciliation between the factions and Paul. This succeeded, to Paul's great relief and joy (2 Cor. 7:5-16), and so he wrote the fourth letter, 2 Corinthians 1—9 (in part), as an expression of gratitude. The great passage on reconciliation, 2 Corinthians 5:16-21, could hardly have been read apart from the very real experience of reconciliation which had just occurred between Paul and the Corinthian church.

The passage opens with a theological reflection on the way reconciliation occurs. In verses 14-15 Paul noted that he no longer has to live for himself, but because of the death of Christ, he is free to live for Christ. As a result of this, he says in verse 16, he no longer needs to judge everyone according to the standards of human self-interest. The phrase Paul uses here is literally "according to the flesh." *Flesh* for Paul means a life directed by one's own (human) standards as opposed to "living by the Spirit," which would be life according to the direction of God. Flesh is not inherently evil, nor does it refer to evil matter. It is an attitude about life which leads us to try to save ourselves rather than give ourselves to God (see Rom. 8:1-17 for the best statement about "flesh"). When Paul says he previously considered someone "according to the flesh," he means he viewed that person from the perspective of human fulfillment or success.

It is not likely that Paul here means he used to look at Jesus as a human but now looks at him as divine. Nor does he mean he once knew the historical Jesus but now knows the resurrected Lord. When Paul wishes to speak about the historical Jesus, which is not often, he uses the name Jesus only (Rom. 8:11; Gal. 6:17) or, especially when referring to the teachings of Jesus, he uses the word *Lord* (1 Cor. 7:10). Paul here means exactly what he says: As a Jew he once expected a Christ who would fulfill the hopes and dreams of the Jewish people, a military-type person who would destroy the enemies of the Jewish people. But Paul was converted. Now he sees the Christ from the divine perspective. The Christ came not to destroy the enemies of Israel but to reconcile them. This is the very heart of the Christian faith. Jesus of Nazareth is the Messiah because God was in him (v. 19), reconciling us through his death on the cross and giving us new life in the resurrection (v. 17). So what we have here in verse 16 is a very important statement by Paul that his confrontation with the crucified and risen Lord transformed his nationalistic Jewish messianic expectations into what we know as the Christian faith. In verse 17 Paul describes this change of perspective in terms familiar to readers of the Old Testament. Even before the period of apocalypticism, which spoke of the destruction of this age and the beginning of a new age (Daniel 7—12, Mark 13), there were prophets who spoke of a coming new creation (Isa. 43:18-21; 65:17). According to Paul those in Christ are such a new creation. What it means to be "in Christ" then becomes very important. In 1 Corinthians 10:2 Paul spoke of the Jews as "in Moses." Presumably, then, those "in Christ" are the Christians. Perhaps the phrase might better be translated: "in the body of Christ." Though for Paul the new age is yet to come (1 Th. 1:10), those who have been freed from the standard of the old age (the flesh) can live in this passing age as a sign of what is coming (the new creation).

All this is possible because God reconciles us in Christ (v. 18), rather than destroying us. And as harbingers of the new creation we have been given the "Christian" task to reconcile others. As he reflected on this fact, Paul then penned that great sentence which has become one of the keystones of the Christian faith, verse 19: The Christ has come, not judging, or destroying, as expected, but doing the reconciling work of God. As a result of that reconciling work, we have received a ministry of reconciliation, both in proclaiming the good news of what Christ has done and in acting to reconcile others to God and to each other. Paul speaks of Christians who have been so commissioned as "ambassadors for Christ," that is, people who have been given the authority to act on Christ's behalf.

In verses 20b-21 Paul gives us a sample of his message. He calls us to be reconciled to God because God, acting in Christ who was innocent of any sin, became sin, nevertheless, so that we might become righteousness. The wording of these sentences has been very puzzling to readers. How did Jesus Christ become *sin* and how do we become God's *righteousness*? If we go back to the basic meaning of sin as alienation, then Paul means God risked allowing his Son to be alienated by sending him into the realm of alienation. He did this so that we might be restored to the side of God in a covenant relationship once again; that is, he offered this (new) covenant to us while we were yet sinners. Through that risk and self-giving, we were brought to a state of righteousness.

This short message, or gospel, must then define what Paul meant by reconciliation. When people are alienated from God through mistrust, or when people are alienated from each other, the Christian ministry is to risk involvement even in that alienation in order to offer to such persons a trustful relationship in the name of Jesus Christ. Such acts are risky because involvement is dangerous, and people may not respond. Nevertheless, that is the Christian ministry. Paul knew that, because he had been reconciled to God and, therefore, could continue to offer himself to those in Corinth who had become alienated from him and the church there.

The Text in Brethren Life

In T. Wayne Rieman's address titled "The Brethren and Biblical Reconciliation," presented at the 1958 Annual Conference during the two hundred fiftieth anniversary celebration, reconciliation is described as "a central tenet" of the Brethren. According to Rieman, "there are many rites, practices, and beliefs which indicate the centrality of the gospel of reconciliation in Brethren life and thought."[1] Among the practices and beliefs related to reconciliation, Rieman notes peacemaking, settling differences according to Matthew 18, anointing for healing, baptism, and the love feast. Thus, it is clear that reconciliation for the Brethren has generally been tied to something else. As a result, Brethren writings prior to the twentieth century do not discuss reconciliation as such. In the twentieth century, however, Brethren began to consider reconciliation as presented in 2 Corinthians 5:16-21 and to reflect on how it permeates many of their beliefs and practices.

An early discussion of 2 Corinthians 5:16-21 is found in D. W. Kurtz's (1879-1949) *Studies in Doctrine* (1919). Kurtz finds verse 19 to be particularly significant. For him it affirms both the incarnation and the meaning of Christ's death. Concerning the meaning of Christ's death, Kurtz says, "But Christ's death did show as nothing else could show the depth of divine love, the suffering of the Heavenly Father, the way in which love bears the sins of the world and suffers to win man back to reconciliation with the Father. 'God was in Christ' (2 Cor. 5:19), loving, suffering, seeking, saving, reconciling man to himself."[2]

Verse 19 was also highly significant to Edward Frantz (1868-1962). Concerning the verse, Frantz says that it is the "clearest and most helpful statement on the subject [of reconciliation] in the whole New Testament."[3] Frantz then goes on to give the three main points presented by verse 19. First, says Frantz, it describes the relationship between God and Christ in the work of reconciliation. God is the doer of the reconciliation, and Christ is the agent of the reconciliation. Second, it explains that reconciliation between God and the world can only come about if there is a change in the world. God's attitude about the world does not have to change, but the world must change its attitude toward God. Third, reconciliation is personal in that the world must be reconciled to God and not to an impersonal system of thought or principle of belief.

While both Kurtz and Frantz emphasize verse 19, neither of them explains what is meant by the words "entrusting the message of reconciliation to us." William Beahm (1896-1964), however, has a good explanation of the words when he writes about 2 Corinthians 5:16-21 and "the ministry of reconciliation" in his book, *Studies in Christian Belief* (1958). Concerning this ministry Beahm says: "It involves the gospel of forgiveness which is the heart of evangelism. It involves the twin efforts of prophetic pronouncement and compassionate welfare. It sets the Christian and the church as ambassadors between God and his estranged and wayward children, seeking by all effective methods available to bring about God's intended reconciliation. It sends Christians out from the inner life of the church into the highways and hedges, out into the areas of sore tension and need, to apply there the healing of God's righteous and redeeming love."[4]

Another text which the Brethren often associate with reconciliation is Matthew 18:15-20, a text already discussed in chapter 5. Usually, when such an association is made, the Brethren present Matthew 18:15-20 as a blueprint for reconciliatory activity. Dale W. Brown, for example, presents it as a biblical model for reconciliation in his book *The Christian Revolutionary* (1971). In the context of his discussion on the relationship of reconciliation to confrontation, Brown points out that reconciliation without confrontation often means the continuation of unjust practices and bad feelings, while confrontation without reconciliation can mean unending retaliation. "Only peace [reconciliation] achieved through confrontation, involving grace and judgment, love and justice, will suffice," says Brown.[5]

Rufus Bowman (1899-1952), writing twenty-six years before Brown, also understands Matthew 18:15-20 as a blueprint for reconciliation. In his book, *Seventy Times Seven* (1945), Bowman presents Matthew 18 as a three-fold technique for reconciliation. First, the innocent party humbly confronts the guilty party in order to effect understanding and love. Second, if the first approach fails, the innocent party takes with him or her one or two friends to confront the guilty party. Third, if there is still no reconciliation, the innocent party asks the church for help in bringing about reconciliation. In all this, says Bowman, unlimited forgiveness is the motive; and if none of the three steps is fruitful, the guilty party "is henceforth to be regarded as an object of conversion."[6]

After presenting this three-fold technique of reconciliation, Bowman illustrates reconciliation with a story about his father:

> When the writer was a boy on a Virginia farm, there was a rogue in the community who would steal our corn and apples. To the dismay of other people, my father would sometimes have this man work for him because he felt that his family needed the money. My father treated this rogue with the utmost kindness and never spoke an unkind word about him. When the man came to die he called for my father, made a confession of how he had lived, and asked for prayer. My father discovered in the man's house a dusty Bible, opened its pages and read Scripture, knelt down and prayed for the man who had wronged him, asked for his restoration to health and to his family, and gripped his hand when he left as friend and brother.[7]

Such a story clearly illustrates that the Brethren practice of reconciliation preceded the Brethren reflections and writings on reconciliation by some two hundred years. However, once the Brethren began to theologize about reconciliation, their concept of reconciliatory activity broadened. They began to realize that reconciliation is needed on more than the individual level. Thus T. Wayne Rieman, in his anniversary address, calls the Brethren to work for reconciliation between nations, between races, and between churches.

In fact, Brethren of the late twentieth century have come to understand reconciliation as one of the primary marks of the church. William Kidwell, writing in *Messenger* in 1977, includes "the reconciling community" as one of the phrases which describe what the church means to him. For Kidwell 2 Corinthians 5:17-18 means that "the church is a community where there can be reconciliation among people of varied feelings, opinions, and backgrounds . . . . Once we do that, then we can turn to working on reconciliation in the wider community; then we can devote our energies to being ambassadors for peace among the nations, the races, the sick and the poor, the downtrodden and the outcasts."[8] William Faw, writing in *Brethren Life and Thought* in 1978, describes the witnesses to peace in the church as "God's agents of reconciliation." After quoting 2 Corinthians 5:18, Faw says, "Those who acknowledge God's work of reconciliation are given the ministry of reconciliation—to discover and proclaim to neighbors and enemies alike the peace that God has worked and is working between us."[9]

Notes

1. T. Wayne Rieman, "The Brethren and Biblical Reconciliation," in *Adventurous Future*, ed. Paul H. Bowman (Elgin, IL: Brethren Press, 1959), 161-162.

2. D. W. Kurtz, "Studies in Doctrine," in *Studies in Doctrine and Devotion* (Elgin, IL: Brethren Publishing House, 1919), 49.

3. Edward Frantz, *Basic Belief* (Elgin, IL: Brethren Publishing House, 1943), 68.

4. William M. Beahm, *Studies in Christian Belief* (Elgin, IL: Brethren Press, 1958), 249-250.

5. Dale W. Brown, *The Christian Revolutionary* (Grand Rapids, MI: Eerdmans, 1971), 130.

6. Rufus D. Bowman, *Seventy Times Seven* (Elgin, IL: Brethren Publishing House, 1945), 76.

7. Ibid., 76-77.

8. William Kidwell, "What the Church Means to Me," *Messenger*, August 1977, 30.

9. William R. Faw, "Christ's Church: God's Colony and Agent of Reconciliation," *Brethren Life and Thought* 23 (Winter 1978):57.

The Text in Today's World

2 Corinthians 5 is important for us to consider because it is a text that marks a basic shift in the Church of the Brethren. The peace position was based primarily on the Sermon on the Mount, not on Paul's concept of reconciliation. 2 Corinthians 5 has become a favorite text only recently, though it surely will grow in importance in the years ahead. Sometime in the earlier part of this century Brethren shifted from a group that opposed war, opposed man's inhumanity to man, opposed violence, and opposed misuse of power for self-aggrandizement, to a group which was willing to reconcile opposing groups and mediate the conflict. It is difficult to determine just where

and when Brethren shifted from opposing war to serving the oppressed (perhaps with the beginning of Brethren service around 1935) and from service to peacemaking. One can see the shift in the titles of two presentations to the World Council by the historic Peace Churches: *War Is Contrary To The Will of God* (1951) and *Peace Is The Will of God* (1953). The first presentation argued against violence. The second argued for Christian peacemaking. In any case, the reconciliation theme is strong in the 250th anniversary statement made by the Brethren to the World Council in 1958 (*The Adventurous Future*, Paul H. Bowman, ed., Brethren Press, 1959, pp. 24-29).

We must be careful with our language. *Reconciliation* is a Latin term meaning to settle disputes by discussing the conflict and making appropriate adjustments. The Greek term *katallage* as used by Paul implies much more the use of one's person (or a group's use of itself) to create a new possibility for peace. Jesus did not form discussion groups but went to the cross, taking human fault with him. By turning the other cheek, Jesus broke the spiral of violence. Paul asks us to continue that kind of ministry.

Reconciliation in the biblical sense is covenant-oriented. It is not concerned primarily about fixing the blame, or the issue of right and wrong, but about enabling alienated parties to discover a new and whole relationship with each other. From a covenantal perspective it is not assumed, therefore, that peace can be achieved merely by adjusting the points of disagreement. Rather, it is supposed that conflict stems from dynamics which come from deep in the history of those involved. In that case change in the dynamics is necessary before peace can be achieved. Brethren concern for reconciliation has shifted in direction toward action aiming at this sort of change. During the Vietnam war, Brethren protested the war, sent relief to both sides, but primarily sought to work at the causes of the conflict. During the drive for civil rights, Brethren protested inequality, sought to aid those hurt in the conflict, but also worked at such causes as prejudice, economic disadvantages, and other deep-seated problems. 2 Corinthians 5 calls for Brethren to continue in this pattern of reconciliation.

The key problem facing us in most conflict situations is aiding the powerless. From the Christian covenant perspective, those who have power (e.g., wealthy industrial nations) can bring peace by using their power for the creation of power and equality among those without power (e.g., underdeveloped nations, minorities, the poor). But if the ones with power in a relationship refuse to share or use their position for others, then what should those without power do? Brethren have agreed that violence does not solve the problem. In days to come, however, Brethren will need to find more ways to help the powerless without, at the same time, creating codependency. The Apostle Paul, the covenant thinker of the New Testament, suggested that the so-called powerless do indeed have much power. In a relational sense the powerless define those with power: Children create parents, workers create industrialists, students create teachers, slaves create masters, the poor create wealthy, and blacks create whites. Those without power could at any time redefine the relationship with the powerful. For example, when blacks declare black more beautiful than white (rather than seek to emulate white ways), they have redefined what it means to be white. Hopefully Brethren of the days to come can explore these situations and find ways to foster positive identities for those who feel disenfranchised.

Case Study

During the Civil Rights movement the Church of the Brethren was very active on the side of African Americans. A number of Brethren participated in marches, sit-ins, and other advocacy actions. Martin Luther King, Jr., used First Church in Chicago as a headquarters for his West Side tenement union. A number of these encounters became violent. However, on behalf of the Church of the Brethren, Ralph Smeltzer, director of peace and social education for the Brethren Service Commission, took on quite a different role. In Selma, one of the most violent situations, Ralph conversed with both sides. According to reporters Ralph worked with segregationists to abandon their absolute position, and he worked with blacks to develop a strong leadership which would work for civil rights in a peaceful manner. His reconciling ministry was considered remarkable in what could be a violent confrontation. Some advocates for civil rights were surprised that Brethren leaders would work with both sides.

1. To what extent do you think Brethren should be involved in justice issues? Should they try to reconcile opposing parties? Or should they side with the oppressed against those who hold for the status quo?

2. How should reconciliation occur? Do you understand reconciliation between opposing parties, like segregationists and integrationists, in the same way God reconciled us through Jesus Christ? Can you describe that?

3. In some areas Brethren are known for their skill in peacemaking and reconciliation. Do you think this reputation is deserved? If so, how does this tradition continue?

On Ecumenical Relationships

Ephesians 4:4-16 (NRSV)

There is one body and one Spirit, just as you were called to the one hope of your calling, [5]one Lord, one faith, one baptism, [6]one God and Father of all, who is above all and through all and in all. [7]But each of us was given grace according to the measure of Christ's gift. [8]Therefore it is said,

> "When he ascended on high he
> made captivity itself
> a captive;
> he gave gifts to his people."

[9](When it says, "He ascended," what does it mean but that he had also descended into the lower parts of the earth? [10]He who descended is the same one who ascended far above all the heavens, so that he might fill all things.) [11]The gifts he gave were that some would be apostles, some prophets, some evangelists, some pastors and teachers, [12]to equip the saints for the work of ministry, for building up the body of Christ, [13]until all of us come to the unity of the faith and of the knowledge of the Son of God, to maturity, to the measure of the full stature of Christ. [14]We must no longer be children, tossed to and fro and blown about by every wind of doctrine, by people's trickery, by their craftiness in deceitful scheming. [15]But speaking the truth in love, we must grow up in every way into him who is the head, into Christ, [16]from whom the whole body, joined and knit together by every ligament with which it is equipped, as each part is working properly, promotes the body's growth in building itself up in love.

Ephesians 4:4-16 (BNT)

There is one body and one spirit, as also you were called in the one hope of your calling, [5]one Lord, one faith, one baptism, [6]one God and father of all, the one who is above all, and through all, and among all. [7]But grace was given to each one of us according to the measure of Christ's gift. [8]Therefore it says:

> When he ascended to the height he
> made captivity itself
> captive,
> and he gave gifts to all people.

[9](And the ascending, what does it mean except that he also descended into the depths of the earth. [10]The one who descended is the one ascended beyond all the heavens, in order that all things might be fulfilled.) [11]And the gifts he gave were that some would be apostles, some prophets, some evangelists, some pastors and teachers, [12]to equip the saints for the work of ministry, for building up the body of Christ, [13]until we all come into the unity of faith and of the knowledge of the Son of God, to maturity, to the measure of the full stature of Christ; [14]so that we are no longer children blown here and there by every wind of doctrine, by human cunning, by their craftiness in deceitful strategies. [15]But being truthful in love, let us grow up in every way into him who is the head, Christ, [16]from whom the whole body, joined and knit together by every ligament with which it is equipped, when each part is working properly, makes the body grow in building itself up in love.

The Text in Its Biblical Setting

As it stands, at some time in the late fifties or early sixties of the first century, Paul sent three letters from prison into the Asia Minor area: Colossians, Philemon, and Ephesians. Philippians was also written from prison, but that letter does not seem the equivalent of Ephesians and Colossians. In Colossians we learn that Tychicus is bearing the letters (Col. 4:7) and will share other news orally. Tychicus was accompanied by Onesimus, a companion of Paul and slave of Philemon. The letter to the Colossians was to be read out loud at the house church(es) there and then taken over to another Asia Minor town, Laodicea (Col. 4:16). The letter for Laodicea was to be read in Colossae. That letter either is lost or may be our canonical letter Ephesians, as some suspect.

As for the letter called Ephesians, there does not seem to be any specific location or context. This has led many to suppose Ephesians was composed to introduce the other more specific letters or, at least, was a general letter which represented all the others. Because of its general nature, perhaps, Ephesians has become the quintessential statement on church unity and high Christology. Through the centuries Christians have turned to it again and again for an understanding of the church universal.

The text begins with a series of affirmations about the oneness of the body of Christ, the Spirit, the Christian hope, the Lord, faith, baptism, and God. Oneness does not mean "single" but rather means "at one," or unified. So the one body may consist of many congregations, many different points of view, but it is held together in a unified faith community. The oneness of the body is held together by one Spirit, a Spirit that creates needed variations.

This oneness in the Spirit has been made possible because Christ has freed us from those things that make us captive. In rising or ascending in victory, Jesus Christ made captivity itself captive and gave to us gifts of the Spirit. These gifts develop and organize the faith community. Paul mentions five specific offices or functions within the faith community. They are apostles, who continue the work of Jesus Christ (see Col. 1:24-25); prophets, who understand the Scriptures and proclaim their meaning (see 1 Cor. 14:3); evangelists, who narrate the good news; pastors or shepherds, who serve and guide the faith community; and teachers, who give instruction (see 1 Th. 2:7-8). These community functions are not to be taken as administrative offices. Verse 12 makes it clear that these gifts have been given to enable the members themselves to perform the functions of ministry and to organize the faith community. Leaders not only facilitate the priesthood of all believers, they encourage every Christian to live according to the fullness of Christ.

In such an atmosphere mature Christians are not led astray by misleading teachings, spurious movements, and persuasive speakers. Rather, Christians can be open and frank with each other. They may differ but still speak the truth in love. In this way the entire church and its congregations grow together into the one who is the beginning and the end, Jesus Christ.

The Text in Brethren Life

Not until the twentieth century did the Brethren begin to cite verses from Ephesians 4 as the basis for ecumenism. Of course, it was not until then that Brethren consciously chose to participate in ecumenical activities. Prior to the twentieth century, Brethren generally opposed cooperative activities with other Christian groups.[1] Such avoidance of ecumenism is not surprising, since the Brethren came into being, in part, because of their opposition to the beliefs and practices of other groups and were persecuted at times for this opposition.

Even though the Brethren did not understand Ephesians 4 as a call to ecumenism until after 1900, they did turn to the chapter for guidance on other issues. Mack (1679-1735) cites Ephesians 4:11-13; 4:12; and 4:5 in his writings. In *Basic Questions* (1713), he refers to 4:11-13 as a goal when he answers the question concerning whether the early Brethren were of one spirit. Mack's *Rights and Ordinances* (1715) lists 4:12 as one of the texts which speak of the church as the body of Christ and quotes 4:5 as testimony that there is one true faith though many adulterated faiths are taught.

Interestingly, Ephesians 4:5 is cited twice in the pamphlet "A Humble Gleam" (1747), written by a Brethren to counter a Quaker booklet. The Quaker booklet criticized those for whom the outward form of baptism was important and espoused the Quaker emphasis on the baptism of the Holy Spirit. Since the Brethren felt that the booklet misinterpreted the Scripture, an unknown member wrote the pamphlet in response. While Ephesians 4:5 does not figure prominently in the pamphlet's arguments, it is noteworthy that the verse is cited in a Brethren publication which sought to emphasize separateness rather than ecumenism.

The Brethren ventured into ecumenical meetings as early as 1742. In that year Count Zinzendorf (1700-1760), a leader of the Renewed Moravian Church, held the Pennsylvania Synods. This series of seven meetings sought to bring the various religious groups of Pennsylvania closer together. While the Count saw the need for unity, he did not seek to do away with diversity. His motto was: "In essentials unity, in nonessentials diversity, in all things charity." Some Brethren leaders attended the first three of these synods—at Germantown, Falckner's Swamp, and Oley. After the third meeting, however, the Brethren decided to withdraw from further attendance. At that meeting three Indian converts were baptized by sprinkling, a mode of baptism of which the Brethren did not approve. Furthermore, some Brethren leaders were suspicious that the synods were only a pretext used by the Moravians to gather new members. At least two Brethren did join the Moravians and traveled with Zinzendorf back to Europe. It is generally thought that the Brethren began holding their Annual Meetings in the same year as the synods, in part as a defensive tactic.

In the opening sentence of his section on the relationship of the Brethren to other groups during the years 1785-1865, Roger Sappington (1929-1989) states: "The period was characterized by intense rivalry and competition among the many different groups in the United States, and the Brethren were not immune to such competition."[2] In general, this competitive relationship continued *throughout* the nineteenth century. Notable expressions of competitiveness were the doctrinal debates. While George Wolfe II (1780-1865) is reported to have debated a Catholic priest in Illinois in 1818, the majority of the doctrinal debates took place in the 1860s, 1870s, and 1880s. The favorite subject for such debates was baptism, however, other topics such as the love feast, the Holy Kiss, and freemasonry were popular. Many Brethren leaders participated in the debates; two of the best known debaters being James Quinter (1816-1888) and R. H. Miller (1825-1892).

In the midst of such competitiveness, Ephesians 4 was not understood as a text on ecumenism. Instead, the chapter sometimes provided a text for claiming the superiority of Brethren practices over those of other Christian groups. For example, a sermon printed in the October 1855 issue of the *Gospel Visitor* uses Ephesians 4:5 as its text. More than half of the sermon focuses on the words *one baptism*, interpreted to mean that all Christians should follow the same mode of baptism. The sermon then claims that the proper mode for all Christians is the trine immersion used by the Brethren.

By the late nineteenth century, the way was being prepared for Brethren participation in the many ecumenical ventures of the twentieth century. Specifically, Brethren missionaries and Brethren leaders in Christian education paved the way. In 1894 the Brethren sent their first missionaries to India and encouraged them to cooperate with missionaries from other denominations. Furthermore, because Brethren Sunday school materials followed the international Sunday school lesson cycle, Brethren editors and writers were making contacts with leaders in other denominations.

In 1919 the Brethren leaders who made up the four boards of the church voted to recommend to Annual Meeting the full participation of the denomination in the Interchurch World Movement. This movement, sponsored in part by the Federal Council of Churches, sought finances from member churches to survey and publish mission opportunities around the world. The Annual Meeting of 1920, however, did not approve the recommendation and the boards were told to withdraw from the movement. Nevertheless, $50,000 had to be paid to the movement because legal papers had been signed by board members pledging that amount. The movement folded soon after.

Even though Brethren participation in the short-lived Interchurch World Movement was not approved, interest in ecumenism continued. In 1925 queries came from two local congregations concerning ecumenical relationships. One query asked for the appointment of a fraternal relations committee to study the uniting of the Church of the Brethren with the Brethren Church, a denomination that came into being as a result of the divisions among the Brethren in the 1880s. The other query asked to have a committee appointed "to confer with and propose a basis of affiliation and union with denominational bodies of similar faith and practice."[3] While neither request was granted that year, the Annual Conference responded by quoting Ephesians 4:4-6 and encouraging friendly relations with evangelical denominations. Eventually a study was made of the possible uniting of the Brethren Church and the Church of the Brethren. The results of the study, which included a reference to Ephesians 4:4-6, were reported to the 1934 conference. In light of the report, the 1934 conference went on record as favoring the reuniting of the two bodies. Also as a result, the Committee on Fraternal Relations became a permanent committee of Annual Conference. In 1968 this committee became known as the Committee on Interchurch Relations.

In 1941 Annual Conference approved membership in both the Federal Council of Churches, which was succeeded by the National Council of Churches of Christ in the USA (NCCC) in 1950, and the World Council of Churches (WCC), which was not actually founded until 1948. Brethren participation in both groups continues to this day. At times opposition to such participation has been voiced, and a committee has been appointed to study the affiliation and report back to Annual Conference, notably in 1945, 1968, and 1981. In all three cases, conference has affirmed continued Brethren involvement in both groups. The 1981 report includes a list of eight concerns about Brethren affiliation with the WCC and the NCCC. Among these concerns are the feeling that the two groups emphasize social concerns over personal salvation, the fear that both groups are infiltrated by communists, and anxiety over the support given by the WCC to violent revolutionary movements.

The very next Annual Conference (1982) adopted a paper titled "A Vision of Unity for the Church of the Brethren in the 1980s." This paper, prepared by the Committee on Interchurch Relations, set the direction for the denomination on ecumenical issues for the coming years. A major portion of the paper is devoted to the biblical basis of ecumenism. Both Ephesians 4:15 and 4:16 are cited. Verse 15 is cited as a call for Christians from different traditions to witness to their respective faiths, and verse 16 is cited to indicate the value of relationships with Christians of other traditions.

Perhaps the ecumenical issue which generated the most debate in the twentieth century was the invitation received by the Brethren in 1965 to participate fully in the Consultation on Church Union (COCU). COCU is the proposal that a "truly evangelical, truly catholic, and truly reformed" church be formed in the US by denominational mergers. At both the 1966 and 1968 Annual Conferences, the invitation was considered. Both times full participation was rejected in favor of an observer-consultant status. Whereas the majority of Brethren leadership on all levels tends to favor ecumenism, the leadership was divided over full participation in COCU. This division is well documented in a special issue of Brethren Life and Thought (Winter 1966), in which two writers supported COCU and three did not. Perhaps it was the division among the leadership which led to the rejection of full COCU participation by such a large majority at the 1966 conference. Edward K. Ziegler (1903-1989) later reflected: "The decision . . . not to enter fully into COCU membership indicated the desire of the church to maintain a strong peace witness and a quality of radical discipleship which did not seem viable within the shape of the uniting church emerging from the consultation."[4]

Brethren writers of the twentieth century have also turned to Ephesians 4 when writing about ecumenism. J. Q. Miller (1899-1983), a Brethren and a leader in both the Federal Council of Churches and the NCCC, refers to Ephesians 4 in several of his published works. His book Christian Unity: Its Relevance to the Community (1957) includes a quotation of Ephesians 4:15-16 in a discussion of the biblical concept of Christian unity. Warren F. Groff, a Brethren representative to the WCC, reminds Brethren that they contribute to the ecumenical paradox. "The Biblical witness and concrete experience within the Christian community testify to the 'oneness' of the church in Christ and yet we live in a divided state, and to this anomaly we contribute as Brethren."[5] Included among the biblical witnesses to oneness, according to Groff, is Ephesians 4:4-6. Finally, Fred Swartz, in his book on how Brethren have related to the quest for Christian unity, quotes Ephesians 4:1-6 as the Apostle Paul's summary of the spirit of unity.[6]

Notes

1. See the section on the temperance movement in the chapter on chemical dependency.

2. Roger Sappington, *The Brethren in a New Nation* (Elgin, IL: Brethren Press, 1976), 103.

3. *Minutes of the Annual Conference of the Church of the Brethren,* held at Winona Lake, IN, 3-10 June 1925, 12.

4. Edward K. Ziegler, "Ecumenical Relations," in *Church of the Brethren: Yesterday and Today,* ed. Donald F. Durnbaugh (Elgin, IL: Brethren Press, 1986), 196.

5. Warren F. Groff, "Guest Editorial: Oberlin Speaks to the Brethren," *Brethren Life and Thought* 3 (Spring 1958):8.

6. Fred W. Swartz, *All in God's Family* (Elgin, IL: Brethren Press, 1977), 96.

The Text in Today's World

It certainly is remarkable that early Brethren used the Ephesian passage as an argument for avoiding those not of the one true faith, and yet modern Brethren use the same text to call for more intense relationships with the worldwide church. Some might call it a contradiction. For those who know the Brethren, however, it does not seem like a contradiction or even a basic paradigm shift (as in Session 20). We are simply dealing with the other side of the coin. As we have indicated before, the existence of a denomination like the Church of the Brethren depends on a sense of pluralism. In medieval times and even through the Reformation, the rule was "the religion of the prince is the religion of the people." Anabaptists and other smaller groups gave their lives to destroy the sense of a state religion. Because of their conviction and sacrifice, they bequeathed to many of us a "freedom of religion."

Brethren must be ecumenical. To fail to recognize the validity of others is to set the stage for our own destruction. At the same time, in a pluralistic world, we cannot find unity in sameness. For that reason Brethren have always been wary of the ecumenical movement. For many years and for many Christians, "one Lord, one faith, one baptism" has meant an agreement in the theology and practice of baptism, eucharist, and ministry. For Brethren the term *one* does not have that connotation. For Free Church types, *one* means a unity among those who differ in faith and practice. In that sense a council of churches makes sense to Brethren, while a "church union" does not.

Historically, Brethren have usually stressed the veracity of their own tradition but have recognized, even rejoiced, in the veracity of other traditions. This attitude makes Brethren very valuable members of the ecumenical movement. They have been able to accept everyone in good faith; therefore, they can often act as bridge persons in cross-denominational situations. Consequently, Brethren often contribute to ecumenical leadership far beyond their proportional representation.

With the continuing deconstruction of the Christian west, Christians are slowly becoming a minority (or weak majority). The Christians of the future will not have the luxury of going their own separate way. Denominations cannot afford their own infrastructures. Brethren have a heavy responsibility to pull together local congregations and denominations for a unified Christian witness and mutual service to others.

Case Study

During the Middle East crisis of 1990, the chair of the Witness Commission brought to Dunkerdale's board meeting notice of an oil-free Sunday. The Church of the Brethren was calling on congregations not to use oil on a designated Sunday in order to call attention to the real cause for conflict in the Middle East. The board was pleased with the idea and responded positively. The celebration of an oil-free Sunday caught the attention of other churches in this southeastern town. The pastors of the Presbyterian church and the Methodist church consulted with the pastor of Dunkerdale. The three of them decided to hold another oil-free Sunday as an ecumenical service. Because the Presbyterian church was larger and better known, it was decided to hold the service there. The service attracted considerable attention. A number of townspeople walked to the service and the local TV station aired much of the service. The news media interviewed the articulate Methodist minister and the television station showed the service inside the Presbyterian church. No mention was made of Dunkerdale Church of the Brethren.

1. Are you pleased that so many Christian people joined in the protest against armed conflict in the Middle East?

2. Are you pleased that the Church of the Brethren could initiate such an outstanding demonstration of Christian unity on an important issue?

3. Are you upset that the Church of the Brethren received no public credit for the event?

4. The next time the Brethren have a good idea would you share it with other Christians in your area?

Session 22

On Biblical Authority

2 Timothy 3:10-17 (NRSV)

Now you have observed my teaching, my conduct, my aim in life, my faith, my patience, my love, my steadfastness, [11]my persecutions and suffering the things that happened to me in Antioch, Iconium, and Lystra. What persecutions I endured! Yet the Lord rescued me from all of them. [12]Indeed, all who want to live a godly life in Christ Jesus will be persecuted. [13]But wicked people and impostors will go from bad to worse, deceiving others and being deceived. [14]But as for you, continue in what you have learned and firmly believed, knowing from whom you learned it, [15]and how from childhood you have known the sacred writings that are able to instruct you for salvation through faith in Christ Jesus. [16]All scripture is inspired by God and is useful for teaching, for reproof, for correction, and for training in righteousness, [17]so that everyone who belongs to God may be proficient, equipped for every good work.

2 Timothy 3:10-17 (BNT)

You have observed my teaching, my conduct, my goal in life, my faith, my patience, my love, my steadfastness, [11]my persecution, my sufferings, the things that happened to me in Antioch, in Iconium, and Lystra, the persecutions I have endured. Yet the Lord rescued me from all of them. [12]Indeed, all who wish to live a godly life in Christ Jesus will be persecuted. [13]Evil people and impostors, deceiving and being deceived, will go from bad to worse. [14]But as for you, stay in what you have learned and believed, knowing from whom you have learned, [15]and that from childhood you knew the sacred writings, which are able through faith in Jesus Christ to make you wise about matters of salvation. [16]Every writing inspired by God is also useful for teaching, for reproof, for correction and for education in righteousness, [17]so that everyone who belongs to God may be skilled, equipped for every good work.

The Text in Its Biblical Setting

2 Timothy purports to have been written by the Apostle Paul to his friend and younger colleague, Timothy. Nearly everyone agrees that the Pastoral Epistles (1—2 Timothy and Titus) do not belong in the same category as the primary letters of Paul (1—2 Thessalonians, 1—2 Corinthians, Romans, Galatians, and Philippians). They simply do not share the same language, the same style, and the same theological perspective. Certainly we should be careful to read the Pastoral Epistles in their own right and not try to compare them with the groundbreaking theology of Romans and Galatians. Many proposals have been offered to explain the differences between the Pastorals and early Paul. At least one explanation merits discussion.

Sociologists of religion have long noticed that all religious ideas, no matter how lofty, must eventually be useful to people where they are. We speak of the context in which people live as the *social matrix*. All universal religions have adapted to the social matrix. Otherwise, they would have died out. Christianity is no exception. The lofty faith perceptions of the Apostle Paul were not immediately useful for the new faith communities of the Mediterranean world. The church needed to modify what Paul had said. The Pastoral Epistles are the product of that modification. So we will read 2 Timothy as instructions to a pastor dealing with a local early Christian faith community.

Speaking at the close of his life, Paul tells Timothy how faith formation occurs. First, there is the power of a model (or hero in the faith). Paul does not tell of his life in order to gain authority over Timothy. Rather, just as Paul has shared his life with Timothy so now Timothy can do the same for others. To be sure, living according to the model of Paul may very well lead to persecutions from neighbors and local authorities.

In addition to model adults, the child needs instruction from the faith community regarding the sacred writings (v. 15). These sacred writings surely included the Hebrew Scriptures, though they may have also included Jewish intertestamental literature. As something of an addition, Paul notes that all such literature is valuable for instruction and correction. Actually the statement in verse 16 seems clear and innocuous: writings that the church calls scripture are useful for instruction. But 2 Timothy 3:16 has become a famous battleground for theological wars over verbal inspiration.

A part of the warfare involves the translation of v. 16. There is no verb "to be" in the verse. So we have to determine for ourselves where the author intended it. Some, usually more conservative, translate it: "all scripture is inspired by God and is useful for teaching." This is a possible translation of the Greek, but seems redundant. If it is scripture then it must be inspired. Surely no reader would have supposed there was a category of uninspired scripture.

Consequently, many others have opted for a second translation: "every writing inspired by God is also useful for teaching." This translation, also true to the Greek, says any inspired writing is useful in the educational process.

The Greek term *theopneustos* occurs only here in the Bible. Basically it means God-breathed. Many translators and readers have assumed the term refers to the person writing the document. This has led to the present day arguments over the nature of inspiration (verbal, infallible, ecstatic). The emphasis on the author has been overdone. The Spirit worked primarily in the life of the community. God working through the Spirit teaches the congregation (1 Th. 4:8-10). According to the Gospel of John it is the Spirit that will lead the faith community into a deeper understanding of what Jesus has said (John 14:25-26). It is not so much a matter of the inspiration of the author as it is the presence of the Spirit in the congregation, or with the readers, as it (they) interprets what has been written. An inspired document then is one that has a proven track record in the faith community. It is not divisive or deceiving (v. 14) and can be trusted to instruct, correct, and train for God's work (vv. 16-17). So understood, the two verses might be translated: "from childhood you have known the sacred writings, which are able through trust in the body of Jesus Christ to make you mature in the way of salvation. For every writing regarded as inspired by God is also useful for teaching."

The Text in Brethren Life

From their very beginnings in 1708, Brethren have emphasized the authority of the Bible in relation to faith and practice. Alexander Mack, Jr., (1712-1803) described how the first eight Brethren "diligently searched the New Testament"[1] before proceeding with the first baptism. Likewise, from the beginning the Brethren have understood the Bible as divinely inspired. For example, a Brethren-authored pamphlet from 1747 stated: "The Holy Scriptures is a letter of God which He has written to the human race through the operation of His Eternal Spirit, etc."[2] Debate over the meaning of inspiration did not begin until the end of the nineteenth century when the Brethren encountered historical criticism (reading the Bible as an historical document). During the next seventy-five years, the question of the nature of biblical inspiration and its effect on biblical authority intensified. By 1977 the debate was so intense that Annual Conference appointed a committee "to prepare a paper on the historical Pietist-Anabaptist and Brethren understandings of the Bible's inspiration and authority."[3]

Over the years since 1708, 2 Timothy 3:15-17, particularly verse 16, has often been cited by Brethren in connection with biblical inspiration and authority. Alexander Mack (1679-1735) himself quoted all three verses when writing about the topic of scripture in his *Rights and Ordinances* (1713). The son begins the conversation by asking about the relationship of faith to scripture. In replying the father says: "A faithful child of God looks only to his heavenly Father, and believes and follows Him in His revealed Word, because he is certain of and believes that God and His spoken Word are completely one . . . Therefore, learn well the true Scriptural distinction in all things, so that you do not become confused, as have, unfortunately, many souls in this day."[4] The father later concludes his reply by quoting 2 Timothy 3:15-17.

In 1845 John Kline (1797-1864) quoted 2 Timothy 3:16 in the midst of making a case for his belief that John's Gospel was written after the other three Gospels but before Paul wrote 2 Timothy. Kline argues that John did not write his Gospel until he recognized the need for a plain and simple presentation of God's ordinances as he (John) had seen them instituted by Jesus. This need was made particularly apparent through the corruption in the Corinthian church. Paul, himself, says Kline, looked to John to learn about the Lord's supper and feetwashing. Paul "therefore includes the Gospel recorded by John in his comprehensive expression that 'all scripture is given by divine inspiration.' In this view of the case, Paul could well insert the words, 'and is profitable for CORRECTION, for INSTRUCTION in righteousness,' because he himself had been corrected and instructed by it."[5]

While Brethren reject the use of a creed, they have been willing, particularly in the last hundred years, to publish manuals which summarize their beliefs as well as their practices. As early as 1887, there appeared *The Brethren's Church Manual*, "containing the declaration of faith, rules of order, how to conduct religious meetings, &c."[6] This manual begins with a statement about the authority of the Bible: "We believe that the Holy Scriptures of the Old and New Testaments have their authority from God and were written by divinely inspired men and that they are a perfect, infallible, and sufficient standard of faith and practice, having truth for their matter and salvation for their end (2 Tim. 3:15)."[7] This manual was very popular and appeared in several revised editions over the next thirty years. Always 2 Timothy 3:15 was cited concerning biblical authority.

During the second decade of the twentieth century, three Brethren authors published books on Brethren doctrine. Interestingly, neither J. H. Moore (1846-1935) in *New Testament Doctrines* (1914) or Otho Winger (1877-1946) in *History and Doctrines of the Church of the Brethren* (1919) cite 2 Timothy 3 when discussing the authority of the Bible. D. W. Kurtz (1879-1949) does cite 2 Timothy 3, but only within a quote from a non-Brethren author.[8]

Edward Frantz (1868-1964) gave the Sunday morning sermon at the 1943 Annual Conference held in McPherson, Kansas. Because 1943 was the two hundredth anniversary of the first printing of the Sauer Bible, the program committee chose "The Bible in Brethren Life" as the topic for the sermon. The sermon was later published in five installments in the *Gospel Messenger* (July 10, July 17, July 24, July 31, and August 7, 1943). For his text, Frantz chose 2 Timothy 3:16. In the sermon Frantz deals with what it means to be "inspired of God," and particularly with the understanding that the original manuscripts of the Bible were free of inaccuracies because the Holy Spirit overpowered the writers so that what they wrote was free of imperfections. Says Frantz: "Such an assumption is the fruitage of well-meant but misguided zeal . . . . The Holy Spirit uses men . . . not by overriding and crushing out their personalities and faculties but in and by means of these very faculties. When . . . they are moved by the Holy Spirit, we know that they speak sincerely, that they speak all the truth they can hold, and that they are on the right road to learn more. We do *not* know that their judgment is thereby made infallible."[9]

The paper on biblical inspiration and authority adopted by the 1979 Annual Conference cites 2 Timothy 3 in three places. Verse 16 is cited twice—once to affirm that the Bible is "inspired of God" and once to acclaim that it is "profitable for teaching, for reproof, for correction, and for training in righteousness." The third citation is in the Appendix, which defines terms. Verses 14-17 are cited as part of the definition of the word *inspiration*.

Included in the task assigned to the committee preparing the paper was the direction to determine representative views among the Brethren on the inspiration and authority of the Bible. This they did with surveys. From the surveys they concluded: "Brethren generally affirm the inspiration of the Bible and the primacy of its authority for faith and practice. Brethren differ on the nature of the inspiration, the equality of authority within the Bible, and the exclusiveness of the Bible's authority in relation to the authority of the church, other inspired writings, and contemporary leading of the Spirit."[10] Thus, the main body of the paper presents the areas of agreement and the areas of disagreement among the Brethren concerning biblical inspiration and authority.

Notes

1. Alexander Mack, Jr., in *European Origins of the Brethren*, comp. and trans. Donald F. Durnbaugh (Elgin, IL: Brethren Press, 1958), 121.

2. "A Humble Gleam," in *Brethren in Colonial America*, ed. Donald F. Durnbaugh (Elgin, IL: Brethren Press, 1967), 430.

3. *Minutes of the Annual Conference of the Church of the Brethren, 1975-1979*, comp. Phyllis Kingery Ruff (Elgin, IL: Brethren Press, 1980), 373.

4. Alexander Mack, *Rights and Ordinances*, in *European Origins of the Brethren*, comp. and trans. Donald F. Durnbaugh (Elgin, IL: Brethren Press, 1958), 383.

5. John Kline, in *Life and Labors of Elder John Kline*, collated from his diary by Benjamin Funk (Elgin, IL: Brethren Publishing House, 1900), 182.

6. H. B. Brumbaugh, *The Brethren's Church Manual* (Huntingdon, PA: Brethren's Publishing Company, 1887), i.

7. Ibid., 5.

8. D. W. Kurtz, "Studies in Doctrine," in *Studies in Doctrine and Devotion* (Elgin, IL: Brethren Publishing House, 1919), 109.

9. Edward Frantz, "How the Bible Came to Us," *Gospel Messenger*, 24 July 1943, 3.

10. *Minutes of the Annual Conference of the Church of the Brethren, 1975-1979*, 559.

The Text in Today's World

The purpose of the biblical canon—to equip persons for good work—has been well defined in verse 17. The Bible is what we call a paradigm for faith and practice. As stated in verse 16, it serves to form Christian life, to educate, and to correct misdirection. The biblical stories tell us how God interacts with us in daily life and forms in us a set of values which guide us from moment to moment. The Bible is not a resource book where we find answers to questions. It is much more the foundation for everyday life. Paul rightly describes our formation as one that results from good role models and an immersion in the sacred or classical writings of the faith community.

Emphasis on the inspiration of the readers of the text alters the meaning of canon. Historically, inspiration of the author can lead to a sense of infallibility or inerrancy. Because of this, some groups of Christians have developed a canon within the canon. Those writings are authoritative which emphasize certain beliefs. For example, Lutherans, who believe in justification by faith, make the writings of Paul their canon within the canon. Other groups believe God would not have inspired contradictions. For them, often of the Reformed tradition, all parts of the canon must agree. Otherwise the Bible is not inspired. But emphasis on the inspiration of the readers makes the canon a paradigm of the community.

For the Free Church, the issue is not to find a specific theme, like justification, or to make the Bible speak with one voice. Members of the Free Church realize there are different understandings and expressions of the gospel. They understand that James emphasizes choice, that Paul emphasizes faith, that John emphasizes perception, that Matthew emphasizes discipleship, that Luke emphasizes servanthood. They rejoice in these different understanding of the gospel. For the Free Church, the canon shows how the Spirit holds together in *one* faith community all these valid, different perceptions of the Christian faith. With growing pluralism in all levels of our society, we very much need the ability to believe firmly in our own perception, yet rejoice in another's perception.

In the early church the formation of the canon was a matter of holding together various regions of the Mediterranean world and their specific understanding of the good news. So, for example, Antioch probably championed Matthew, Ephesus promoted John, Rome claimed Mark, Jerusalem liked James. The canon enabled everyone to belong to the one Christian community, yet hold to their own perception of the faith.

The formation of the canon was the first attempt to define ecumenicity. It did not define the one faith but defined the way various groups could live and work in unity. Heresy was not so much a belief system outside the canon (although Gnosticism might have qualified), as it was the insistence on being correct to the exclusion of others. Through the ages most Christian aberrations have been just that, building a whole system on only a part of the New Testament.

While today we would do well to base our ecumenicity on the whole canon rather than any more narrow creed, we also realize that most denominations now are ecumenical movements in their own right. As Brethren enter a period of growth and inclusion of others, there must be a basis for our unity as a denomination. That basis will be the canon of the New Testament. It will be the accepted authority because it has been read by a community inspired by the Holy Spirit.

Case Study

The doorbell rang at the home of Sarah and Alexander Kline. A pleasant, well-dressed couple stood on the porch. "Are you Christians?" the woman asked. "Yes," responded Brother Kline. "Do you worship on Sunday?" "Yes," responded Sister Kline. "But in the book of Genesis it says that God blessed the seventh day and hallowed it, because on it God rested from all the work that he had done in creation," said the man. Before the Klines could answer the woman added, "And in the Ten Commandments we are told to keep the Sabbath day holy. You do believe in the Ten Commandments, don't you?" Sarah Kline intervened quickly, "Oh yes, we Brethren take the Ten Commandments quite seriously." "Then," asked the man, "why don't you worship on the seventh day, the real Sabbath, like we do?"

How would you respond to the couple? What do you think of these very different responses:

1. We Brethren do not consider the Old Testament to be inspired of God, so we do not take it as authoritative. Therefore, we do not keep the Sabbath.

2. We Brethren take the Old Testament to be inspired, but as a faith community we have not taken it to be authoritative. So we do not keep the Sabbath.

3. We Brethren believe the Old Testament was inspired and was authoritative for Jews, but as Christians we interpret the Old Testament through the New Testament. The first Christians worshiped on Sunday. So we worship and rest on Sunday.

4. We Brethren believe Jesus was the ultimate revelation of God. Jesus died on the cross and was raised on the first day of the week. So we celebrate the first day, Sunday, as the beginning of new life. The Sabbath represents the last day of the old age. When we come together for worship on Sunday, we give thanks that the old is passing away and the new is here. Would you like to join us for church this Sunday morning?

Session 23

On Faith and Works

James 2:18-26 (NRSV)

But someone will say, "You have faith and I have works." Show me your faith apart from your works, and I by my works will show you my faith. [19]You believe that God is one; you do well. Even the demons believe—and shudder. [20]Do you want to be shown, you senseless person, that faith apart from works is barren? [21]Was not our ancestor Abraham justified by works when he offered his son Isaac on the altar? [22]You see that faith was active along with his works, and faith was brought to completion by the works. [23]Thus the scripture was fulfilled that says, "Abraham believed God, and it was reckoned to him as righteousness," and he was called the friend of God. [24]You see that a person is justified by works and not by faith alone. [25]Likewise, was not Rahab the prostitute also justified by works when she welcomed the messengers and sent them out by another road? [26]For just as the body without the spirit is dead, so faith without works is also dead.

James 2:18-26 (BNT)

But, someone may say, "You have faith, but I have works." Show me your faith apart from works, and I will show you my faith which arises from works. [19]You believe that God is one? The demons also believe and their response is to shudder with fear. [20]Do you want to see, you empty person, that faith apart from works is sterile? [21]Was not our father Abraham justified by works when he placed his son Isaac on the altar? [22]Do you not see that his faith went right along with his works, and faith was completed by works? [23]And the scripture was fulfilled which says, "Abraham believed God, and he was considered righteous." And he was called a friend of God. [24]Do you see that a person is justified from works, and not from faith only. [25]And likewise was not Rahab the harlot justified by works when she received the messengers and then sent them out by another way. [26]For as the body apart from the spirit is dead, so also faith apart from works is dead.

The Text in Its Biblical Setting

The Letter of James has no equivalent in the New Testament. First of all, it hardly has the form of a letter. Those who have read the letters of Paul will miss the extended greetings, prayers, thanksgivings, exhortations, and final salutations. After a short address, the book of James instead jumps rapidly from topic to topic without any self-evident order to the material. A number of reasons have been offered for this peculiarity. Some have suggested that James was not a letter, but a speech or discussion in which the material we have is the answer of the author to questions we no longer possess. Another excellent possibility is that James represents the single complete piece of wisdom literature in the New Testament (see 1:5). In wisdom literature, as is evident in the book of Proverbs, the subject can shift very quickly without transitions.

Secondly, James presents a style of faith which differs markedly from that of any other writer in the New Testament. It reflects the outlook of certain Jewish groups in the New Testament period who saw the problem of life as a struggle between good and evil within the person. They thought that all people had within them a good impulse and a bad impulse. Religious people were ones who subdued or controlled the bad impulse and allowed the good impulse to rule their lives and daily decisions. God gave believers strength to follow the good impulse. In James 1:12-15 the author speaks of temptation as a person's own desire. It is this desire or impulse which gives rise to sin (v. 15). The real problem for a person would be uncertainty about the good impulse and how it differs from the bad impulse. Such uncertainty was called "doublemindedness" or doubt. The person who lacks wisdom (regarding the two impulses) lives in doubt and so is tossed to and fro (Jas. 1:5-8). Presumably, then, the Letter of James was written so that Christians might have the wisdom of God necessary to recognize and follow the good impulse in everyday decisions.

Because of this Jewish emphasis on decision making and daily practice, the book of James stands over against what might be called cheap grace. The author doubts that faith alone can create a sense of well-being and acceptance (righteousness) with God or with others. Righteousness derives from a sense of wholeness in life (v. 26).

This particular section (2:18-26) illustrates very well the style and intent of the author. The one-sided conversation with the foolish person is fairly clear: there is a question about faith and works (v. 18); a question about faith in the oneness of God (v. 19); and a question about faith alone (v. 20).

The reader needs to be very careful here. Some, including many early Protestant scholars, have assumed the faith-works conflict reflects an early Judaizing reaction to Paul's emphasis on faith (Rom. 1:16-17). That probably is not true. It is likely James was written before Paul became popular, so they can hardly have locked horns. Furthermore, the faith mentioned in v. 18 has little to do with Paul's notion of faith.

By faith Paul meant trust. For him trust was an active, relational stance toward God and others. By the word *faith*, James does not mean trust. He is referring to belief as a system or proposition. *Faith* here is belief in the existence and power of God, not trust and communion as in Paul. From this perspective we can see that even the demons can believe in the existence of God (v. 19). We also can understand that such belief systems are of little value unless they express themselves in our lives (v. 18).

James uses Abraham as an example or proof of his position. He claims that Abraham did believe in God, but it was not until he was willing to sacrifice his son Isaac that his faith was completed by works. Then it could be said that it (his faith) was reckoned to him as righteousness (Gen. 15:6). Several of the New Testament writers used Abraham as an example. In Romans 4:1-5, Paul, defining faith in his own way, understood the same text in Genesis to mean that Abraham was justified by faith alone. In yet another way, the author of Hebrews defined faith as moving toward the promise without knowing where to go. Faith was total trust in God's leading. Because Abraham, in obedience to God, left his father's house in Haran, he was a man of faith (Heb. 11:8).

Rahab (Josh. 2:1-21) presents more difficulties. Despite the fact that Rahab was a prostitute, or perhaps because of it, early Christians saw in her an analogy of grace. She was justified because of her role in the taking of the promised land. Matthew, who included four "irregular" women in the genealogy of Jesus (Tamar, Rahab, Ruth, and Bathsheba), spoke of Rahab as the mother of Boaz, second husband of non-Jewish Ruth. Although the author of Hebrews generally extolled those who ventured forth in faith, he praised Rahab for her hospitality to the Hebrew spies. Despite the obvious "grace" involved, James argues that she was justified for her work in facilitating the destruc-

tion of Jericho (v. 25). Just as a corpse has no life, so faith is also dead
without resultant action (v. 26).

The Text in Brethren Life

Since the time of Martin Luther (1483-1546), there has existed a
debate over whether salvation is by faith or by works. One of Luther's
primary tenets was that justification is by faith alone. Thus, it is not
surprising that he placed little value on the letter of James with its
emphasis on works. Brethren, however, have a fondness for James.
For them faith and works cannot exist independent of one another.
No doubt this understanding of faith and works comes, in part, from
their roots in Radical Pietism and Anabaptism. For the Pietists, faith
must be active in love. For the Anabaptists, faith always results in
obedience.

Alexander Mack (1679-1735) tackled the faith/works debate in his
Basic Questions (1713). Question 21 asks: "If baptism is made an
absolutely necessary commandment for salvation, will this not introduce a new papacy, and bring about salvation by works?" In reply
Mack affirms that salvation is "by faith in Christ alone." Then he
continues: "If it is to be a saving faith, it must produce works of
obedience. Where that faith is not present which produces obedience
(not according to the pope's doctrine and command but rather by the
command of Jesus the crucified), then no salvation is promised for a
single work done without faith."[1] Thus Mack early laid down the
Brethren understanding that faith is made known by works, the view
found in James 2.

Peter Nead (1796-1877) elaborated further on the relationship of
faith to works. His 1834 *Primitive Christianity* states: "Mere Faith will
save no man; for James tells us that 'Faith without works is dead.' . . .
Yea, it is vain, and will profit us nothing: therefore, in order to
salvation, when one believes in the Gospel, he ought to yield obedience to the same; and then it is, that his Faith will save his soul."[2] Later
in 1845 Nead published a large pamphlet which included an essay
titled "Faith Alone and Prayerless Doctrine Considered." In this essay
Nead argues "that it is an error to teach, that man is saved by faith
only."[3] To prove his argument Nead quotes biblical texts which show
that there is more to salvation than faith. Among the texts quoted is
James 2:14-20. After quoting James, Nead says: "Now it is very plain
that the faith commanded in the Gospel, is the parent and principle

of obedience. It is a working and not a fruitless faith. When faith is not united to obedience, it is imperfect or dead, being alone."[4]

John Kline (1797-1864) presented the Brethren view of his day in a sermon preached on November 4, 1848. Kline begins by noting that he is sometimes accused of teaching "a doctrine of works." In his reply to this accusation, he says:

> We as Brethren believe and teach that "faith without works is dead." All good works are done in faith. And no man can believe in the Lord Jesus Christ with his heart, without loving him; because faith is loving acceptance of all the truth revealed by the Lord to man. Our heartfelt reception of that truth leads to obedience, and obedience to good works.[5]

The Brethren emphasis on works of obedience clearly lies behind a pamphlet by J. H. Moore (1846-1935) titled "The Perfect Plan of Salvation; or Safe Ground" (1874). While the primary purpose of the pamphlet is to convince non-Brethren of the necessity of Brethren practices—trine immersion, the love feast, and the Holy Kiss—the opening pages link these practices to obedience as part of the plan of salvation. Included in Moore's divine system of religion is "ONE FAITH, made perfect by works, of which Jesus is the author and finisher."[6]

One year after the publication of Moore's pamphlet, another pamphlet titled "True Evangelical Obedience" appeared. This pamphlet, written by J. W. Stein (1842-1908), at that time a recent convert to the Brethren, focuses on the importance of obedience in the life of faith. Stein begins by making a clear distinction between works of the law, which are useless, and "*works* of gospel obedience, which are indispensable constituents of living faith, (Jas. ii:14-20) and *by which a man is justified* (Jas. ii:24)."[7] While Stein affirms Paul's words that a person is justified by faith and not deeds in the introduction, he spends the remaining thirty-one pages explaining why works of obedience are necessary.

In the twentieth century, Brethren moved away from the use of the word *obedience*, when describing the relationship of faith and works, to use of the word *service*. The process of this shift can be seen in a 1919 study of doctrine by D. W. Kurtz (1879-1949). When defining faith Kurtz discusses three activities of the mind: (1) belief, (2) trust and love, (3) obedience. Kurtz's discussion of obedience begins by citing James 2:17-20. These verses from James, says Kurtz, show that even in the early church there existed the false notion that faith is only belief in doctrines. Continuing on, Kurtz says: "Faith in Christ means to surrender to him or obey him. This does not mean to 'give up the will,' but to use the will, and purely choose the way, the truth, and the life. But choosing Christ and following him is obedience. It means service."[8] Kurtz begins with obedience and ends with service.

By 1943 Edward Frantz (1868-1964) had totally abandoned the word *obedience* in favor of the word *service* when writing about faith and works in his book *Basic Beliefs*. Frantz's discussion of doctrine and service includes the following: "The value of what a man believes concerning any fundamental doctrine of Christian faith is shown not by what he says about it but by what he does about it . . . . It [service] shows what aspects of doctrine have real bearing on soundness in faith . . . . Service is *not* more basic than belief in determining character, but it is the index to the value of the belief behind it."[9] While the primary text which Frantz cites when discussing doctrine and service is Matthew 25:31-46, he also includes James 2:18 in his Scripture index for the discussion.[10]

The late-twentieth century Brethren understanding of faith and works as presented in James 2 is well summed up by Willard Dulabaum in an article about volunteer service:

> James 2, of course, is a delight for service-minded Brethren! We take pride in our emphasis upon making love practical and tangible . . . . Perhaps we do not witness well enough in word, or claim as much credit for our deeds as some would have us. But our real strength has been service designed to get the job done, with as much joy in creating partnerships as in taking credit. If others can be found to help in the job, fine. The call continues to go out: "Faith, by itself, if it has no works, is dead."[11]

Notes

1. Alexander Mack, *Basic Questions*, in *European Origins of the Brethren*, comp. and trans. Donald F. Durnbaugh (Elgin, IL: Brethren Press, 1958), 335-336.

2. Peter Nead, *Primitive Christianity, or a Vindication of the Word of God* (Staunton, VA: Kenton Harper, Printer, 1834), 37.

3. Peter Nead, *Theological Writings, or a Vindication of the Word of God* (Dayton, OH: the author, 1850), 313.

4. Ibid., 314.

5. John Kline, *Life and Labors of Elder John Kline*, collated from his diary by Benjamin Funk (Elgin, IL: Brethren Publishing House, 1900), 242.

6. J. H. Moore, "The Perfect Plan of Salvation; or Safe Ground" (Urbana, IL: G. W. Flynn & Co., 1874), 7.

7. J. W. Stein, "True Evangelical Obedience" (Danville, IL: Illinois Printing Co., 1875), 1.

8. D. W. Kurtz, "Studies in Doctrine," in *Studies in Doctrine and Devotion* (Elgin, IL: Brethren Publishing House, 1919), 76.

9. Edward Frantz, *Basic Belief* (Elgin, IL: Brethren Publishing House, 1943), 92-94.

10. Ibid., 171.

11. Willard E. Dulabaum, "Putting It All Together," *A Guide for Biblical Studies* 92 (March-May 1977), 82.

The Text in Today's World

Few texts more exemplify the heart of the Church of the Brethren than this one. As can be seen from the exegesis and the history, the issue is not that of salvation by works. That is not to say Brethren and similar groups have not drifted toward salvation by works. There is always that temptation to believe right action will gain approval, and we have done that. On the other hand, though, we need to note that many peculiarities of the Church of the Brethren have been community marks, rather than works of salvation (dress codes, feetwashing, love feast, prayer veil). The insistence on works signifies a wholistic understanding of life. While the moment of faith may be the beginning of action, without that action faith becomes a spiritual gnosticism. Earlier theologians spoke of a faith (*fiducia*) which results in concrete faith action (*credentia*). To be sure, one may enter the moment of faith without acting on it, but we consider that spiritually sick. One may speak of love without marriage, but we think of such persons as Don Juans. James argues against such partitions. Brethren today will resist the same temptations. Those who call on us to believe in Jesus Christ or to accept the infallibility of Scriptures or to experience rebirth—all must be asked about wholeness. Is it only faith? Or does that faith you proclaim lead to membership in the faith community, lead to care for others, lead to sharing of resources, lead to love of peace?

In more recent times, yet another perspective strikes us. Sociologists of knowledge and linguistic philosophers argue that in communication first comes action, then symbols, and finally language. Granted, action arises from some conviction (faith); the language of faith that we speak actually arises from the actions of faith that we do. The language of faith may change from time to time, but the action of faith remains steady. Because of this, Brethren can well argue that faith and Christian formation derive more from working together than from thinking together, or even experiencing together. We are not speaking of salvation by works but of basic formation for living.

Brethren have nearly always argued for the practical approach to faith. Workcamps, service projects, and disaster teams may appear on paper as care for others, but Brethren know that working together forms faith. Working together makes for a peace not based on argument or creed. Like potlucks (rather than catered meals), the church needs work days, repair jobs, and service projects simply because the church must work together. A church which has common physical labor to do will likely find a common denominator in its fellowship more quickly than one that does not. People will even develop new skills in order to join the "labor force" (if that is where community is formed).

Case Study

To the sorrow of everyone in Sauer Memorial Church, the Brumbaugh family has been moved by Sister Brumbaugh's accounting firm. They will go to the Butte, Montana branch of the firm. The Brumbaugh's have talked at length to the pastor about the transfer. There is no Church of the Brethren close enough to Butte for them to consider. The pastor offered to call one of her friends who was a United Church of Christ pastor in that city. "No," said Brother Brumbaugh, "we are going to join the Mormon church there." "Oh no," responded the pastor, "They consider the Book of Mormon more important than the New Testament. How could you, such a well-known Brethren family, become Mormons?"

To this Sister Brumbaugh replied, "We don't know much about the Book of Mormon and their beliefs, but we are surprised by your objections. They have a strong family life, like the Brethren. They believe in adult baptism, like the Brethren. They oppose the use of drugs, even coffee and tea, like the Brethren. They have a program of overseas witness by their youth, just like the Brethren. They have a strong sense of community, like the Brethren; and they dislike ritual and liturgy, just like the Brethren. Why would you object to our joining the Mormons?"

1. If you were the pastor at Sauer Memorial, how would you respond?

2. Would you consider the Mormons, if you were transferred to a place where there was no Church of the Brethren?

3. If you were to choose a new church, to what extent would the beliefs of the church affect your choice?

Session 24

On Anointing for Healing

James 5:13-16 (NRSV)

Are any among you suffering? They should pray. Are any cheerful? They should sing songs of praise. [14]Are any among you sick? They should call for the elders of the church and have them pray over them, anointing them with oil in the name of the Lord. [15]The prayer of faith will save the sick, and the Lord will raise them up; and anyone who has committed sins will be forgiven. [16]Therefore confess your sins to one another, and pray for one another, so that you may be healed. The prayer of the righteous is powerful and effective.

James 5:13-16 (BNT)

Are there any among you who are depressed? Let them pray. Are any cheerful? Let them sing. [14]Are there any among you sick? Let them summon the elders of the church, and let the elders pray over them, anointing them with oil in the name of the Lord. [15]Prayer offered in good faith makes whole those who are sick. The Lord will restore them, and if any have committed sins, he will forgive them. [16]So then confess your sins to each other, and pray for each other, so that you may be healed. The prayer of a righteous person works with profound effect.

The Text in Its Biblical Setting

The wisdom of James is preeminently congregational. True religion is visiting the widows and orphans (1:27). The royal law coming from the scripture is to love one's neighbor (2:8). Gossiping does more than anything else to destroy the community (3:6). Quarrels come from giving in to the evil impulse (4:1-10). Gaining riches creates dissension in the community (5:1-6; 2:1-7). So the passage 5:13–16 should also be understood in a community context. Verse 13 suggests that individuals with problems may participate in the "services" of the faith community. Those who are depressed would do well to join in the prayers. Those who are happy and cheerful, on the other hand, should join in the singing. In Colossians 3:12-17 we have an excellent description of the kind of life in the early church which made this possible: The church was bound together by forgiveness, love, and the peace of God. Its "service" was the presentation of the word in teaching and preaching (admonishing), and the singing of psalms, hymns, and songs (Col. 3:16). The author of James suggests, therefore, that individual moods can be celebrated or caught up in the regular structure of community worship. Likewise, illness should be handled in the context of the faith community. The elements of the community's service to the sick were: a visit from the elders; a prayer by the elders (or the church members, see v. 16); anointing by the elders; and confession of sins.

In the ancient world, the direct association of healing with divine activity was assumed. There was a somewhat scientific or non-cultic approach to medicine in the Greek world, starting with Aristotle, but the Roman world held doctors in a rather low repute. Consequently, the major healing institutions of the New Testament period were still religious groups, primarily that of Asklepios. Asklepios was the Greek god of medicine, and his shrines were places of healing. At his temples were priests skilled in healing, although much was accomplished simply by having the patient sleep overnight (with the god) in the temple (incubation). Accounts of miraculous cures by incubation can be found in all parts of the Roman empire. In the third century B.C., a snake in which Asklepios was said to reside was brought to Rome to avert a deadly epidemic, and a temple was built on an island in the Tiber River. That temple may still be seen with the snake on a staff, the symbol of modern medicine.

The Judeo-Christian approach to healing was somewhat different from that of Asklepios. The God of Israel was also a healing god and the temple priests made judgment on such matters (Mark 1:43). But the Judeo-Christian faith was much more psychosomatic and community-minded in its understanding of illness. We see, especially in the psalms, that illness, sin, and alienation from the community are all the same thing. Look, for example, at the remarkable description in Psalm 102:3-11. In the New Testament and the early church, illness was directly associated with alienation from the faith community. In 1 Corinthians 11, Paul ascribes the cause of illness and even death in the Corinthian church community to the fact that some do not properly discern the body of Christ. They, therefore, participate in love feast and communion on a false basis (v. 30). Early in the first century, another Christian, Ignatius of Antioch, struggled with schismatics who refused to participate in the communion of the church. He claims that breaking bread together is the medicine for eternal life, an antidote against death itself (Ignatius to the Ephesians [20:2]). According to Ignatius, being schismatic obviously creates illnesses, and full participation in the life of the church is a "medicine." Little wonder then that the author of James advises the ill person to call upon the church. It seems probable, though not certain, that James would suppose the illness to be due to some friction with other members of the church. At least he assumes the necessity of a confession. In any case the order is as follows:

1. **Call upon the elders.** Elders were older natural leaders in the Near Eastern world. According to Acts, elders were functioning as leaders in the Jerusalem church where tradition says that James himself was resident (11:30). At the same, time elders were also appointed by Paul and Barnabas in Hellenistic churches (Acts 14:23), so this form of organization was fairly universal. To call upon the elders was to call upon the whole church through its representatives.

2. **Pray.** We have already noted how frequently the power of the faith community is stressed in these twenty-six texts. In Matthew 18 (see Session 5), we were informed that whatever the community decided had already been determined in heaven. Here we discover the same thing. The prayer of the elders, acting on behalf of the faith community, will have the power to heal. In verse 16b, James states emphatically that a person at one with the congregation and the Lord ("a righteous person") has much power in prayer.

3. **Anoint with oil.** Oil was used for a variety of solemn occasions such as coronation (1 Sam. 10:1) or at death (Mark 16:1). It was also used to signify healing, as a balm for wounds (Isa. 1:6), or as a sign of the healing action of God (Mark 6:13). Here we have the solemn use of oil to signify the concern of the church. The phrase "in the name of the Lord" refers not just to the power of the example of Jesus but to the continuing power of the Lord's community (Acts 3:5-6).

4. **Confess sin.** If illness is associated with alienation from the community of God, there must be a moment when the sick person confesses that alienation. There is no exact parallel to this practice elsewhere in the New Testament, though in Matthew 5 the disciple is urged to become reconciled with members of the congregation before "going to church" (5:23-24). In any event, confessing one's brokenness is a prerequisite to experiencing healing.

The Text in Brethren Life

While it is generally affirmed that the Brethren practiced anointing since their beginning in 1708, there is no documentation of the anointing among the Brethren prior to 1770. Writing about 1770, Morgan Edwards (1722-1795), a Baptist pastor and historian, included the Brethren in his multi-volume work about the Baptists in America. Edward's description of Brethren practices contains the following reference to anointing: "They anoint the sick with oil for recovery."[1] The first mention of anointing by the Brethren themselves is in the minutes of the 1797 Annual Meeting: "From James 5:14, etc., the brethren testified unanimously, 'That the sick who desire and call for it should be anointed, according to the word of the holy apostle, in the name of the Lord.' "[2] Unfortunately, the query giving rise to this affirmation of the anointing service is not stated in the minutes.

Two specifications about anointing are noted in the minutes for 1812. First, the anointing is to be administered only if the person being anointed seeks no further aid from physicians. Second, there is no biblical reason why a person, having been anointed and recovered, cannot again be anointed if again taken ill. The minutes of 1827 outline the anointing service. First, a few verses are sung and a prayer is spoken.

> Then (there should always be two brethren) the one reaches forth his hand and the other poureth the oil on it, and the first puts the same on the head of the sick, and says the words, which the Apostles James teaches (chap. 5:14), "Thou art anointed in the name of the Lord." and thus three times, but the words only once said. Then both brethren lay their hands upon the head of the sick, and pray over him, for it is not considered to be intended only

an inward unction, but an outward anointing, whereof the apostle speaks, as mentioned before.[3]

A more detailed outline of the service is found in the minutes for 1860.

The Annual Meeting minutes indicate that two basic questions concerning anointing arose in the nineteenth century: Who in the church should preside at the anointing service, and who could receive the anointing? In response to the first question, the Annual Meetings repeatedly said that ordained elders (bishops) were to preside at anointings except in cases of necessity where two elders could not be obtained. The basis for this reply was, of course, the reference to elders in James 5:14. Regarding who could be anointed, the minutes of 1850 stated that only members of the church could receive anointing, and the minutes of 1852 said that anointing was meant for sick persons. It should also be noted that by 1860 the minutes indicate that a person might continue to use medicine after receiving the anointing. This seems to be a reversal of the 1812 statement that a person should not enlist further aid from physicians after being anointed.

Peter Nead (1796-1877), presents anointing as more than a service based upon the example of James 5:14-15. Nead, writing in 1834, says: "Now, all those who desire to have this holy work [the anointing] performed upon them ought to be perfectly reconciled unto the will of God—in particular as it respects their recovery from a bed of affliction. Yes, they ought to make a complete surrender of themselves into the hands of the Lord."[4] With this statement Nead characterizes the anointing as more than a petition for physical healing. It is an act whereby the sick person accepts the will of God, whether that be health, continued sickness, or death.

L. W. Teeter (1845-1927), in a late nineteenth-century tract titled "Anointing the Sick," presents further interpretative comments about the anointing service. There are, says Teeter, a primary design and a secondary design of the service. The primary design is physical restoration of the body. The secondary design consists of three blessings or promises based upon verse 15. First, "the prayer of faith will save the sick." The full extent of this salvation is known only to God. Second, "the Lord will raise them up." While, as in the first promise, the exact nature of the raising up is not known, the sick person can be sure that it will be what is best in his or her situation. Third, "anyone who has committed sins will be forgiven." This, says Teeter, is a clear promise that all sins of the sick person will be forgiven, not just those sins which may have brought on the present illness. Teeter completes his tract with an explanation as to why the *laying on of hands*, which is also part of ordination and baptism among the Brethren, follows the actual anointing as part of the service. According to Teeter, the phrase "pray over them" in verse 14 implies that the elders will lay their hands upon the head of the sick person and offer a special prayer on his or her behalf. To support the association of laying on of hands with anointing, Teeter cites Mark 6:13; 16:18; and Acts 28:8.

A popular discussion of anointing in the twentieth century is the booklet titled "Anointing for Healing" by Warren D. Bowman (1894-1987), a pastor and college president. Originally written in 1942, Bowman revised it twice and it was reprinted many times. In addition to describing the anointing service and its expected results, Bowman answers several questions about anointing. First, concerning whether children should be anointed, Bowman says: "While a child may understand the anointing only in part, or perhaps not at all, the prayers of the ministers and others . . . could have a powerful effect."[5] Second, concerning whether people near death should be anointed, Bowman concludes: "While not denying this service to our aged saints who desire it as a spiritual blessing, we should emphasize that this is not the main function of anointing, that its main function is for healing."[6] Third, as to whether an unconscious patient should be anointed, Bowman points to the fact that anointing often gives great comfort to the sick person's relatives and "that Jesus performed some of his greatest miracles of healing because of the faith of the patient's relatives."[7]

A 1963 report to Annual Conference includes a discussion of the biblical basis of anointing, consideration of the relationship of anointing to modern medicine, a statement of the place of anointing in spiritual health, and a presentation of the procedures of the anointing service. Concerning the effect of anointing on sick persons, the report says: "Individuals who were fearful or under strain have found peace and contentment within God's will and have been led to commit themselves wholly to God's loving care. With it have also come forgiveness of sins, a strengthened faith, and, in many instances, some most remarkable in character, the healing of body, mind and emotions, as well as the restoration of social relationships. In cases where full physical healing was not experienced, the service has helped the persons involved to say with Christ, 'Not my will, but Thine be done.' "[8] Concerning the relationship of the anointing to contemporary healing sciences, the report states: "The anointing service should not be expected to take the place of but work in cooperation with the proper use of medicine in treatment of bodily ills, of psychology or psychiatry in dealing with emotional ills, or of psychiatric social work in treatment of ruptured personal relationships."[9]

The theme of the 1987 Annual Conference was ANOINTED. During the conference the various uses of anointing in the Bible were highlighted, including "hospitality, holiness, consecration, installation, leadership, and gladness and festivity as well as healing."[10] In connection with the emphasis on anointing in 1987, a new pamphlet was published titled "Anointing: A Biblical Teaching as Practiced by the Church of the Brethren" by Dean M. Miller. According to Miller the service of anointing can properly be used in the following situations: physical illness, accident or sudden trauma, impending surgery, critical decisions, risk and vulnerability, reconciliation, emotional pain, and spiritual renewal.

Notes

1. "Morgan Edwards on Pennsylvania Congregations," in *Brethren in Colonial America*, ed. Donald F. Durnbaugh (Elgin, IL: Brethren Press, 1967), 174.

2. *Minutes of the Annual Meetings of the Church of the Brethren, 1778-1909* (Elgin, IL: Brethren Publishing House, 1909), 19.

3. Ibid., 50.

4. Peter Nead, *Primitive Christianity, or a Vindication of the Word of God* (Staunton, VA: Kenton Harper, Printer, 1834), 142.

5. Warren D. Bowman, "Anointing for Healing" (Elgin, IL: Church of the Brethren, 1942), 21-22.

6. Ibid., 23.

7. Ibid., 24-25.

8. *Minutes of the Annual Conferences of the Church of the Brethren, 1955-1964*, comp. and ed. Ora W. Garber (Elgin, IL: Brethren Press, 1965), 280.

9. Ibid., 283.

10. Phyllis Kingery Ruff, "Secretary's Report," in *Minutes of the Annual Conference of the Church of the Brethren, 1985-1989*, comp. Annual Conference Office (Elgin, IL: Brethren Press, 1990), 349.

The Text in Today's World

It may be that the modern, scientific world view has eroded the meaning of one of the richest of the Brethren practices, the anointing for healing. During the nineteenth century, concern for anointing shifted from healing to the problem of proper order. During the more recent decades of this century, interest has centered on the psychological or psychosomatic function of confession, prayer, and anointing. As the focus of our concern has shifted in these ways, some of the original importance of the practice was lost. We lost sight of the truth that illness can derive from alienation. Our biblical heritage states strongly that personhood derives from community involvement. To lose that community involvement either by separation, alienation, or isolation can and likely does result in some form of illness. The Bible even speaks of severe alienation as death. But we have tended to speak of illness as a physical phenomenon which can be diagnosed and controlled scientifically. Or when we have spoken psychosomatically, we have tended to think of healing in the context of an individual patient-therapist relationship rather than in terms of the faith community. James 5 points us to reconciliation in the community as a means of dealing with illness.

Faith healing is coming back in our day. The practice of anointing will likely become popular, once again. Brethren may be tempted to go the direction of "faith healing" in which one person prays with power that God will intervene in the life of sick persons to make them whole. James 5 should lead us in quite another direction. The elders represent the church and pray in the name of the Lord. They were not persons of unusual gifts or abilities. In fact, the author of James notes that his example, Elijah, was a person just like us (5:17). So though persons who need healing may call on the elders to represent the church, they also can confess to each other and pray for each other. The Brethren of this century could well move to recapture this priesthood of all believers in the realm of healing. Some churches have organized lay ministries for the sick, which catch up the meaning of James 5. Visiting by lay persons is not just a courtesy. For people who are sick the power of the faith community praying in the name of the Lord is enormous. It is indeed a healing ministry.

This is not to deny that there are particular persons who have specific gifts or skills to share in the healing of the sick. Whether in the medical community, the psychological community, or the religious community, there are those equipped to contribute in special ways to the ministry of healing. In the final analysis, however, healing is a function of the faith community. Only as we experience the support and fellowship of a caring community of love can we discover the strength to be truly whole.

Case Study

A doctor in the Cove (Middle Pennsylvania) had a patient of Pennsylvania German extraction who was six months pregnant. She was newly married and this was her first child. However, she showed every sign of a possible miscarriage. The doctor, a member of a local Church of the Brethren congregation, was puzzled. There was no sign of a physical problem. He strongly suspected his patient was having psychosomatic problems. So he spoke to the young woman about the Brethren anointing service and asked if she would like to have the anointing for her and her baby. The woman said she would. So the doctor called in the woman's pastor and his own pastor. The two represented her congregation and her larger community in the service. When she came to the point of confession, she became nearly hysterical and said that her parents strongly disapproved of the man she had married and by whom she was pregnant. She simply could not bring herself to disobey her parents (and the words of Jesus). The two pastors anointed her, spoke of God's love in Jesus Christ, promised to speak to her parents, and assured her of the complete support of her faith community. She carried the baby full term.

1. Do you believe her physical problem could have been caused by her faith and family crisis?

2. Do you believe the anointing service could have "cured" her, or do you think she just passed through a difficult time of her pregnancy?

3. The woman was not Brethren. Do you consider the anointing service valid for anyone in the context of their own community. Or would it be valid without any community?

4. Had you been the doctor would you have used a religious service to help your patient?

5. When there is such a health problem in your church (or community) do you have support groups to help?

Session 25

On Doing as Jesus Did

1 Peter 2:18-25 (NRSV)

Slaves, accept the authority of your masters with all deference, not only those who are kind and gentle but also those who are harsh. [19]For it is a credit to you if, being aware of God, you endure pain while suffering unjustly. [20]If you endure when you are beaten for doing wrong, what credit is that? But if you endure when you do right and suffer for it, you have God's approval. [21]For to this you have been called, because Christ also suffered for you, leaving you an example, so that you should follow in his steps. [22]"He committed no sin, and no deceit was found in his mouth." [23]When he was abused, he did not return abuse; when he suffered, he did not threaten; but he entrusted himself to the one who judges justly. [24]He himself bore our sins in his body on the cross, so that, free from sins, we might live for righteousness; by his wounds you have been healed. [25]For you were going astray like sheep, but now you have returned to the shepherd and guardian of your souls.

1 Peter 2:18-25 (BNT)

You who are domestic slaves, respectfully submit to your masters, not just to those who are good and kind, but also to those who are harsh. [19]It would be most appropriate if, because of your God-consciousness, any of you endured pain though suffering unjustly. [20]For what value is there in it if you *do wrong* and take the beating patiently? But if you *do good* and suffer patiently, that is appropriate in the eyes of God. [21]For this is why you were called, because even Christ suffered on your behalf, leaving you a pattern so that you could trace his steps. [22]He never committed a sin, and deceit was never found on his lips. [23]Though he was abused he did not answer back, and though he suffered he did not threaten retaliation, but entrusted himself to the one who judges justly. [24]He himself bore our wrongdoing in his body on the tree, in order that we might not take part in sin any longer, but might live in righteousness. By his lashings you were healed. [25]Once you were like so many sheep wandering around aimlessly, but now you have turned to the one who is the shepherd, the one who takes care of your personal lives.

The Text in Its Biblical Setting

Like the Apostle Paul, Peter understood the function of Jesus as that of a reconciler and our Christian life as a calling to continue that task of reconciliation. However, there are sharp differences between the two writers. Paul sees the reconciler as one who aggressively seeks to bring about reconciliation by certain acts of love or by telling the good news. Paul was "evangelistic." Peter, in this letter at least, does not describe such missionary zeal. Peter sees the world in conflict between those who live in obedience to the truth, who love one another, and who have been born anew(1:22-23) on the one hand, and those who live in "futile ways" (1:18) on the other. In this conflict it is the responsibility of the Christian to stand between the lines, so to speak, exhibiting the innocence and good deeds of a believer but taking abuse and attack from the forces of evil. There seems to be no deliberate attempt to convert others, though Peter does hope, if not assume, that eventually this posture will result in a change for the non-believers (2:12). In this respect 1 Peter reads much like the Gospel of Mark where we learn of a Jesus who must suffer many things (Mark 8:31-34; 1 Pet. 2:24). There is more of an emphasis on the cross than on the new life of the resurrection. It is generally supposed the letter of 1 Peter actually contains a baptismal sermon designed to encourage new Christians in their faith.

This being the case, it is not surprising that the "house code" in 1 Peter does not have the same function as it did for Paul. For Paul the household codes discouraged that self-seeking for freedom and equality (the end-time expectation) which could be spiritually self-destructive. The codes were a means of expressing ultimate values within the limitations of the present social milieu. The codes in Paul describe life "between the times." For Peter the codes describe what it means to suffer innocently. This is especially true of the master-slave section found in 2:18-25. Peter does not assume that both master and slave are Christian. To the contrary, he speaks to the probable situation where a Christian slave might well be owned by a hostile master. He advises such a slave to submit to the regulations and orders of the master. This is necessary because if the master is hostile for good reason, then the redemptive role of the slave has been destroyed. But if slaves do not deserve the hostility, then they, as the supposedly powerless persons, can have considerable effect on the supposedly powerful master.

Peter uses this example as a stepping stone into his Christology. The Christ was not a warrior type, nor one who used "power" to achieve the will of God. Rather, he became powerless like the slave, suffering like the slave. Through it all, he was innocent of any charges brought against him and did nothing to deserve the hostility he received. In shifting from the household code to Christology, the author also shifted to a more general audience. All Christians should adopt the "pattern" left by Jesus the Christ (2:21). For Brethren it is verse 21 which has been so important in determining the nature of Christian life.

Clearly the author urges us to follow in the steps of Jesus Christ. But in what sense are we to walk in those steps? Peter speaks of Jesus as a *hypogram*. A hypogram was an educational device used in the Hellenistic world to teach a child to write. A blank piece of paper was placed over *(hypo)* a letter of the alphabet *(gram)* so the student could trace it. So understood, the *hypogram of* 1 Peter 2:21 comes closer to an example, or, as we have translated, "pattern," than the "paradigm" we saw in John 13:15 (see Session 12). The life of Jesus, especially his innocent suffering, comes to us then as a pattern which we may trace out in our present lives (walking). Probably no book of the New Testament stresses so much the function of Jesus as an example as does 1 Peter. In 3:17 his death is used as an illustration of how we might suffer for doing right. Verse 4:1 expresses much the same sentiment. And in 1:15-16 the author uses Leviticus (11:44-45) as a call for us to be holy as the Lord is holy.

The prevalence of the example or imitation theme takes on even more importance when we note that 1 Peter was written to persons who had just become Christians. They are newborn babes (2:2) whose lives have just been purified (1:22). For new Christians who might well ask what life looks like in the "resurrected" state, that is, in the new age, Peter answers that Jesus is the pattern. In him we can see what it means to live in this age but march to a different drummer.

For Jesus that pilgrimage between the times leads to the cross (v. 24). In speaking of the cross Peter picks up here a common theme in the New Testament—the cross as a tree or piece of wood. In the early preaching of Acts (5:30), Jesus was said to have been hung on a tree. Paul explained this in Galatians 3:13 by pointing out how Jesus became a curse for us on the tree, for, according to Deuteronomy

21:22-23, execution by hanging on a tree is the death of one accursed. Jesus did not just die; he was shamed, insulted, accursed. By bearing this abuse innocently, Jesus annulled our evil; he took away our sins. This understanding of the meaning of Jesus' death has much in common with the suffering servant motif in Isaiah 53. And indeed the author of 1 Peter shifts in 2:24b-25 to the words and intent of the servant song. Quoting Isaiah 53:5 he says it is by that abuse, the stripes or the wounds on Jesus' back, that we are healed. The word translated "stripes" in the RSV refers to the wounds received in a whiplashing. Though taken from Isaiah 53, the words fit well with the context in 1 Peter, since slaves would likely receive such beatings as a punishment.

The author then returns to the theme of following Jesus, the one abused. He was more than a mediator or redeemer. He led the way; he showed us the appropriate life for this age. In his passion, abuse, and death he also became our leader. Quoting Isaiah 53:6, Peter says that his readers once were wandering sheep, but now in Jesus Christ they have found a guide and shepherd. Again we have touched on a theme often found in 1 Peter. Apparently the readers were Gentiles (1:14). Peter speaks of these Gentile Christians as persons who once were no people, but now have become God's own people, a chosen race, a royal priesthood, and a holy nation (2:9-10), terms heretofore applied only to the Jews.

Though Peter advises us to trace the footsteps of Jesus, he does not often indicate what that would mean specifically (though see 4:3 and 4:7-11). His key word for describing the Christian life is "doing good" (2:14, 15, 20; 3:6, 11, 17; 4:19). Doing good appears to be doing whatever is "right," as the NRSV translates it. Only in doing good can Christians in their daily lives be a means of redemption and reconciliation in the face of conflict (2:12).

The Text in Brethren Life

Among the Brethren it is not unusual to find Jesus referred to as an example or to hear phrases such as *follow Jesus, seek the mind of Jesus,* and *follow in Jesus' steps.* Therefore, it is not surprising when Vernard Eller, writing about discipleship in the *Brethren Encyclopedia* (1983), says: "All Brethren distinctive doctrines can be interpreted as outgrowths from and necessary implications of a basic commitment to the following of Jesus."[1] In the same discussion Eller also emphasizes the importance of the concept of *Nachfolge*, the German word for "a following after," among the Brethren.

Earlier W. Harold Row (1912-1971), who headed the Brethren Service Commission for twenty years, had used the concept of *Nachfolge* in his address titled "The Brethren and Biblical Ethics," at the two hundred fiftieth anniversary celebration in 1958. At that time Row said: "Prominent in the writing of the early Brethren was the concept of following Jesus (*Nachfolge*—following after). This *imitatio Christi* motif is deeply rooted in our history, as it was in the New Testament."[2] The accuracy of Row's statement is easily seen in Alexander Mack's (1679-1735) *Rights and Ordinances* (1713). In his discussion of the Lord's supper, Mack says: "Observe well, that the true believers and lovers of the Lord Jesus have always looked steadfastly and single-mindedly to their Lord and Master in all things. They follow Him gladly in all of His commands, just as He has told them to do, and He has shown them by His own example."[3]

Peter Nead (1796-1877) quotes 1 Peter 2:21 to support his argument that men should have beards. While Nead admits that there is no direct commandment in the New Testament that men should have beards, he asserts that Jesus and his disciples wore beards and that since men are to follow Jesus' example, as stated in verse 21, men should wear beards.[4] Christian Hope (1844-1899), the first Brethren missionary (see chapter 8) ends his tract titled "The Atoning Blood of Christ" with a reference to the concept of Jesus as an example. Says Hope: "In closing, please take a glance at Christ and his people. He was, while here, poor, despised, persecuted; a man of sorrow for the sins of others, and finally killed. Isaiah 53. So are they in every land and nation when they fully imitate him."[5]

Moving into the twentieth century, C. C. Ellis (1874-1950), president of Juniata College from 1930 to 1943, combines the concept of Jesus as example in 1 Peter 2:21 with the concept of seeking the mind of Christ in Philippians 2:5. While contemporary biblical scholars may shudder at equating a Petrine concept with a Pauline concept, it is easy to understand why Ellis, writing in 1919 from a Brethren perspective, would make such a combination. Ellis first presents Jesus' life as "the best example of the spiritual life that the world has ever known."[6] Next he moves to the concept of the mind of Christ in Philippians and presents his understanding of the nature of Christ's mind by describing the three qualities of Jesus—humility, unselfishness, and sincerity. While Ellis does not explain how he arrives at these three qualities, it is certain he has distilled them from his understanding of the New Testament.

As the Brethren moved further into the twentieth century, some of them began to question the biblical appropriateness of a Christology which understands Jesus as a moral example to be imitated. Harold Row, in the previously mentioned anniversary address, after affirming the roots of the *imitatio Christi* motif among the Brethren, says: "Perhaps we have at times stressed this too much, too mechanically. Christ calls us to obedience, not merely to outward imitation."[7] William Beahm (1896-1964), however, writing in his *Studies in Christian Belief* (1958), eloquently defends the concept of Jesus Christ as a moral example in the following paragraph:

> Through the centuries and today the high moral example of Jesus has been variously discounted. Some have objected to "example-ism" in order to make clear that we are saved by faith and not by works. Others have objected to such a view of Christ's example as perfectionism. It overlooks the depths of sin in man's nature, it is argued, and, at best, it covers up by hypocrisy the pride of moral achievement which besets those who pretend to follow in his steps. Underlying these objections is the assumption that Jesus Christ is divine and we are human and therefore he cannot serve as our moral example. But the Biblical record is explicit and the logic is clear. The man Christ Jesus is our moral example.[8]

In spite of some questioning of the concept of Jesus as example during the mid-twentieth century, the concept remains central to the Brethren. In particular, it continues to be included in materials designed for new members of the Church of the Brethren. The 1964 guide to church membership known as *Becoming and Belonging* has a section presenting Jesus as the example for Christians: "Jesus gives the power of his own example. He asks us to live in a way he himself lived. We follow in his steps not by copying every precise act of his, but by becoming his disciples and living in keeping with the spirit of his life and example."[9] More recently, a manual specifically dedicated to "new Brethren . . . to those who come from other traditions and other cultures, even from other nations," takes its title from 1 Peter 2:21—*To Follow in Jesus Steps*. Included in the manual are chapters on such Brethren beliefs and practices as believers' baptism, the love feast, anointing, and pacifism.

Notes

1. Donald F. Durnbaugh and Dennis D. Martin, eds. *Brethren Encyclopedia* (Phila-delphia: The Brethren Encyclopedia, Inc., 1983), s.v. "Discipleship," by Vernard Eller.

2. W. Harold Row, "The Brethren and Biblical Ethics," in *Adventurous Future*, ed. Paul H. Bowman (Elgin, IL: Brethren Press, 1959), 135-136.

3. Alexander Mack, *Rights and Ordinances*, in *European Origins of the Brethren*, comp. and trans. Donald F. Durnbaugh (Elgin, IL: Brethren Press, 1958), 364.

4. Peter Nead, *Primitive Christianity, or a Vindication of the Word of God* (Staunton, VA: Kenton Harper, Printer, 1834), 168.

5. Christian Hope, "The Atoning Blood of Christ," in *The Brethren's Tracts and Pamphlets* (Elgin, IL: Brethren Publishing House, 1900).

6. C. C. Ellis, "Studies in Christian Living," in *Studies in Doctrine and Devotion* (Elgin, IL: Brethren Publishing House, 1919), 215.

7. Row, 136.

8. William M. Beahm, *Studies in Christian Belief* (Elgin, IL: Brethren Press, 1958), 47-48.

9. Ercell V. Lynn, ed., *Becoming a New Person in Christ and Belonging in the Christian Fellowship* (Elgin, IL: Brethren Press, 1964), 2:44.

10. C. Wayne Zunkel, *To Follow in Jesus' Steps* (Elgin, IL: Brethren Press, 1991), 1.

The Text in Today's World

If there is any "canon within the canon" for Brethren, it would be 1 Peter. In it are references to the simple life, to the priesthood of all believers, to the love feast, to witnessing before the governmental authorities, and most of all to following Jesus. Following Jesus was very important to the early Brethren, in a way that distinguished them from the major Reformation bodies. Whereas the mainline Reformers wanted to restore the primitive *faith* of Christianity, Brethren and similar groups sought to return to the *life* of the early community.

For the early Brethren following Jesus was simply taking seriously the way the early church described the Christian life in terms of Jesus' acts and sayings. During the latter part of the nineteenth century and the first part of this century, however, scholars began to focus on Jesus in a different sort of way. Using the tools of historical research in a rather questionable manner, they came up with a picture of a simple "liberal" Jesus, who had little in common with the theology of the early church, and urged Christians to emulate this supposedly "historical" Jesus. This distorted understanding of following Jesus had an enormous impact on the Church of the Brethren in our century. Fortunately, that has run its course. We realize now that the real Jesus must have been a much more complex person than the kindly man of Nazareth described in many popular books on Jesus' life. We also realize that it is mistaken to play Jesus off against the faith of the early church, since it is only through the witness of the church that we have access to Jesus. Because we have Jesus through the earliest disciples, it would be correct to say that there is no easy distinction between Jesus and the first faith community.

There is, however, a way of looking to Jesus as one to follow which is biblically valid. In trying to describe the life of those who live by the power of the resurrection as they anticipate the end, the early Christians made use of the life and teaching of Jesus. For models the church might have, at first, turned to leaders such as Peter, Paul, James, and John (see 1 Cor. 4:16-17), but eventually the church turned to material which had been passed on from Jesus (1 Cor. 7:10). So, likewise, may we. The Brethren concern for the Christian life and especially for the life of the community of faith will lead us to seek our Lord—not only the Lord of the continuing community (the Spirit of Christ) but also the visible form of that Lord: Jesus of Nazareth. Our life and faith may not derive from the historical Jesus but rather from the church's faith in him. Just as the early church discovered, so the community today must look to some specific example of faith in life: how to deal with brother and sister, how to work through marriage and family problems, how to deal with conflict, how to treat enemies or outsiders, how to understand possessions and responsibilities. Jesus provides us with such an example.

Brethren may be tempted to "leave" Jesus in order to make dogmatic considerations primary or in order to make the present experience (Spirit) primary. But insofar as Jesus remains central to Brethren church life, Brethren will continue to have a practical faith which seeks to reconcile others and mediate violence, just as Jesus finally did on the cross. For this reason and in this sense, for Brethren, 1 Peter 2:18-25 still remains the most important passage in the New Testament.

Case Study

During the intense cold war with Russia (1960s) the Church of the Brethren made, through the Brethren Service Commission, several successful overtures to Russian Orthodox church leaders. One such overture resulted in two exchange visits (1963, 1967). Both visits received considerable attention. When one exchangee, Archpatriarch Nikodim of Moscow, came to Bethany Theological Seminary, he was greeted by a number of right-wing and East European demonstrators. They carried protest signs around the edge of the Bethany campus. While it was not completely known at the time, the protest did considerable "damage." In conservative DuPage county, it put Bethany Seminary in a bad light. Furthermore, Bethany Hospital had just arranged to purchase land for a hospital in Downers Grove. Some wealthy citizens of DuPage county were financing the purchase. After the visit of Nikodim, the Church of the Brethren and Bethany Seminary were labelled "communist sympathizers." The purchase of the land for Bethany Hospital never materialized. (It is now Good Samaritan Hospital of the Evangelical Health System.) Some "biased" observers suspect the visit of Nikodim undermined the move of Bethany Hospital. Had you been part of the administration of Bethany Theological Seminary and/or Bethany Hospital would you have:

1. Asked the Brethren Service Commission not to send Archpatriarch Nikodim to DuPage County, Illinois?

2. Called the DuPage sheriff's department and asked to have the protestors removed before the media arrived?

3. Encouraged the students and faculty to serve the protestors coffee and donuts?

4. Done nothing?

Actually the students and faculty did serve coffee and donuts. In any case, Bethany Hospital did not move—a fact that changed the history of Brethren health care and deeply affected health delivery in the city of Chicago.

On Slavery

Revelation 18:9-14 (NRSV)

And the kings of the earth, who committed fornication and lived in luxury with her, will weep and wail over her when they see the smoke of her burning; [10]they will stand far off, in fear of her torment, and say,

"Alas, alas, the great city,
Babylon, the mighty city!
For in one hour your judgment has come."

[11]And the merchants of the earth weep and mourn for her, since no one buys their cargo anymore, [12]cargo of gold, silver, jewels and pearls, fine linen, purple, silk and scarlet, all kinds of scented wood, all articles of ivory, all articles of costly wood, bronze, iron, and marble, [13]cinnamon, spice, incense, myrrh, frankincense, wine, olive oil, choice flour and wheat, cattle and sheep, horses and chariots, slaves—and human lives.

[14]"The fruit for which your soul longed
has gone from you,
and all your dainties and your splendor
are lost to you,
never to be found again!"

Revelation 18:9-14 (BNT)

And the kings of the earth, who committed fornication and lived in sensual luxury with her, will weep and wail when they see the smoke rising from her fires. [10]Standing at a distance, afraid because of the torture befallen her, say,

Alas, alas, the great city,
Babylon, the powerful city!
Because your judgement has come in one hour.

[11]And the merchants of the earth will weep and mourn for her, because no one will buy their cargo anymore, [12]cargo of gold, and silver, and precious stones, and pearls, and fine linen, and purple and silk and scarlet, and all kinds of scented wood,

and various articles of ivory, and articles of precious wood, and
bronze, and iron, and marble, ¹³and cinnamon, and spice, and
incense, and myrrh, and frankincense, and wine, and olive oil,
and fine flour, and wheat, and cattle, and sheep, and horses,
and chariots, and people, body and soul.

> ¹⁴And the fruit for which your very being longed
>   has gone from you.
> And all your luxuries and splendors
>   are lost for you,
>   and never will they be found again.

The Text in Its Biblical Setting

The book of Revelation stands at the end of the Bible as a sign of
the fulfillment of God's promises. The work revealed to John on
Patmos (1:9) points to the end of the old age and the beginning of the
reign of God. The suffering of the age will have ended. God will dwell
with us enthroned in the holy city, Jerusalem (21:1-4). Because of its
powerful vision of the splendid end-time, the book of Revelation has
brought comfort to and inspired many Christians caught in oppression or seemingly hopeless circumstances. Just as the beginning of the
new age centers in the new Jerusalem, so the end of the old age is also
marked by the destruction of this evil time, Rome (chapter 18).

The term *apokalypsis* in Greek (translated here "revelation") refers
to a type of literature that arose during the Jewish exile (598 B.C.). We
often think of Daniel as the primary example. It was a type of faith
which saw history as the present evil age in which we live and hope
in a coming new age in which God's promises (as in Isa. 65:17-25) will
be fulfilled. In the New Testament the teachings of Jesus and Paul are
based on this way of seeing history. The reign of God is at hand, and
we can anticipate a new life. Indeed, we stand now at the threshold.

Late in the first century of the Christian era, apocalyptic literature
turned in two other directions. On the one hand it was spiritualized
so that the end-time became a heavenly reality and the old age was
identified with the created world. Salvation came through denial of
creation and identification with the spiritual. We call that Gnosticism.

Apocalyptic literature also turned geographic. It can best be seen
in the book of Revelation (though much the same shift is visible in the
apocalyptic literature of an Apostolic Father, see *Hermas* Sim. IV). In
the geographical shift, the evil age is associated with an oppressive

city or state while the new age is identified with a religious city or church. In so far as the book of Revelation places the ultimate conflict between Rome and Jerusalem, it is no longer apocalypticism as we find it in Jesus (e.g., Mark 13) or Paul (1 Th. 5:1-11).

The passage 18:9-14 stands within the great description of the fall of Rome, named here the epitome of evil power, Babylon (see 1 Pet. 5:13). Hatred for Rome is expressed in two charges: fornication and a luxurious lifestyle. The charge of national fornication reflects similar attacks in the Hebrew Scriptures on any nation which would compromise itself for political gain. The exilic prophet claimed Israel had prostituted herself with Assyria (Ezek. 16:28; cf. Rev. 17). The power and glitter of Rome caused the kings of the world to make agreements and contracts which compromised their own national integrity (18:9).

Like the prophets before him the author also attacks Rome for its sensual and excessive lifestyle (Amos 6:4). None of the wares listed in Revelation 18:12-13 could be considered essential for life. To be sure, Rome built an empire on the backs of slaves and captive people, but more offensive to the author was living a life of luxury at the expense of the poor (v. 13).

After describing the destruction in the form a dirge or funeral song (like Jer. 50—51), the author in verse 14 turns to a lament sung by the kings and merchants who have profited by the opulence and power of Rome.

Rome was the imperial capital. To keep the empire together it furnished administrative structure and military might. Consequently, it imported from the provinces food and materials. These were unloaded primarily at the harbor in Ostia (the offices and warehouses can be seen to this day). This list of items shipped is a remarkable reflection on the wealth of the empire. At the end of the list, probably deliberately behind cattle, sheep and horses, we find human beings also for sale.

In many respects Rome was built on the backs of slaves. It is estimated by modern demographers that the populace of Rome itself was about 65 percent slave. If one includes those once slave, but now free, it surely was even higher. These slaves were, for the most part, captives from conquered territories. They often included well trained administrators and educators. The administration of the Roman Empire likely depended on these slaves who worked for the senate and the emperor. Other slaves were born in captivity or they sold themselves into slavery as a way of dealing with personal bankruptcy.

As an addendum it should be noted that Rome actually was not destroyed at the time that Revelation was written. In fact, Christian-

ity was named the official religion of Rome by Constantine (313 A.D.).
Roman Christians of those first three centuries did not countenance
the institution of slavery. In early pre-Constantinian Christian funeral
inscriptions, one can identify slaves only by their names, not by social
rank.

The Text in Brethren Life

Between the years 1782 and 1865, the issue of slavery was considered at thirteen different Annual Meetings. Every time the issue was
considered, the minutes clearly indicate that the Brethren were opposed to slavery. At various places in the minutes, slavery is described
as "unchristian" (1782); "in no wise . . . justified . . . according to the
Gospel" (1837); and "contrary to the doctrine of Christ" (1863). Interestingly, only three of the thirteen statements in the minutes include
a biblical text as support for the Brethren opposition to slavery. In each
case a different text is cited: Revelation 18:13 (1813); Matthew 7:12
(1862); and Luke 6:31 (1865).

The most extensive application of a biblical text to the issue of
slavery is for the Revelation 18:13 text. Concerning this text the 1813
minutes read:

> With regard to the slave trade and slave holding, It is
> unanimously considered that it is wrong, and that it be-
> longs to the iniquities of Babylon, making merchandise of
> souls of men (Rev. 18:13), and that it is carried on by the
> spirit of this world, and is contrary to the good and holy
> Spirit of God, by whom all the faithful souls dedicated to
> God are ruled and led into all truth, and are to come out,
> according to the counsel of God, of Babylon, not touching
> the unclean thing, that they be not partakers of her sins,
> and receive not of her plagues.[1]

References to the other two texts are as follows: "It [defending and
justifying slavery] is utterly wrong for any brother to do so, according
to Matt. 7:12."[2] "It [entertaining proslavery principles] is considered
not right, according to Luke 6:31."[3]

Since the Revelation text was the first to be cited in the minutes and
since the citation is so lengthy, one might expect that the Brethren
most often used it as the basis for their opposition to slavery. Not so!
As far as can be determined from surviving records, the Brethren did
not often cite biblical texts to support their antislavery view. But when

they did, they most often cited the Golden Rule, as found in either Matthew 7:12 or Luke 6:31. The Golden Rule, of course, is also one of the texts which the Brethren used to support their opposition to gambling. (See chapter 9.)

Christopher Sauer, Jr., (1721-1784) strongly opposed slavery, as did his father. In 1761 Sauer, Jr., who had been ordained a minister in the Germantown congregation in 1753, published an antislavery editorial in his newspaper *Pennsylvanische Berichte*. The occasion for the editorial was the fact that Sauer had learned that three ships had left Philadelphia for Africa to obtain slaves. Concerning this event Sauer writes:

> It is with the utmost regret that we learn that Germans are to engage in the nefarious slave traffic. Though they are well paid for everything they sell, they still begrudge laborers, servants, or maidservants their pay. This godless traffic could find, up to the present, no safe footing in Pennsylvania, owing to the abhorrence the Germans still have for it. But for some years now, even some of them have begun to take part in this great injustice.... May God be merciful to our country before its measure of iniquity is full and the vials of His wrath are poured out upon it![4]

Throughout the minutes of Annual Meeting, it is clear that those who owned slaves had to set the slaves free before they could join a Brethren congregation and that a member who chose to purchase slaves could not remain a member. This was obviously true even before the minutes of Annual Meeting are known to have been recorded. In June 1775, John van Laschet from the Conestoga congregation wrote a letter to the Germantown congregation. In the letter Laschet begs forgiveness for having been a slave holder saying: "I find myself needing to beg you, all together, brethren and sisters, in anything where I may have sinned against you or angered you, be it in words or works, or otherwise in my conduct. I fervently beg your forgiveness and hope in the future with the help of God to conduct myself better and more carefully."[5] Laschet also says in the letter that he has freed the black woman and her son. Evidently there was some problem with this claim since the minutes of the 1782 Annual Meeting specifically mention Laschet by name and the fact that he has a black woman as a slave and that she has four children. In the minutes Laschet is told to set her free n the presence of other Brethren as witnesses.

Included in the 1782 minutes are detailed instructions as to when and how Laschet was to set free the woman and her children. Similar instructions also appear in the 1797, 1813, and 1854 minutes. In general, these instructions are as follows: (1) Adult slaves were to be given an outfit of new clothes and set free at once; (2) Children were to be kept as servants and be given food, clothes, and an education until they reached adulthood; (3) Adulthood was understood to be 21 for men and 18 for women, but the 1797 minutes list the age as 25, evidently for both men and women.

In 1853 the Annual Meeting had to deal with the fact that in some states slave owners could not legally manumit slaves "in safety, without transporting them beyond its [the state's] limits." Since this was a difficult issue, a committee was appointed to solve the problem. At the 1854 meeting, the committee presented it solution, which was adopted only after lengthy discussions. According to the solution, slave holders were to pay adult slaves a sum of money or goods when setting them free. This sum was understood as compensation for their services and could be used to finance their travel to a state where they could be free. Local congregations were to judge what a fair amount of compensation would be in each case.

The very first volume of the *Gospel Visitor*, which began publication in April 1851, contains an antislavery article. Included in the article is a reference to the Golden Rule as the reason why slavery is contrary to God's laws. Immediately following the article are some remarks by Henry Kurtz (1796-1874), the editor. Kurtz first affirms the Brethren opposition to slavery. Then, however, he says that articles about slavery have no place in the *Visitor* because it "was never intended to be the channel, through which the turbid waters of political warfare should flow."[6] In spite of this intention, Kurtz continued to print articles about slavery in the paper. The September 1853 issue contains a letter written by Philip Boyle (1807-1872), a Brethren elder in Maryland, to Lewis Tappan, the secretary of the American and Foreign Anti-Slavery Society. Tappan had written to Boyle asking for the Brethren position on slavery. Boyle replied and sent a copy of his reply to the *Visitor*. Kurtz decided to print the reply because it provided such a good summary of the Brethren position. The biblical basis given by Boyle for the Brethren opposition to slavery is Matthew 7:12. Later articles about slavery in the *Visitor* also cited the Golden Rule. For example, in the August 1861 issue, James Quinter (1816-1888) quoted the Golden Rule as the text for Brethren opposition to slavery.

Even though the Brethren were always opposed to slavery, they were not free of racial prejudice. Furthermore, even though Annual

Meeting had affirmed as early as 1835 that color made no difference when it came to receiving people into the church, "the Brethren were not at all eager to have black persons as members of the church, and consequently very few blacks became Brethren in the years before 1865."[3] A particular problem was that some white members did not want to salute black members with the Holy Kiss. (See chapter 16.) In spite of such prejudice, a few blacks did join the Brethren. One notable example prior to the Civil War was Samuel Weir (1812-1884). Weir was born a slave in Virginia but was freed by Andrew McClure when McClure joined the Brethren in 1843. A few months later Weir also joined the church, being baptized by Peter Nead. When Weir moved to Ohio, he was welcomed as a member in some congregations but not in all. In 1849 he was licensed to the ministry, and in 1881 he was ordained an elder. Both his licensing and his ordination were understood to be for work among other blacks.

Notes

1. *Minutes of the Annual Meetings of the Church of the Brethren, 1778-1909* (Elgin, IL: Brethren Publishing House, 1909), 31.

2. Ibid., 207.

3. Ibid., 239.

4. "Editorial Statement of Christopher Sauer II," in *Brethren in Colonial America*, ed. Donald F. Durnbaugh (Elgin, IL: Brethren Press, 1967), 207-208.

5. "John van Laschet to the Germantown Congregation," in *Brethren in Colonial America*, 208.

6. Henry Kurtz, "Remarks of the Editor," *Gospel Visitor*, January 1852, 159.

7. Roger E. Sappington, *Brethren in a New Nation* (Elgin, IL: Brethren Press, 1976), 276.

The Text in Today's World

Many of us are surprised by the intense hatred for Rome found in this passage. We have been taught to forgive our enemies seventy times seven. Jesus said love of enemies was the supreme mark of a Christian, a kind of maturity found in God (Matt. 5:43-48). Under what circumstances could we have in the same New Testament such a relentless hatred? Or worse yet, how could the New Testament rejoice in another's destruction (*Schadenfreude* in German)? To be honest, if this passage represents the actual feelings of Christians at the end of the century, then we must revise our estimate of the early

church. That is not likely the case. Rome had not been destroyed at
the time Revelation was written. We are reading a vision, not an
historical account. The apocalyptic vision places a city which represents the culminated evil of the old age against a city which represents
the presence of God in the new age. Such a city was Babylon, and now
it is Rome. On the other hand, the heavenly city, Jerusalem (21:2),
surely refers to the church, not the actual city of Jerusalem.

Is visionary hatred permissible? Perhaps each reader will have to
make that decision. Surely the present-day Christian ought to state
plainly that the old age will pass away. Fallen, fallen is the disregard
for life that characterizes the Rome of our day. Fallen, fallen are the
forces that destroy our very social fabric. Fallen, fallen is that which
makes us abuse each other in word and deed. Fallen, fallen are
systems that allow a few to live off the labor of the many. Fallen, fallen
is the old age.

Slavery is not so apparent to us today. There are slaves in the world,
but not many are literally owned by someone else. Much more
prevalent is the issue raised by the text: some in society live in luxury
at the expense of many others who barely exist without even basic
necessities. We can see the problem everywhere. In South Africa a
great culture has been built on the shoulders of black men who labor
in places like the mines and black women who serve as domestics.
Neither receive enough wages to advance up the economic ladder.
They must spend so much time at work there is no possibility of
family life or enjoyment.

But we need not shift to South Africa. In the United States, Native
Americans feel that the powerful US has been built at the expense of
the people who first lived here. African-Americans feel the southern
way of life and northern industry have been built on their labor. They
have yet to enjoy fully the fruits of their labor. The text speaks directly
to these situations. The vision of the end-time anticipates the cessation
of such systems which allow one group of people to use another for
its own benefit. The author of Revelation saw vividly the fall of such
systems and saw the consternation of those who cooperated and
profited with that great prototype, Rome. We share in that vision.

Case Study

The National Council of Churches, in cooperation with several
Native American groups, declared 1992 a year of mourning for what

the white European settlers did to the native population. Instead of celebrating Columbus's discovery of America, Americans were called to apologize. Along with the celebration of the 500th anniversary of the discovery of America by Europeans, many native Americans were protesting the desecration of Indian burial grounds. Potawatomi Church of the Brethren, in southern Ohio, displayed in its narthex a number of arrowheads, axheads, and bones collected from various farms in the area. George Tallchief, one of the few native Americans living near the Potawatomi church, came to the church board and asked for the artifacts to be returned to his tribe. As a member of the board at Potawatami would you:

1. Argue that the ones who found the archaeological material should keep possession of it? Otherwise all museums would be destroyed.

2. Ask George Tallchief to help design at a tasteful display of artifacts and drawings at Potawatami which would help people understand and appreciate the life of early native Americans?

3. Give all the artifacts to George Tallchief with a written note of apology to the Potawatomis?

4. Send the artifacts to the Cincinnati museum and ask them to arbitrate the matter with the Potawatomis?